The Kitchen Yearbook

Marshall Cavendish

Edited by Renny Harrop
Designed by Caroline Austen

Published by Marshall Cavendish Books Limited
58, Old Compton Street,
London W1V 5PA

Some of this material has previously appeared
in the partwork *Supercook*

First printing 1978
Second printing 1981

Printed in Hong Kong

ISBN 0 85685 443 3

Introduction

Throughout the year, as the seasons change, so do our needs and tastes for food. A bleak winter conjures up thoughts of steaming soups and piping hot stews. The Spring brings new flavours, crisp vegetables, fresh fish, and poultry. The lazy salad days of Summer mean long evenings and eating out of doors. The rich harvests of Autumn bring fruits, fish and game. Inevitably, as the nights grow shorter, the cycle moves on and Winter frost returns. These natural events are taken for granted, but even in our urbanized society, our tastes are still guided by the natural elements and our ancient instincts. Rich, warming food to keep out the chill and sustain us in our work; the fresh, healthy Spring vegetables; in warmer days, cool salads; and as the harvest comes in, with its abundant produce, it also brings our deep-rooted and traditional enjoyment of all the natural gifts the land still provides.

Note: Measurements are given in Metric and Imperial, separated by an oblique stroke. These should not be used interchangeably when following a recipe as they are not direct conversions. Follow either one or the other.
Herbs when in season are specified as fresh. If they are not available, dried herbs may be substituted using one-third of the quantity given. For example, for 1 tablespoon freshly chopped basil, use 1 teaspoon dried basil.
All flour is plain and all sugar granulated unless otherwise specified. Ovens should be preheated to the temperature given in the recipe.

CONTENTS

Spring

Summer

Autumn

Winter

Feast Days

Spring

The arrival of spring has always been an excuse for feasting. As the days gradually lengthen, and the appearance of the sun becomes less unpredictable, new life (much of it edible!) suddenly becomes apparent wherever we look. Tender young lambs, fresh green vegetables, fruit blossom—all reflect not only the change in our surroundings but also a change in our eating habits. We want to eat food that is lighter in colour and flavour, to lose some of the weight we put on in the winter, and, as the season progresses, to make the most of the fresh scenery by eating outside. So spring food has to be flexible, making the best of what's around but using it both in cold and hot dishes, for picnics or for chilly evenings. Spring is above all a gay and carefree time so whatever you're eating, enjoy it.

What's best in season

Fruit:	Apples	Grapes	Mandarins	Pineapples
	Apricots	Grapefruit	Melons	Rhubarb
	Bananas	Lemons	Oranges	Tangerines
	Gooseberries	Limes	Pears	

Vegetables:	Artichokes	Cauliflowers	Leeks	Radishes
	Asparagus	Celery	Lettuces	Spinach
	Avocados	Chicory	Mushrooms	Spring onions
	Beetroot	Cucumbers	Onions	Swedes
	Broad beans	French beans	Parsnips	Tomatoes
	Cabbages	Globe artichokes	Peas	Turnips
	Carrots	Kale	Potatoes	Watercress

Herbs:	Basil	Coriander	Marjoram	Sage
	Bay	Dill	Mint	Summer savory
	Chervil	Fennel	Parsley	Tarragon
	Chives	Lemon balm	Rosemary	Thyme

Nuts:	Almonds			

Fish:	Bass	Haddock	Plaice	Trout
	Brill	Halibut	Prawns	Turbot
	Carp	Herring	Salmon	Whitebait
	Cockles	Lobster	Sardines	Whiting
	Crab	Mackerel	Shrimps	
	Crayfish	Oysters	Sole	

Poultry:	Available fresh or frozen all year round

Game:	Pigeon	Quail	Rabbit

Meat and offal:	Available fresh or frozen all year round

Appetizers

Sicilian stuffed tomatoes

8 large tomatoes
6 Tbsp olive oil
2 medium onions, finely chopped
1 garlic clove, crushed
125g/4oz fresh breadcrumbs
8 anchovy fillets, chopped
3 Tbsp black olives, stoned and chopped
2 Tbsp parsley, freshly chopped
2 tsp oregano, freshly chopped
3 Tbsp Parmesan cheese, grated
1 Tbsp butter, cut into 8 pieces

Cut off the tops of the tomatoes. Scoop out and discard the seeds, being careful not to pierce the skins.

Heat the oil in a frying pan. Add the onions and garlic and fry until the onions are soft but not brown. Remove from the heat and stir in the breadcrumbs, anchovies, olives, parsley and oregano. Fill the tomatoes with the anchovy mixture, piling it up slightly. Place the tomatoes side by side in a baking dish. Sprinkle over the Parmesan cheese and put a piece of butter on each tomato.

Bake in a moderate oven (180°C/350°F or Gas Mark 4) for 20 to 25 minutes or until the tops are lightly browned. Serve hot straight from the oven, or allow to cool and serve chilled.
Serves 4

Sardine Eggs

6 eggs, hard-boiled
175g/6oz can sardines, drained
4 Tbsp mayonnaise
1 Tbsp lemon juice
1 Tbsp parsley, freshly chopped
salt and white pepper

Cut the eggs in half lengthways. Cut a thin slice off the bottom of each one so they will sit flat. Remove the yolks and press through a sieve into a small mixing bowl.

Add the remaining ingredients with seasoning to taste to the egg yolks and mash together well. Fill the whites with the sardine mixture. Serve chilled with brown bread and butter.
Serves 6

Sicilian Stuffed Tomatoes make a colourful and appetizing first course, served hot or cold.

Oysters Kilpatrick – simple to prepare and exotic to taste.

garlic clove, tarragon, anchovies, parsley, cayenne and seasoning to taste. Add three-quarters of the prawns to the mayonnaise and mix well. Chill in the refrigerator.

Cut the stalks off the artichokes. Pull off any bruised or tough outer leaves, then slice off the top third of the artichokes. Trim the tips of the remaining leaves using scissors. Rub the cut edges with the remaining lemon juice to prevent discoloration.

Half fill a large saucepan with water and add 1 teaspoon salt. Bring to the boil. Place the artichokes in the water and simmer for 30 minutes or until tender. Test by pulling out a leaf. Remove the artichokes from the pan and place upside-down on kitchen paper towels to drain and cool.

Pull the leaves of each artichoke apart and remove the yellow inner core. Scrape out the hairy choke and discard it. Fill the centres with the prawn mayonnaise. Garnish with the remaining prawns.

Serve on individual plates garnished with lemon slices. Serve any extra sauce separately.
Serves 6

Oysters Kilpatrick

50g/2oz butter, softened
32 oysters, top shells removed
2 tsp Worcestershire sauce
12 lean bacon rashers, grilled
until crisp and crumbled
2 Tbsp parsley, freshly chopped

Carefully spread a thin layer of butter over each oyster. Sprinkle with the Worcestershire sauce and bacon. Grill the oysters for 2 minutes. Serve hot, garnished with the parsley.
Serves 4

Globe artichokes with prawns and spicy mayonnaise

600ml/1 pint mayonnaise
4 Tbsp lemon juice
2 Tbsp chives, finely chopped
1 tsp capers, chopped
1 garlic clove, crushed
1 Tbsp tarragon, freshly chopped
6 anchovies, finely chopped
2 Tbsp parsley, freshly chopped
pinch cayenne pepper
salt and pepper
250g/8oz prawns (shelled weight),
deveined
6 globe artichokes
2 lemons, sliced

Mix together the mayonnaise, 1 tablespoon of the lemon juice, the chives, capers,

Fried shrimp balls

700g/1½lb shrimps (shelled weight),
deveined and finely chopped
25g/1oz fresh brown breadcrumbs
1 garlic clove, crushed
1 small onion, finely chopped
3 Tbsp ginger wine
black pepper
75g/3oz dry breadcrumbs
vegetable oil for deep frying
lemon wedges to serve
FRITTER BATTER
50g/2oz flour
¼ tsp salt
pinch sugar
4 Tbsp water
2 tsp vegetable oil
1 egg white

Mix the shrimps with the fresh breadcrumbs, garlic, onion, ginger wine and pepper to taste. With floured hands form the mixture into 24 balls.

To make the fritter batter, sift the flour, salt and sugar into a mixing bowl. Stir in the water and oil to make a smooth batter. Beat the egg white until it will form a soft peak and fold into the batter. Dip the shrimp balls in the batter, then roll them in the dry breadcrumbs to coat on all sides. Shake off any excess.

Half fill a deep-frying pan with oil and heat to 190°C/375°F on a deep-fat thermometer, or until a cube of stale bread dropped into the oil turns light brown in 35 seconds.

Put the shrimp balls, five or six at a time, in the frying basket and lower into the oil. Fry, shaking occasionally, for 3 to 5 minutes or until crisp and golden brown. Drain the shrimp balls on kitchen paper towels and keep hot while you fry the remaining shrimp balls.

Serve hot, garnished with the lemon wedges.

Serves 4-6

Kipper pâté

375g/12oz kipper fillets, boned
25g/1oz butter, melted
1 Tbsp sweet sherry
4 Tbsp double cream
1 tsp Worcestershire sauce
black pepper
25g/1oz clarified butter, melted

Put the kippers in a bowl and pour over boiling water. Leave for 15 minutes, then drain well. Skin the fillets and flake the flesh. Put the flesh in a blender with the melted butter, sherry, cream, Worcestershire sauce and pepper to taste. Blend, off and on, for 1 to 2 minutes or until the mixture is smooth. Alternatively, pound the ingredients together with a pestle in a mortar until they are smooth.

Spoon the pâté into a small serving dish and smooth the top. Pour over the clarified butter and chill for at least 2 hours before serving, with Melba toast.

Serves 4

Deep-fried whitebait

50g/2oz flour
salt and black pepper
1 Tbsp parsley, freshly chopped
500g/1lb whitebait
vegetable oil for deep frying
lemon wedges for serving

Mix together the flour, salt and pepper to taste and the parsley in a polythene bag. Add the whitebait to the bag and shake well to coat them with the seasoned flour.

Half fill a deep-frying pan with oil and heat to 185°C/360°F on a deep-fat thermometer, or until a cube of stale bread dropped into the oil turns golden brown in 50 seconds. Put half the whitebait in the frying basket and lower into the oil. Fry for 2 to 3 minutes or until crisp and light brown. Shake the basket occasionally. Drain the fried whitebait on kitchen paper towels and keep hot white you fry the remaining whitebait.

Serve hot with lemon wedges and tartare sauce.

Serves 4

Kipper Pâté, served in individual dishes, makes a tasty start to a meal.

Soups

Creamy asparagus soup

25g/1oz butter
1 medium onion, finely chopped
3 Tbsp flour
1.2l/2 pints chicken stock
salt and white pepper
½ tsp celery salt
¼ tsp grated nutmeg
500g/1lb asparagus, chopped
300ml/10floz single cream

Melt the butter in a saucepan. Add the onion and cook until soft but not brown. Remove from the heat and sprinkle over the flour. Stir well, then gradually stir in the chicken stock. Add salt and pepper to taste, the celery salt, nutmeg and asparagus. Return to the heat and bring to the boil, stirring constantly. Cover and simmer gently for 20 to 30 minutes or until the asparagus is very tender.

Remove from the heat. Purée the soup in a blender or foodmill or rub it through a strainer using the back of a wooden spoon, or pass through a food mill. If you are serving the soup hot, return it to the saucepan and reheat gently. Stir in the cream just before serving.

Creamy Asparagus Soup makes a rich, delicately flavoured first course to a dinner party, served hot or cold.

To serve the soup cold, stir the cream into the purée and chill for at least 2 hours before serving.
Serves 4-6

Iced watercress and almond soup

1 bunch watercress, finely chopped
1 celery stalk, finely chopped
300ml/10floz single cream
grated rind of 1 lemon
300ml/10floz milk
450ml/15floz chicken stock
3 Tbsp ground almonds
2 Tbsp butter
2 Tbsp flour
salt and black pepper

Put the watercress, celery, cream, lemon rind and milk in a large saucepan and bring to just under boiling point. Remove from the heat and stir in the stock and almonds. Blend the butter with the flour to make a smooth paste (beurre manié) and stir into the soup in small pieces. Return to the heat and cook for 2 to 3 minutes, stirring constantly, or until the soup is thick and smooth. Season to taste and cook gently for a further 2 minutes.

Remove from the heat and chill for at least 1 hour before serving.
Serves 4

Minestrone

900ml/1½ pints water
125g/4oz dried kidney beans
50g/2oz chick-peas
175g/6oz salt pork, cut into cubes
4 Tbsp olive oil
2 medium onions, finely chopped
1 garlic clove, crushed
2 medium potatoes, peeled and diced
4 carrots, scraped and cut into
1cm/½in lengths
4 celery stalks, cut into 1cm/½in lengths
½ small cabbage, finely shredded
6 medium tomatoes, peeled, seeded
and chopped
2.5l/4 pints chicken stock
1 bouquet garni
salt and black pepper
250g/8oz green peas (shelled weight)
125g/4oz macaroni
50g/2oz Parmesan cheese, finely grated

Bring the water to the boil in a saucepan.
Add the beans and chick-peas and boil for
2 minutes. Remove from the heat and

leave to soak for 1½ hours.

Return to the heat and bring back to the
boil. Simmer for 1½ hours or until the
beans and chick-peas are almost tender.
Drain well.

Fry the salt pork in a large saucepan
until it is golden brown and has rendered
most of its fat. Remove the salt pork cubes
from the pan. Add the oil, onions and
garlic to the pan and fry until the onions
are soft but not brown. Stir in the potatoes,
carrots and celery and continue to cook for
5 minutes, stirring. Add the cabbage and
tomatoes and cook for a further 5 minutes.

Add the stock, bouquet garni, chick-
peas, beans, salt pork and salt and pepper
to taste. Bring to the boil, then cover and
simmer for 35 minutes.

Discard the bouquet garni. Add the peas
and macaroni and continue to simmer,
uncovered, for 10 to 15 minutes or until
the macaroni is *al dente*, or just tender.

Ladle the soup into bowls and sprinkle
with the Parmesan. Serve hot.
Serves 8

*Iced Watercress and Almond Soup –
a creamy spring appetizer.*

Avgolemono is a traditional Greek soup with an unusual and delicious lemon flavour.

Avgolemono

75g/3oz long-grain rice
1.8l/3 pints chicken stock
4 eggs
juice of 2 lemons
pepper
2 Tbsp parsley, freshly chopped

Wash the rice, then soak in cold water for 30 minutes. Drain. Place the rice in a saucepan with the stock. Bring to the boil. Reduce heat, cover and simmer for 15 minutes or until the rice is tender. Remove from the heat.

Beat the eggs together in a mixing bowl. Gradually beat in the lemon juice, then a few spoonsful of the stock mixture. Stir the egg mixture into the remaining stock mixture in the saucepan.

Return to the heat and cook gently for 2 to 3 minutes. Do not let the soup boil or it will curdle. Add pepper to taste. Serve hot, sprinkled with parsley.

Serves 6

Herb and potato soup

4 medium potatoes, peeled and chopped
25g/1oz butter
2 medium onions, thinly sliced and
pushed out into rings
1 Tbsp chervil, freshly chopped
2 Tbsp parsley, freshly chopped
2 Tbsp chives, freshly chopped
salt and black pepper
1.2l/2 pints chicken stock

Cook the potatoes in boiling salted water until they are tender. Drain well, then rub through a sieve into a mixing bowl.

Melt the butter in a large saucepan. Add the onions and cook until they are soft but not brown. Remove from the heat and stir in the potato purée, chervil, parsley, chives and salt and pepper to taste.
Gradually stir in the stock. Return to the heat and bring to the boil, stirring frequently. Cover and simmer gently for 30 minutes. Serve hot.

Serves 4

Green pea and sausage soup

1 Tbsp butter
500g/1lb green peas (shelled weight)
4 lettuce leaves, shredded
3 spring onions, chopped
½ tsp sugar
salt and black pepper
1.2l/2 pints water
300ml/10floz milk
1 Vienna sausage, thinly sliced
300ml/10floz double cream

Melt the butter in a large saucepan. Add the peas, lettuce, spring onions, sugar and salt and pepper to taste. Cook, stirring, for 2 minutes. Add the water and milk and bring to the boil. Simmer gently for 15 minutes or until the peas are tender. Remove from the heat.

Purée the soup in a blender or foodmill, or by pushing through a sieve, and then strain. Alternatively, rub the soup through a strainer using a wooden spoon.

Return the puréed soup to the saucepan and bring to the boil, stirring. Add the sausage and simmer gently for 2 minutes. Stir in the cream and heat through without boiling. Serve hot.

Serves 6

Spinach soup

25g/1oz butter
1 large onion, finely chopped
2 Tbsp flour
1.2l/2 pints chicken stock
salt and black pepper
½ tsp paprika
½ tsp grated nutmeg
2 Tbsp lemon juice
700g/1½lb spinach, coarsely chopped
6 Tbsp double cream
6 lean bacon rashers, grilled until
crisp and crumbled

Melt the butter in a large saucepan. Add the onion and fry until it is soft but not brown. Remove from the heat and sprinkle over the flour. Stir well, then gradually stir in the stock. Add salt and pepper to taste, the paprika, nutmeg, lemon juice and spinach and return to the heat. Bring to the boil. Cover and simmer for 20 to 25 minutes or until the spinach is very tender.

Purée the soup in a blender or foodmill, then return to the saucepan. Reheat gently, stirring frequently. Ladle into soup bowls and top each serving with a tablespoon of cream and crumbled bacon. Serve hot.

Serves 6

Green Pea and Sausage Soup is an economical and filling start to a meal.

Main Dishes

Whiting stuffed with prawns

juice of 1 lemon
6 medium whiting, boned and cleaned
salt and black pepper
125g/4oz butter
300g/10oz button mushrooms, sliced
300g/10oz prawns (shelled weight)
deveined
6 Tbsp parsley, freshly chopped

Sprinkle the lemon juice over the fish, then rub inside and out with salt and pepper.

Melt 25g/1oz of the butter in a frying pan. Add the mushrooms with salt and pepper to taste and fry for 2 to 3 minutes. Stir in the prawns and parsley and cook for 2 to 3 minutes longer. Remove from the heat. Stuff the cavities in the whiting with the mushroom mixture. Cut half the remaining butter into small pieces and dot over the bottom of a baking dish. Place the whiting in the dish, side by side, and dot with the remaining butter.

Bake in a moderate oven (180°C/350°F or Gas Mark 4) for 20 to 30 minutes or until the fish is cooked. Test with a fork: the flesh should flake easily.

Serve hot.

Serves 6

Plaice with artichoke sauce

1kg/2lb plaice fillets, skinned
salt and black pepper
1 small onion sliced and pushed out into rings
1 celery stalk, chopped
1 mace blade
1 bouquet garni
6 white peppercorns, crushed
300ml/10floz fish stock
175ml/6floz dry white wine
1 Tbsp lemon juice
1 Tbsp parsley, freshly chopped
SAUCE
3 globe artichokes
juice of 1 lemon
25g/1oz butter
25g/1oz flour
salt and white pepper
pinch cayenne pepper
4 Tbsp double cream

First prepare the artichokes for the sauce. Snap the leaves off the artichokes and cut off the stalks. Trim the base of all pieces of green to expose the white heart. As each heart is prepared, drop it into a saucepan of water to which the lemon juice has been added. Bring the water to the boil and simmer for 30 to 40 minutes or until the artichoke hearts are tender.

Plaice with Artichoke Sauce makes a satisfying and delicious main course.

Meanwhile, rub the plaice fillets with salt and pepper. Lay them in a flameproof casserole and add the onion, celery, mace blade, bouquet garni and peppercorns. Pour over the stock, wine and lemon juice. Bring to the boil, then cover and cook gently for 8 to 12 minutes or until the fish is cooked. Test with a fork: the flesh should flake easily.

Transfer the fish fillets to a warmed serving dish. Fold them over or roll up and keep hot. Strain the cooking liquid and reserve 300ml/10fl oz.

Melt the butter in a saucepan. Stir in the flour to make a smooth paste and cook for 1 minute, stirring. Remove from the heat and gradually stir in the reserved cooking liquid. Return to the heat and cook, stirring, for 2 to 3 minutes or until the sauce is thickened and smooth. Stir in salt and pepper to taste and the cayenne. Remove from the heat.

Drain the artichoke hearts and chop finely. Add to the sauce with the cream. Heat through gently without boiling, then pour over the fish fillets. Sprinkle with the parsley and serve.
Serves 6

Fillets of sole with spinach and Mornay sauce

700g-1kg/1½-2lb sole fillets, skinned
salt and black pepper
125ml/4floz fish stock, boiling
125ml/4floz white wine, boiling
1kg/2lb spinach
50g/2oz butter
SAUCE
25g/1oz butter
4 Tbsp flour
300ml/10floz milk
300ml/10floz fish stock
50g/2oz Parmesan cheese, grated
50g/2oz Gruyère cheese, grated
4 Tbsp double cream
salt and white pepper

Lay the sole fillets in a baking dish. Sprinkle with salt and pepper and pour over the boiling fish stock and wine. Cover the dish and bake in a moderate oven (180°C/350°F or Gas Mark 4) for 8 to 12 minutes or until the fish is cooked.

Meanwhile, put the spinach in a saucepan. Do not add any water. Cook for about 6 minutes or until the spinach is tender.

While the spinach is cooking, make the sauce. Melt the butter in a saucepan. Stir in the flour and cook, stirring, for 1 minute. Gradually stir in the milk, then the fish stock and bring to the boil, stirring constantly. Simmer, stirring, until the sauce is thick and smooth. Remove from

the heat and add the Parmesan, Gruyère, cream and seasoning to taste. Stir well and keep hot.

When the spinach is cooked, drain it, pressing to remove all excess moisture. Chop the spinach and add the butter and salt and pepper to taste. Mix well. Spread the spinach over the bottom of a flameproof serving dish. Top with the drained sole fillets and pour over the sauce. Grill until the top is lightly browned.

Serve hot.
Serves 4

Halibut steaks with cucumber and soured cream sauce

300ml/10floz dry white wine
2 Tbsp lemon juice
1 Tbsp dill, freshly chopped
1 small onion, halved
4 peppercorns, coarsely crushed
salt
4 medium halibut steaks
1 small cucumber, peeled, seeded and finely chopped
50g/2oz flour
1 tsp paprika
black pepper
150ml/5floz soured cream
25g/1oz butter
1 Tbsp vegetable oil

Put the wine, lemon juice, dill, onion, peppercorns and 1 teaspoon salt in a shallow dish. Add the fish steaks and marinate for 2 hours, basting occasionally.

Put the cucumber in a colander, sprinkle with salt and leave to drain for 30 minutes. Rinse and pat dry with paper towels.

Mix together the flour, paprika, a pinch of black pepper and ¼ teaspoon salt. Remove the halibut steaks from the marinade and coat with seasoned flour.

Discard the onion from the marinade. Put the marinade in a saucepan and add the cucumber. Bring to the boil and boil until it has reduced to about 150ml/5fl oz. Strain into a bowl, rubbing the cucumber through the strainer until only a dry pulp remains. Discard the pulp.

Return the strained mixture to the saucepan and stir in the soured cream. Heat through gently, stirring occasionally.

Meanwhile, melt the butter with the oil in a frying pan. Add the halibut steaks and fry for about 8 minutes on each side or until the fish is cooked. Test with a fork: the flesh should flake easily. Transfer the steaks to a warmed serving dish and pour over the cucumber sauce. Serve hot.
Serves 4

Spinach is a healthy, colourful accompaniment to many dishes, and is particularly good with fish.

Grilled Sardines with Watercress Sauce is a simply cooked dish with a special flavour.

Fried trout with soured cream and mushroom sauce

75g/3oz flour
salt and black pepper
6 medium trout, cleaned and eyes removed
125g/4oz butter
2 Tbsp vegetable oil
375g/12oz button mushrooms, halved
1 tsp lemon juice
1 tsp paprika
300ml/10floz soured cream
1 Tbsp parsley, freshly chopped

Mix the flour with salt and pepper to taste in a polythene bag. Add the fish and shake gently to coat them with the seasoned flour.

Melt 50g/2oz of the butter with the oil in a frying pan. Add the fish, in batches, and fry for about 5 minutes on each side or until lightly browned and cooked. Test with a fork: the flesh should flake easily.

Transfer the fish to a warmed serving dish and keep hot.

Melt the remaining butter in a saucepan. Add the mushrooms and cook for 3 minutes. Stir in the lemon juice, paprika, soured cream and salt and pepper to taste and cook, stirring, for 2 to 3 minutes or until the mixture is hot but not boiling.

Pour the sauce over the fish and sprinkle with the parsley. Serve hot.
Serves 6

Baked salmon steaks with hollandaise sauce

1 Tbsp butter, softened
4 salmon steaks, thick
salt and black pepper
1 bouquet garni
12 large mushrooms
125ml/4floz dry white wine
300ml/10floz fish stock
8 large prawns, shelled and deveined
6 parsley sprigs
SAUCE
3 Tbsp dry white wine
2 large egg yolks, lightly beaten
125g/4oz unsalted butter, diced
2 tsp lemon juice
salt and pepper

Grease a flameproof dish with the softened butter. Rub the salmon steaks with salt and pepper and place in the dish. Add the bouquet garni. Remove the mushroom stalks from the caps and add the stalks to the dish. Reserve the mushroom caps. Pour the wine and the stock over the salmon. Bring to the boil, then transfer to a moderate oven (180°C/350°F or Gas Mark 4). Bake for 30 minutes, basting the

Grilled sardines with watercress sauce

12 sardines, cleaned
2 Tbsp olive oil
1 bunch watercress, finely chopped
1 Tbsp parsley, freshly chopped
250ml/8floz mayonnaise
salt and black pepper

Arrange the sardines, in one layer, in a shallow flameproof casserole or serving dish. Brush with half the olive oil. Grill for 3 to 5 minutes or until lightly browned. Turn the sardines and brush the other sides with the remaining oil. Grill for a further 3 to 5 minutes or until lightly browned and cooked. Test with a fork: the flesh should flake easily.

Meanwhile, mix together the watercress, parsley, mayonnaise and salt and pepper to taste. Put this sauce into a serving bowl.

Serve the sardines hot with the sauce.
Serves 4

salmon twice during the cooking period.

Arrange the mushroom caps and prawns around the salmon and bake for a further 5 minutes or until the salmon is cooked.

Transfer the salmon steaks to a warmed serving dish. Arrange the mushroom caps and prawns around and on top. Keep warm while you make the sauce.

Pour the wine into a heavy pan and boil rapidly until it has reduced by one third. Cool. Place the egg yolks in the top of a double boiler, or a heatproof bowl placed over a pan filled one-third full with simmering water. Beat until thick and creamy and pale yellow in colour. Add the wine and whisk again. Add the butter, piece by piece, whisking constantly until each piece has melted. When the sauce will just hold its shape, remove from the heat and whisk in the lemon juice and season to taste with salt and pepper. Spoon a little of the sauce over the steaks and serve the rest separately in a sauceboat. Garnish with the parsley sprigs and serve.
Serves 4

Beef and cheese roll with tomato sauce

3 thick white bread slices, crusts removed
4 Tbsp milk
700g/1½lb minced beef
2 eggs, lightly beaten
2 tsp dry mustard
salt and black pepper
1 tsp thyme, freshly chopped
1 onion, finely chopped
2 Tbsp parsley, freshly chopped
1 Tbsp flour
250g/8oz Mozzarella cheese, thinly sliced
25g/1oz butter, melted
SAUCE
40g/1½oz butter
2 onions, finely chopped
1 garlic clove, crushed
500g/1lb tomatoes, peeled and quartered
1 tsp sugar
salt and black pepper
4 Tbsp red wine

Put the bread in a bowl and pour over the milk. Soak for 3 minutes. Gently squeeze the bread and pour off any excess milk. Add the beef, eggs, mustard, salt and pepper to taste, the thyme, onion and parsley. Knead well together, then turn out on to a piece of greaseproof paper or foil that has been sprinkled with the flour. Using a fork, press the meat out into a thin rectangle. Cover and chill for 1 hour.

Cover the top of the meat rectangle with the cheese slices. Roll up the meat like a Swiss roll, using the paper to lift it. Place

in a shallow roasting tin with the join underneath and brush with the melted butter. Bake in a moderate oven (180°C/350°F or Gas Mark 4) for 50 minutes.

Meanwhile, make the sauce. Melt the butter in a saucepan and add the onions and garlic. Fry until the onions are soft but not brown. Add the tomatoes, sugar, salt and pepper to taste and the red wine. Simmer for 45 minutes, stirring occasionally.

Transfer the meat roll to a warmed serving dish and pour over the sauce, or serve it separately in a sauceboat.
Serves 4-6

Beef carbonnade

50g/2oz flour
salt and black pepper
1kg/2lb chuck steak, cut into 2.5cm/1in cubes
4 Tbsp vegetable oil
6 medium onions, thinly sliced
2 garlic cloves, chopped
550ml/18floz beer
1 Tbsp brown sugar
1 bouquet garni

Sift the flour and salt and pepper to taste into a polythene bag. Add the steak cubes and shake the bag to coat them.

Heat the oil in a flameproof casserole. Add the meat cubes and brown quickly on all sides. Remove from the casserole. Add the onions and garlic to the casserole and fry until the onions are soft but not brown. Return the meat to the casserole with the beer, brown sugar and bouquet garni. Cover and simmer for 2 hours or until the meat is tender.

Thirty minutes before the end of the

Above : Beef and Cheese Roll with Tomato Sauce makes a wholesome and tasty supper dish.

Overleaf: Marinated Beef Tenderloin – succulent and satisfying served with new potatoes and broccoli.

cooking, remove the lid so that the liquid will reduce. Discard the bouquet garni and serve hot, from the casserole, with buttered noodles.
Serves 4

Fillet steaks teriyaki

4 fillet steaks, about 6mm/¼in thick
25g/1oz butter
1 Tbsp vegetable oil
MARINADE
4 Tbsp sweet sake or pale dry sherry
2 Tbsp soy sauce
1 garlic clove, crushed
4 Tbsp chicken stock

Mix together the ingredients for the marinade in a shallow dish. Add the steaks and baste them well with the marinade. Leave to marinate for 30 minutes, basting occasionally.

Remove the steaks from the marinade and pat dry with kitchen paper towels. Reserve 4 tablespoons of the marinade.

Melt the butter with the oil in a frying pan. Add the steaks and fry for 1 minute on each side. Pour off all but a thin film of fat from the pan and add the marinade. Fry the steaks for a further 3 minutes on each side, basting occasionally with the pan juices. This will produce rare steaks; increase the time for medium or well done steaks.

Transfer the steaks to warmed serving dishes and spoon over the pan juices. Serve hot.
Serves 4

Marinated fillet of beef

2kg/4lb fillet of beef
salt and black pepper
8 streaky bacon rashers
MARINADE
300ml/10floz red wine
125ml/4floz tarragon vinegar
1 tsp grated nutmeg
1 tsp ground cloves
2 bay leaves
1 onion, sliced and pushed out into rings
½ lemon, thinly sliced
1 large carrot, scraped and thinly sliced
SAUCE
2 Tbsp vegetable oil
2 onions, finely chopped
1 large carrot, scraped and finely chopped
375ml/12floz beef stock
1 bouquet garni
40g/1½oz butter
1 Tbsp flour

Rub the beef with salt and pepper and place in a shallow dish. Mix together all the marinade ingredients and pour over the beef. Leave to marinate for 24 hours, turning occasionally.

Remove the beef from the marinade and pat dry with kitchen paper towels. Place the beef in a roasting tin. Strain the marinade and reserve 125ml/4fl oz.

Lay the rashers of bacon over the meat and roast in a hot oven (220°C/425°F or Gas Mark 7) for 1 hour. This will produce rare meat. If you prefer it well done, increase the cooking time by 30 minutes.

Meanwhile, make the sauce. Heat the oil in a saucepan. Add the onions and carrot and fry until the onions are soft but not brown. Stir in the reserved marinade and bring the liquid to the boil. Boil until the liquid has reduced to one-third the original quantity. Add the stock, bouquet garni and salt and pepper to taste. Cover and simmer for 30 minutes.

Blend ½ tablespoon of the butter with the flour to make a smooth paste (beurre manié). Add in small pieces to the sauce, stirring constantly, and cook until the sauce is thickened and smooth. Discard the bouquet garni and stir in the remaining butter. Pour the sauce into a sauceboat.

Discard the bacon and serve the meat with the sauce.
Serves 8

Spiced meatballs

1kg/2lb veal or beef, finely minced
1 medium onion, very finely chopped
50g/2oz fresh white breadcrumbs
1 egg, lightly beaten
2 Tbsp parsley, freshly chopped
1 Tbsp mint, freshly chopped
2 tsp oregano, freshly chopped
2 garlic cloves, crushed
½ tsp mixed spice
salt and black pepper
2 Tbsp olive oil
1 Tbsp wine vinegar
125g/4oz flour
125ml/4floz vegetable oil

Mix together the meat, onion, breadcrumbs, egg, parsley, mint, oregano, garlic, mixed spice and salt and pepper to taste. Add the olive oil and vinegar and knead together with your hands. Shape the mixture into 32 walnut-sized balls. Coat the balls with half the flour, then chill for 1 hour.

Coat the balls with the remaining flour. Heat the vegetable oil in a frying pan. Add the balls, in batches, and fry for 6 to 8 minutes or until browned and cooked through. Drain on kitchen paper towels.

Serve hot, with a tomato sauce.
Serves 4

Veal Rolls Stuffed with Chicken Livers and Herbs makes an unusual and sophisticated supper dish.

Veal rolls stuffed with chicken livers and herbs

500g/1lb veal escalopes, pounded thin
6 Tbsp flour
40g/1½oz butter
2 Tbsp vegetable oil
250ml/8floz Marsala
250ml/8floz chicken stock
STUFFING
25g/1oz butter
125g/4oz chicken livers, finely chopped
50g/2oz Proscuitto ham, chopped
1 small onion, finely chopped
1 tsp chives, freshly chopped
1 tsp parsley, freshly chopped
1 tsp marjoram, freshly chopped
1 tsp thyme, freshly chopped
salt and black pepper

First prepare the stuffing. Melt the butter in a saucepan. Add the chicken livers and fry until they are lightly browned but still soft. Remove from the heat and add the remaining stuffing ingredients with salt and pepper to taste. Mix well and leave to cool.

Cut the escalopes into 10cm/4in squares. Place a heaped tablespoonful of the chicken liver filling in the centre of each square and roll up, tucking in the sides. Tie with cotton thread. Coat the veal rolls with the flour.

Melt the butter with the oil in a frying pan. Add the rolls, in batches, and fry for about 10 minutes or until they are well browned on all sides. Remove the rolls from the pan.

Pour off all but 1 tablespoon of the fat from the pan. Add the Marsala and chicken stock and bring to the boil. Return the veal rolls to the pan and simmer gently for 15 minutes or until the meat is very tender.

Transfer the veal rolls to a warmed serving dish and keep hot. Boil the cooking liquid for about 10 minutes or until it has reduced to about 125ml/4fl oz.

Pour the liquid over the veal rolls and serve immediately.
Serves 4

Greek roast veal

3kg/6lb shoulder of veal, boned
1 garlic clove, thinly sliced
salt and black pepper
finely grated rind of 1 lemon
finely grated rind of 1 orange
1 Tbsp marjoram, freshly chopped
25g/1oz butter
1 Tbsp olive oil
2 Tbsp lemon juice
2 Tbsp orange juice
300ml/10floz dry white wine (preferably resinated Greek wine)
1 bay leaf, crumbled
lemon wedges to garnish

Lay the veal flat on a working surface. Make incisions all over the meat and insert the garlic slivers. Rub the meat with salt and pepper and sprinkle with the orange and lemon rinds and marjoram. Roll up the meat and tie with string at 2.5cm/1in intervals.

Melt the butter with the oil in a flameproof casserole. Put the veal roll in the casserole and brown on all sides. Remove from the heat.

Mix together the lemon and orange juice, the wine and bay leaf and pour over the veal. Return to the heat and bring to the boil. Cover and simmer gently for 2 hours or until the veal is tender.

Transfer the veal to a carving board. Remove the string. Garnish with the lemon wedges. Keep hot.

Skim any fat off the surface of the cooking liquid and strain it into a saucepan. Boil until it has reduced to half its original quantity. Pour into a sauceboat and serve with the meat.
Serves 6

Cantonese roast pork

1kg/2lb pork fillet
2 Tbsp vegetable oil
2½ Tbsp clear honey
MARINADE
4 Tbsp soy suace
1 Tbsp sugar
3 Tbsp dry sherry
½ tsp cinnamon
½ tsp rosemary, freshly chopped
½ tsp marjoram, freshly chopped
½ tsp monosodium glutamate (optional)
salt and black pepper
SAUCE
125ml/4floz soy sauce
4 Tbsp chilli sauce

Cut the pork fillet along the grain into strips about 15cm/6in long and 2.5cm/1in wide. Mix together the ingredients for the marinade, with salt and pepper to taste, in a shallow dish. Add the pork strips and turn them over in the marinade until well coated. Leave to marinate for 3 hours, turning the strips every 20 minutes.

Put enough water in a roasting tin to make a 2.5cm/1in layer. Place a wire rack in the tin. Arrange the pork strips on the rack, reserving the marinade. Roast in a hot oven (220°C/425°F or Gas Mark 7) for 12 minutes.

Mix the oil into the reserved marinade and brush this mixture over the pork strips. Reduce the oven temperature to moderate (180°C/350°F or Gas Mark 4) and roast the pork for a further 10 minutes.

Brush the pork strips with the honey and continue roasting for 5 minutes.

To make the sauce, mix the ingredients together well and pour into a serving bowl.

Cut the pork strips crosswise into 1cm/½in slices and serve hot with the sauce, rice and hot mustard.
Serves 4

Pork fillets with vermouth and soured cream sauce

4 medium pork fillets, beaten flat
salt
50g/2oz butter
1 garlic clove, crushed
6 black peppercorns
300ml/10floz dry vermouth
2 tsp cornflour
150ml/5floz soured cream
1 Tbsp chives, freshly chopped

Rub the fillets with the salt. Melt the butter in a frying pan. Add the pork fillets, in batches, and fry until they are lightly browned on all sides. Transfer the fillets to an ovenproof casserole.

Sprinkle the garlic and peppercorns over the fillets and pour over all but 1 tablespoon of the vermouth. Cover and bake in a moderate oven (180°C/350°F or Gas Mark 4) for 45 minutes or until the fillets are tender.

Transfer the fillets to a warmed serving dish and keep hot. Skim off any fat from the surface of the cooking liquid and strain it into a saucepan. Dissolve the cornflour in the reserved tablespoon of vermouth. Stir a little of the cooking liquid into it. Pour into cooking liquid in a thin stream, stirring, for 2 minutes or until thickened and smooth. Add the soured cream and stir well. Heat through gently without boiling.

Pour the sauce over the fillets and sprinkle with the chives.

Serve hot.
Serves 4

Fresh orange juice is just one of the ingredients in the piquant and refreshing recipe for Greek roast veal.

Pork chops with white wine and herbs

1 Tbsp oregano, freshly chopped
1 Tbsp marjoram, freshly chopped
1 garlic clove, crushed
salt and black pepper
4 large pork loin chops, about
2cm/¾in thick
50g/2oz butter
125ml/4floz dry white wine
1 tsp cornflour
1 Tbsp parsley, freshly chopped

Mix together the oregano, marjoram, garlic and salt and pepper to taste. Coat the pork chops with the herb mixture.

Melt the butter in a frying pan. Add the chops and fry for 3 minutes on each side, using tongs to turn them. Pour in half the wine and bring to the boil. Cover and cook for 30 to 40 minutes or until tender.

Transfer the chops to a warmed serving dish and keep hot. Dissolve the cornflour in the remaining wine. Stir in a little of the hot liquid and add to the pan, stirring constantly. Bring to the boil, stirring well. Simmer for 3 to 5 minutes or until thickened and smooth and pour over the chops. Sprinkle with the parsley and serve.
Serves 4

Pork and pineapple casserole

1kg/2lb pork fillets, beaten thin
1 garlic clove, halved
salt and black pepper
1 Tbsp finely grated orange rind
1½ tsp marjoram, freshly chopped
1½ tsp sage, freshly chopped
25g/1oz butter
2 medium green peppers, pith and seeds removed and cut into thin strips
300ml/10floz dry white wine
125g/4oz canned pineapple cubes, drained
1 Tbsp cornflour
2 Tbsp orange juice

Rub the pork fillets (escalopes) with the cut sides of the garlic and with salt and pepper. Discard the garlic. Lay the fillets flat on a working surface and sprinkle over the orange rind, marjoram and sage. Roll up the fillets and tie with string.

Melt the butter in a flameproof casserole. Add the green pepper strips and fry for 4 minutes, stirring frequently. Remove from the casserole.

Add the pork rolls to the casserole and brown on all sides. Add the wine, pineapple, green pepper strips and salt and pepper to taste. Bring to the boil, then

cover and simmer for 30 to 40 minutes or until the pork is cooked and tender.

Transfer the pork rolls to a warmed serving dish. Remove the string. Arrange the pineapple pieces and green pepper strips around the pork rolls. Keep hot.

Skim any fat off the surface of the cooking liquid, then strain into a saucepan. Dissolve the cornflour in the orange juice. Stir a little of the hot cooking liquid into this mixture. Return the mixture to the saucepan and stir into the cooking liquid. Bring to the boil and simmer for 5 minutes or until thickened and smooth. Pour the sauce over the pork rolls and serve.
Serves 4

Lamb with cider sauce

1 best end neck of lamb, consisting of 8 chops (carre d'agneau)
salt and black pepper
1 garlic clove, halved
2 Tbsp olive oil
2 carrots, scraped and chopped
2 small turnips, peeled and quartered
2 leeks, white part only, chopped
2 small onions, chopped
2 streaky bacon rashers, chopped
2 tsp chervil, freshly chopped
300ml/10floz chicken stock
300ml/10floz cider
4 Tbsp fresh white breadcrumbs
25g/1oz butter
2 Tbsp flour

Rub the lamb with salt and pepper and the cut sides of the garlic. Discard the garlic. Heat the oil in a large flameproof casserole. Put the meat in the casserole and brown on each side. Remove the meat.

Add the carrots, turnips, leeks, onions and bacon to the casserole and fry for 10 minutes, stirring frequently. Return the meat to the casserole and add the chervil. Pour in the stock and cider and bring to the boil. Cover and transfer to a moderate oven (180°C/350°F or Gas Mark 4). Bake for 1 hour.

Remove the casserole from the oven and transfer the meat to the rack in the grill pan, fat side up. Coat with the breadcrumbs and grill for 5 minutes or until the crumbs are evenly browned.

Meanwhile, strain the cooking liquid from the casserole into a saucepan. Discard the vegetables. Blend together the butter and flour to make a smooth paste (beurre manié) and add in small pieces to the cooking liquid. Cook, stirring constantly, for 5 minutes or until the sauce thickens and is smooth. Serve the meat on a warmed dish with the sauce.
Serves 4

Pork and Pineapple Casserole is a deliciously flavoured combination of fruit and meat which makes an ideal lunch or supper dish.

Loin of Lamb with Peas and Beans is a fresh tasting dish which tastes as good as it looks.

Loin of lamb with peas and beans

50g/2oz butter
1 Tbsp olive oil
1 medium onion, thinly sliced
125g/4oz streaky bacon, cut into strips
2kg/4lb loin of lamb, chined
500g/1lb green peas (shelled weight)
250g/8oz green beans, trimmed
150ml/5floz soured cream

Melt the butter with the oil in a roasting tin. Add the onion and bacon and fry until the onion is soft but not brown and the bacon has rendered its fat. Add the lamb and brown on all sides.

Transfer to a fairly hot oven (200°C/ 400°F or Gas Mark 6) and roast for 20 minutes.

Add the peas and beans to the roasting tin and reduce the oven temperature to warm (170°C/325°F or Gas Mark 3). Roast for a further 1 hour 10 minutes, or until the meat and vegetables are tender.

Transfer the lamb to a carving board. Strain off all but about 1 tablespoon of fat from the roasting tin. Stir the soured cream into the vegetable mixture and spoon into a warmed serving dish.

Carve the meat into thick slices and serve with the vegetables.
Serves 4-6

Saddle of lamb with mint

3kg/6lb saddle of lamb
salt and black pepper
8 lemon thyme sprigs
50g/2oz fresh brown breadcrumbs
2 Tbsp mint, freshly chopped
1 small onion, grated
15g/½oz butter, melted
175ml/6floz chicken stock
½ Tbsp butter
1 Tbsp flour

Rub the meat with salt and pepper. Insert the lemon thyme sprigs between the meat and the fat. Place the saddle, fat side uppermost, on a rack in a roasting tin.

Mix together the breadcrumbs, mint, onion and salt and pepper to taste. Stir in the melted butter. Spread this mixture evenly over the fat on the saddle.

Roast in a moderate oven (180°C/350°F or Gas Mark 4) for 1 hour. Reduce the oven temperature to cool (150°C/300°F or Gas Mark 2) and continue roasting for a further 1 to 1¼ hours or until the meat is cooked and tender. Transfer the meat to a carving board and keep hot.

Skim any fat from the surface of the cooking juices in the roasting tin. Strain the juices into a saucepan and stir in the stock. Bring to the boil. Blend the butter with the flour to make a smooth paste (beurre manié) and add to the saucepan in small pieces. Cook, stirring, until the sauce is thickened and smooth. Pour the sauce into a warmed sauceboat and serve with the meat.
Serves 6-8

Roast leg of lamb with lemon and broad bean sauce

2kg/4lb leg of lamb
4 garlic cloves, cut into slivers
salt and black pepper
2 Tbsp vegetable oil
2 egg yolks
4 Tbsp lemon juice
250ml/8floz chicken stock
500g/1lb broad beans (shelled weight)
2 tsp thyme, freshly chopped

Make slits in the lamb and insert the garlic slivers. Rub the meat with salt and pepper and place on a rack in a roasting tin. Pour over the oil and roast in a moderate oven (180°C/350°F or Gas Mark 4) for 1½ hours or until the lamb is cooked. Baste occasionally with the dripping in the roasting tin.

Meanwhile, mix together the egg yolks, lemon juice and stock in a small bowl. Cook the broad beans in boiling salted water for 10 to 15 minutes or until just tender. Drain well.

Transfer the lamb to a carving board. Remove the garlic slivers, if you like. Keep hot.

Skim off any fat from the cooking juices in the roasting tin. Add the juices to the egg yolk mixture and pour into a saucepan. Add the broad beans, thyme and salt and pepper to taste and cook gently, stirring occasionally, until the sauce is thickened and smooth. Do not let the sauce boil or it will curdle. Pour the sauce into a sauceboat and serve with the lamb.

Serves 6

Gammon with tarragon cream sauce

2kg/4lb gammon, soaked overnight
and drained
2 bay leaves
6 peppercorns
2 thyme sprigs
SAUCE
1 medium onion, finely chopped
4 Tbsp white wine
50g/2oz butter
2 Tbsp flour
300ml/10floz chicken stock
1 Tbsp tarragon, freshly chopped
salt and white pepper
150ml/¼ pint double cream

Put the gammon in a saucepan with the bay leaves, peppercorns and thyme sprigs. Cover with cold water and bring slowly to the boil. Simmer for 2 hours, skimming off any scum that rises to the surface and adding more water if necessary. Turn off the heat and leave the gammon in the water for 30 minutes.

Meanwhile, prepare the sauce. Put the onion and wine in a saucepan and bring to the boil. Simmer until the wine has evaporated, then remove from the heat.

Melt 40g/1½oz of the butter in another saucepan. Remove from the heat and stir in the flour to make a smooth paste. Gradually stir in the stock. Return to the heat and cook, stirring, for 3 to 4 minutes or until the mixture is thickened and smooth. Stir in the onion and tarragon with salt and pepper to taste. Cook for 2 minutes, stirring constantly.

Stir in the cream and remaining butter and heat through without boiling. Keep warm.

Remove the gammon from the pan. Peel off the skin and fat and carve the meat into thin slices. Arrange on a warmed serving dish and pour over the sauce. Serve hot.

Serves 6-8

Marinated liver in red wine sauce

75ml/3floz olive oil
300ml/10floz dry red wine
1 garlic clove, crushed
1 bay leaf
salt and black pepper
1kg/2lb calf's or lamb's liver,
thinly sliced
125g/4oz lean bacon, very thinly
sliced into strips
1 Tbsp parsley, freshly chopped

Mix together 4 tablespoons of the oil, the wine, garlic, bay leaf and salt and pepper to taste in a shallow dish. Add the liver slices and marinate for 30 minutes.

Heat the remaining oil in a frying pan. Add the bacon and fry until it is crisp. Drain on kitchen paper towels and keep hot. Remove the liver slices from the marinade and pat dry with kitchen paper towels. Add to the pan, in batches, and fry until lightly browned on all sides. Transfer to a warmed serving dish and keep hot.

Add the marinade to the pan. Bring to the boil and boil for 10 minutes or until reduced to about one-third of the original quantity. Add the bacon to the liver and strain over the marinade. Sprinkle with the parsley and serve hot.

Serves 4

A well-known Portuguese dish, Marinated Liver in Red Wine Sauce tastes simply delicious.

Spiced chicken with honey

50g/2oz butter
125ml/4floz clear honey
4 Tbsp prepared German mustard
1 tsp salt
1 tsp mild curry powder
2kg/4lb chicken, cut into 8 serving pieces

Spiced Chicken with Honey is very simple to prepare but tastes magnificent. Serve for lunch or supper.

Melt the butter in a saucepan and stir in the honey, mustard, salt and curry powder. Pour half the mixture into a roasting tin. Place the chicken pieces in the tin and pour over the remaining honey mixture.

Bake in a fairly hot oven (190°C/375°F or Gas Mark 5) for 1 hour or until the chicken is tender. Baste the chicken with the honey

mixture in the tin at least twice during the cooking period.

Transfer the chicken to a warmed serving dish and spoon over any honey mixture in the tin. Serve hot.
Serves 4

Mozzarella chicken

2 Tbsp vegetable oil
1 medium onion, finely chopped
500g/1lb tomatoes, peeled and chopped
2 Tbsp tomato purée
3 Tbsp water
1 Tbsp oregano, freshly chopped
salt and black pepper
6 streaky bacon rashers
25g/1oz butter
1 tsp tarragon, freshly chopped
6 chicken breasts, skinned and boned
125g/4oz Mozzarella cheese, sliced

Heat the oil in a saucepan. Add the onion and fry until it is soft but not brown. Add the tomatoes, tomato purée, water, oregano and salt and pepper to taste. Simmer for 20 minutes, stirring occasionally.

Meanwhile, fry the bacon in a frying pan until it is crisp. Drain on kitchen paper towels. Add the butter to the bacon fat in the pan. When it has melted stir in the tarragon. Add the chicken breasts and fry for 15 to 20 minutes or until tender and cooked through.

Transfer the chicken breasts to a flameproof serving dish. Place a slice of bacon on each breast and pour over the tomato sauce. Cover with the cheese slices. Grill for 4 to 5 minutes or until the cheese has melted and is lightly browned. Serve hot.
Serves 6

Chicken with prawns and asparagus

25g/1oz butter
2.5kg/5lb chicken, cut into 8 serving pieces
2 small onions, finely chopped
3 Tbsp flour
450ml/15floz chicken stock
salt and black pepper
½ tsp paprika
¼ tsp cayenne pepper
2 tsp dill, freshly chopped
1 bay leaf
2 Tbsp Madeira
500g/1lb asparagus
250g/8oz prawns (shelled weight), deveined
150ml/5floz double cream

Melt the butter in a flameproof casserole. Add the chicken pieces, in batches, and brown on all sides. Remove from the casserole.

Add the onions to the casserole and fry until they are soft but not brown. Remove from the heat and sprinkle over the flour. Stir well, then gradually stir in the stock. Add salt and pepper to taste, the paprika, cayenne, dill, bay leaf and Madeira and mix well. Return to the heat and bring to the boil, stirring.

Return the chicken pieces to the casserole. Cover and cook for 30 minutes. Add the asparagus and prawns to the casserole. Re-cover and cook for a further 30 minutes or until the chicken is tender.

Transfer the chicken pieces to a warmed serving dish. Arrange the asparagus around the chicken. Keep hot.

Stir the cream into the casserole and heat through without boiling. Discard the bay leaf and pour the sauce over the chicken and asparagus.

Serve hot.
Serves 4-6

Chicken stuffed with chicken livers, cream cheese and herbs

75g/3oz butter, softened
1 large onion, finely chopped
1x2.5kg/5lb chicken or capon
4 chicken livers, finely chopped
2 tsp thyme, freshly chopped
2 tsp marjoram, freshly chopped
2 tsp chervil, freshly chopped
1 Tbsp parsley, freshly chopped
125g/4oz cream cheese
50g/2oz fine dry breadcrumbs
salt and black pepper
SAUCE
150ml/5floz dry white wine
150ml/5floz chicken stock
150ml/5floz single cream

Melt 25g/1oz of the butter in a frying pan. Add the onion and fry until it is soft but not brown. Add the chicken livers, thyme, marjoram, chervil and parsley. Fry for a further 3 minutes, stirring frequently. Remove from the heat and allow to cool slightly, then stir in the cream cheese, breadcrumbs and salt and pepper to taste.

Stuff the chicken with the cream cheese mixture and truss. Place the chicken in a roasting tin and rub with salt and pepper. Spread with the remaining butter. Roast in a medium oven (190°C/375°F or Gas Mark 5) for 1½ hours.

Mix together the wine, stock and cream and pour into the tin around the chicken 30 minutes before the end of the cooking time.

Transfer the chicken to a warmed

serving dish and untruss. Skim any fat from the surface of the cooking liquid, adjust the seasoning and pour into a sauceboat. Serve this sauce with the chicken.
Serves 6

Marmalade duck

1x2.25kg/5lb duck
salt and black pepper
1 orange, peeled and quartered
1 bouquet garni
500g/1lb marmalade
juice of 2 oranges
1 Tbsp brandy
1 tsp cornflour
1 Tbsp water
GARNISH
2 large oranges, sliced
8 watercress sprigs

Rub the cavity in the duck with salt and pepper. Put the orange quarters and bouquet garni inside and truss the duck. Place it on a large piece of aluminium foil and spread the duck with the marmalade. Wrap the foil loosely around the duck and place on a rack in a roasting tin. Make several cuts in the bottom of the foil to allow the duck fat to drip into the roasting tin.

Roast in a very hot oven (220°C/425°F or Gas Mark 7) for 15 minutes. Reduce the oven temperature to moderate (180°C/350°F or Gas Mark 4) and continue roasting for 1½ hours, or until the juices run clear when the thigh is pierced.

Remove the foil 20 minutes before the end of roasting to allow the skin to brown. Transfer the duck to a warmed serving dish. Untruss and keep hot.

Skim any fat off the surface of the liquid in the roasting tin. Stir in the orange juice and brandy and place over heat on top of the stove. Bring to the boil, stirring. Boil for 5 minutes. Dissolve the cornflour in the water and stir a little of the hot liquid into the mixture. Stir back into the sauce. Simmer for 2 minutes, stirring, or until thickened and smooth. Strain the sauce into a sauceboat.

Arrange the orange slices and watercress around the duck and serve with the sauce.
Serves 4

Marmalade Duck – succulent duck roasted with bitter sweet marmalade and served with an orange and brandy sauce is the perfect dinner party dish.

Vegetables

Souffléd carrots

600ml/1 pint chicken stock
500g/1lb carrots, scraped and quartered
salt and white pepper
2 tsp marjoram, freshly chopped
1 tsp flour
3 eggs, separated

Bring the stock to the boil in a saucepan. Add the carrots and cook for 10 to 15 minutes or until they are tender. Drain the carrots, reserving 2 tablespoons of the stock. Purée the carrots in a blender or foodmill or push them through a sieve into a mixing bowl. Alternatively, use a potato masher. Season the carrot purée well and stir in the marjoram, flour and reserved stock. Lightly beat the egg yolks together and stir into the carrot mixture.

Beat the egg whites until they will hold a stiff peak. Fold them into the carrot mixture. Spoon into a buttered shallow baking dish and bake in a moderate oven (180°C/350°F or Gas Mark 4) for 15 minutes.

Serve hot, from the dish.
Serves 4

French beans with tomato sauce

25g/1oz butter
1 Tbsp olive oil
1 garlic clove, crushed
1 onion, finely chopped
1 small red pepper, pith and seeds removed and chopped
1 small carrot, scraped and chopped
700g/1½lb tomatoes, peeled and chopped
1 tsp sugar
salt and black pepper
500g/1lb French beans
1 Tbsp parsley, freshly chopped

Melt the butter with the oil in a saucepan. Add the garlic, onion, red pepper and carrot and fry until the onion is soft but not brown. Add the tomatoes, sugar and salt and pepper to taste. Simmer gently for 40 minutes.

Fifteen minutes before the sauce is ready, cook the beans in boiling salted water for about 10 minutes or until they are just tender. Drain well and stir them into the tomato sauce. Simmer for a further 2 minutes.

Pour the beans and sauce into a warmed serving dish and sprinkle with the parsley. Serve hot.
Serves 4

Mixed vegetables in cream sauce

1 small cauliflower, broken into flowerets
125g/4oz green peas (shelled weight)
125g/4oz green beans
4 small carrots, diced
250g/8oz asparagus
4 small button mushrooms
40g/1½oz butter
2 Tbsp flour
300ml/10floz single cream
150ml/5floz milk
salt and white pepper
2 tsp chervil, freshly chopped
1 tsp lemon juice

Cook the cauliflower, peas and beans in boiling salted water for 10 to 15 minutes or until they are tender. Add the carrot dice after about 7 minutes cooking. Meanwhile, cook the asparagus, with the tips just above the water, in gently simmering water for 10 to 15 minutes or until tender. Do not overcook the vegetables; they should be tender but still firm.

Meanwhile, cook the mushrooms in 15g/½oz of the butter in a small saucepan for 2 to 3 minutes.

Drain all the vegetables. Cut the asparagus into 2.5cm/1in pieces. Put all the vegetables in a warmed serving dish and keep hot.

Melt the remaining butter in a saucepan. Stir in the flour and cook for 1 minute. Remove from the heat and gradually stir in the cream and milk. Return to the heat and simmer, stirring constantly, until the sauce is thickened and smooth. Stir in salt and pepper to taste and the chervil.

Remove from the heat and stir in the lemon juice. Pour the sauce over the vegetables and mix well. Serve hot.
Serves 4

Rice with peas, Venetian style

1 Tbsp olive oil
175g/6oz lean bacon, chopped
50g/2oz butter
1 onion, thinly sliced
500g/1lb green peas (shelled weight)
500g/1lb Italian rice, such as Avorio
75ml/3floz dry white wine
1.2l/2 pints chicken stock, boiling
salt and black pepper
125g/4oz Parmesan cheese, grated

Heat the oil in a saucepan. Add the bacon and fry until it is crisp and golden brown. Drain the bacon on kitchen paper towels and set aside.

Fresh, crunchy carrots and cauliflowers are ideal for serving with spring dishes.

Salsify Sauteed with Herbs is an unusual vegetable dish but one that's well worth trying.

Add 25g/1oz of the butter to the fat in the pan and when it has melted add the onion. Fry until the onion is soft but not brown. Add the peas and rice and cook gently, stirring, for 5 minutes. Stir in the wine and about one-third of the boiling stock. Regulate the heat so that the mixture is bubbling all the time, and stir occasionally with a fork. When the rice swells and the liquid has been absorbed, add another one-third of the boiling stock. Add the remaining stock when that has been absorbed.

Stir in the bacon, remaining butter, salt and pepper to taste and the cheese. Mix well and cook gently for 1 minute.

Transfer to a warmed serving dish and serve hot.
Serves 4-6

Salsify sautéed with herbs

500g/1lb salsify, scraped and cut into
7.5cm/3in pieces
25g/1oz butter
1 garlic clove, crushed
1 tsp chervil, freshly chopped
1 tsp oregano, freshly chopped
2 Tbsp parsley, freshly chopped
salt and black pepper
1 tsp lemon juice

Cook the salsify in boiling salted water for about 20 minutes or until it is just tender. Drain well and keep warm.

Melt the butter in a frying pan. Add the garlic and fry for 1 minute. Add the salsify, chervil, oregano, parsley and salt and pepper to taste and fry, stirring, for 6 to 8 minutes or until the salsify is lightly browned.

Transfer to a warmed serving dish and sprinkle over the lemon juice. Serve hot.
Serves 4

Chinese fried cucumber and pineapple

2 medium cucumbers, thinly sliced
2 Tbsp vegetable oil
$\frac{1}{2}$ tsp salt
1 Tbsp vinegar
$\frac{1}{2}$ small pineapple, peeled, cored and cut into cubes
175ml/6floz water
2 tsp flour
1 tsp sugar
1 tsp soy sauce

Salt the cucumber slices and leave for 30 minutes in a colander. Rinse, drain and pat the cucumber slices dry with kitchen paper towels. Heat the oil in a frying pan.

Add the cucumber slices, salt and vinegar and cook for 4 minutes. Add the pineapple and cook for 2 minutes longer.

Mix together the water, flour, sugar and soy sauce in a small bowl, stirring well to dissolve the flour. Pour into the frying pan and cook, stirring constantly, for a further 5 minutes or until the liquid has thickened. Serve hot.

Serves 4

Spinach baked with noodles

125g/4oz butter
2 onions, finely chopped
1.5kg/3lb spinach
salt and black pepper
2 eggs, lightly beaten
375g/12oz egg noodles, cooked
75g/3oz Parmesan cheese, grated
75g/3oz dry white breadcrumbs
SAUCE
40g/1½oz butter
3 Tbsp flour
450ml/15floz milk

Melt half the butter in a frying pan. Add the onions and fry until they are soft but not brown.

Meanwhile, put the spinach in a saucepan. (Do not add any water: there should be enough left on the leaves after washing.) Cook for about 6 minutes or until the spinach is tender.

Drain the spinach well, pressing to remove all excess moisture. Chop the spinach finely and add to the onions with salt and pepper to taste. Stir in the eggs and cook gently, stirring, for 2 minutes or until the eggs are just beginning to set. Remove from the heat.

Arrange half the egg noodles in a baking dish. Sprinkle with half the cheese and cover with half the spinach mixture. Add layers of the remaining egg noodles, cheese and spinach mixture.

To make the sauce, melt the butter in a saucepan. Stir in the flour and cook, stirring, for 1 minute. Gradually stir in the milk and bring to the boil, stirring constantly. Simmer, stirring, until the sauce is thickened and smooth. Add salt and pepper to taste, then pour over the top of the spinach and noodle mixture.

Melt the remaining butter in a frying pan. Add the breadcrumbs and remove from the heat. Spoon over the sauce. Bake in a fairly hot oven (190°C/375°F or Gas Mark 5) for 20 minutes or until the breadcrumb topping is golden brown. Serve hot, from the dish.

Serves 4-6

Spinach Baked with Noodles makes a filling lunch or supper dish, ideal for vegetarians.

Above : Mangetout are a variety of pea of which the pod is also eaten.
Right : Thinly sliced pickled cucumbers in a vinegar and dill dressing can be used as a garnish, or served with meat and poultry dishes.

Salads

Pickled cucumber salad

3 cucumbers
salt and white pepper
1 Tbsp sugar
125ml/4floz white vinegar
1 Tbsp lemon juice
3 Tbsp dill, freshly chopped

Score down the skin of the cucumbers with a fork to make ridges. Cut the cucumbers into very thin slices. Put the slices in a shallow dish and sprinkle generously with salt. Cover and leave for 1 hour.

Meanwhile, mix together the sugar, vinegar, lemon juice and salt and pepper to taste. Stir well to dissolve the sugar.

Drain the cucumber slices and pat dry with kitchen paper towels. Arrange the slices in a serving dish and pour over the vinegar dressing. Sprinkle with the dill and chill for at least 3 hours before serving.
Serves 4

Mangetout salad

4 dried Chinese mushrooms, soaked in cold water for 30 minutes
1 Tbsp vegetable oil
175g/6oz can bamboo shoots, drained and thinly sliced
375g/12oz mangetouts
1 celery stalk, cut into 5cm/2in pieces
1 tsp salt
½ tsp sugar
1 tsp white wine vinegar

Drain the mushrooms, reserving 1 tablespoon of the soaking liquid. Thinly slice the mushrooms. Heat the oil in a frying pan. Add the mushroom slices and bamboo shoots and fry for 2 minutes, stirring constantly. Add the mangetouts and celery and cook, stirring, for 2 minutes.

Sprinkle the salt, sugar, vinegar and reserved soaking liquid over the vegetables. Cook, stirring, for a further 2 minutes or until the liquid has evaporated.

Transfer the vegetables to a serving dish and allow to cool. Then chill for at least 1 hour before serving.
Serves 4

Avocado chervil salad

4 avocados
125ml/4floz lemon juice
salt and black pepper
1 Tbsp chervil, freshly chopped

Halve the avocados and remove the stones. Peel off the skin and cut the flesh into thin slices. Place the slices in a shallow glass dish and pour over the lemon juice. Season with salt and pepper and toss the slices so they are well coated with the lemon juice.

Sprinkle with the chervil and serve.
Serves 4

Fennel, chicory and tomato salad

1 head Florence fennel, thinly sliced
1 head chicory, thinly sliced
4 tomatoes, thinly sliced
4 Tbsp olive oil
2 Tbsp white wine vinegar
1 garlic clove, crushed
salt and black pepper

Put the fennel, chicory and tomato slices in a salad bowl. Mix together the oil, vinegar, garlic and salt and pepper to taste in a screwtop jar and shake well. Pour this dressing over the vegetables and toss to coat them. Chill before serving.
Serves 4-6

Picnic Fare

Veal cake

500g/1lb lean veal, cut into 1cm/½in cubes
500g/1lb cooked ham, cut into 1cm/½in cubes
salt and black pepper
2 Tbsp parsley, freshly chopped
1 tsp celery salt
2 tsp thyme, freshly chopped
6 hard-boiled eggs, sliced
450ml/15floz jellied veal or chicken stock

Mix together the veal, ham, salt and pepper to taste, the parsley, celery salt and thyme in a mixing bowl. Layer the meat mixture and egg slices in a 1l/2 pint pudding basin, beginning and ending with the meat mixture. Pour over the stock. Cover with foil and secure with string.

Put the basin in a saucepan and add enough water to come halfway up the sides. Bring to the boil and simmer for 2 hours, adding more water when necessary.

Remove the basin from the pan and take off the foil cover. Cool, then chill for at least 4 hours or until set. Dip the bottom of the basin quickly in hot water and turn out the cake on to a plate. Wrap carefully and chill until you leave for the picnic.

Serves 6

Meat loaf

1.5kg/3lb lean beef, minced
4 bason rashers, finely chopped
2 tsp thyme, freshly chopped
salt and black pepper
1 garlic clove, crushed
4 Tbsp red wine
1 Tbsp wine vinegar
1 tsp prepared French mustard

Mix together the beef, bacon, thyme, salt and pepper to taste, the garlic, wine, vinegar and mustard in a mixing bowl. Knead well together with your hands. Put the meat mixture into a greased 1kg/2lb loaf tin and smooth the top. Place the tin in a roasting tin and add enough water to come half way up the tin.

Bake in a warm oven (170°C/325°F or Gas Mark 3) for 1 hour. Cover the loaf tin with foil to prevent the top browning too much and continue baking for 30 minutes.

Remove the tin from the oven and pour off any fat. Leave to cool for 1 hour, then turn out of the tin and wrap in aluminium foil. Chill for at least 6 hours before packing in the picnic basket.

Serves 6-8

Bean salad

250g/8oz dried red kidney beans, soaked overnight
175g/6oz dried white beans, such as haricot or butter beans, soaked overnight
125g/4oz dried chick-peas, soaked overnight
1 red pepper, pith and seeds removed and chopped
8 spring onions, chopped
1 garlic clove, crushed
3 Tbsp chives, freshly chopped
2 Tbsp white wine vinegar
6 Tbsp olive oil
1 Tbsp lemon juice
salt and black pepper

Drain the beans and chick-peas and put in a saucepan. Cover with fresh water and bring to the boil. Simmer for 40 minutes or until the beans and chick-peas are tender.

Drain well and allow to cool.

Put the beans and chick-peas in a salad bowl and add the red pepper, spring onions, garlic and chives. Mix together the vinegar, oil, lemon juice and salt and pepper to taste in a screwtop jar. Shake well and pour over the bean mixture. Toss well so all the ingredients are coated with the dressing.

Spoon into a plastic container and chill for at least 30 minutes before packing into the picnic basket.

Serves 6-8

Ideal for a spring picnic, this cold Meat Loaf goes well in sandwiches or with salads.

Potato salad with herbs

500g/1lb potatoes
8 spring onions, chopped
1 Tbsp parsley, freshly chopped
2 tsp marjoram, freshly chopped
1 tsp lemon thyme, freshly chopped
1 tsp chervil, freshly chopped
6 Tbsp olive oil
2 Tbsp wine vinegar
salt and black pepper
½ tsp sugar

Cook the potatoes in boiling salted water until tender, then drain well and slip off the skins. Allow to cool until you are able to handle them comfortably. Cut the potatoes into 1cm/½in cubes.

Put the potato cubes in a mixing bowl and add the spring onions, parsley, marjoram, lemon thyme and chervil. Mix together the oil, vinegar, salt and pepper to taste and the sugar in a screwtop jar, shaking well to dissolve the sugar. Pour this dressing over the potato mixture and toss well until all the potato cubes are coated.

Pack into a polythene container and chill well before putting in the picnic basket.
Serves 4

Pissaladières

PASTRY
250g/8oz flour
½ tsp salt
75g/2oz butter
50g/2oz vegetable fat
3-4 Tbsp iced water
FILLING
4 Tbsp olive oil
6 medium onions, thinly sliced
2 garlic cloves, crushed
3 large tomatoes, peeled, seeded and finely chopped
1 Tbsp tomato purée
50g/2oz can anchovies, drained and chopped
27 black olives, stoned
salt and black pepper

First make the pastry cases. Sift the flour and salt into a mixing bowl. Add the butter and vegetable fat and cut them into small pieces, then rub into the flour until the mixture resembles breadcrumbs. Mix in enough water to form a dough. Chill for 30 minutes.

Roll out the dough to an oblong about 2cm/¾in thick. Cut out nine circles using a 10cm/4in pastry cutter. Use the circles to line nine greased tartlet tins. Place the tins on a baking sheet, line each with crumpled greaseproof paper and fill with enough

Delicious savoury tartlets, Pissaladières are ideal for picnics but make tasty snacks any time of the day.

baking beans to cover the base.

Bake the tartlet cases in a fairly hot oven (190°C/375°F or Gas Mark 5) for 10 minutes, then remove the greaseproof paper and beans. Bake for a further 5 minutes or until the pastry is golden brown. Cool in the tins for 5 minutes, then carefully remove and cool completely on a wire rack.

Meanwhile, make the filling. Heat the oil in a frying pan. Add the onions and garlic and fry until the onions are soft but not brown. Stir in the tomatoes, tomato purée, anchovies, olives and salt and pepper to taste. Cook for a further 2 to 3 minutes.

Remove from the heat and spoon the filling into the pastry cases. Allow to cool before wrapping in foil for the picnic.
Makes 9 tartlets

Picnic patties

40g/1½oz butter
½ small onion, finely chopped
125g/4oz mushrooms, sliced
2 Tbsp flour
salt and black pepper
¼ tsp grated nutmeg
1 tsp oregano, freshly chopped
¼ tsp Tabasco sauce
125ml/4floz single cream
250g/8oz cooked chicken, diced
125g/4oz cooked ham, diced
PASTRY
350g/12oz flour
¼ tsp salt
300g/10oz butter
6-7 Tbsp iced water
1 egg yolk
2 Tbsp milk

First make the pastry. Sift the flour and salt into a mixing bowl. Add 50g/2oz of the butter and cut it into small pieces with a knife. Rub the butter into the flour until the mixture resembles breadcrumbs. Stir in enough of the water to bind the mixture, then knead to a dough. Chill for 15 minutes.

Roll out the dough to an oblong about 6mm/¼in thick. Place the remaining butter, in an oblong piece about 6mm/¼in thick, in the centre of the dough. Fold over the dough in half to enclose the butter. Turn so the open end faces you and roll out to an oblong. Fold the oblong in three and turn again so the open end faces you. Roll out to an oblong once again and fold in three. Chill for 15 minutes.

Repeat the rolling, folding, turning and chilling twice.

During the final chilling, prepare the filling. Melt 25g/1oz of the butter in a

saucepan. Add the onion and fry until it is soft but not brown. Add the mushrooms and cook for 3 to 4 minutes. Remove the vegetables from the pan.

Add the remaining butter to the pan. When it has melted, stir in the flour, salt and pepper to taste, the nutmeg, oregano and Tabasco. Cook, stirring, for 1 minute. Remove from the heat and gradually stir in the cream. Return to the heat and cook, stirring, until the mixture is thickened and smooth. Remove from the heat.

Stir the cooked onion and mushrooms into the sauce with the chicken and ham. Leave to cool slightly.

Roll out the dough to a circle about 3mm/⅛in thick. Cut out twelve 13cm/5in circles with a pastry cutter. Mix together the egg yolk and milk. Brush around the edges of the circles.

Spoon equal amounts of the mushroom filling on to the centre of each pastry circle and fold over the dough to make half-moon shapes. Press the edges together to seal. Brush with the egg yolk glaze.

Place the patties on a baking sheet and bake in a hot oven (220°C/425°F or Gas Mark 7) for 20 to 25 minutes or until the pastry is puffed up and golden brown.

Cool on a wire rack before wrapping.
Makes 12 patties

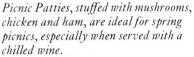

Picnic Patties, stuffed with mushrooms, chicken and ham, are ideal for spring picnics, especially when served with a chilled wine.

Stuffed cucumbers

2 cucumbers, peeled and halved lengthways
salt and black pepper
125g/4oz can tuna fish, drained and flaked
125g/4oz cooked ham, diced
2 hard-boiled eggs, finely chopped
50g/2oz cream cheese
4 pickled onions, finely chopped
2 Tbsp mayonnaise
1 Tbsp prepared mustard

Scoop the seeds from the cucumber using the point of a teaspoon. Cut away some of the flesh, leaving a shell about 6mm/¼in thick. Rub the cucumber shells with salt and leave for 15 minutes.

Meanwhile, mix together the tuna fish, ham, eggs, cream cheese, pickled onions, mayonnaise, mustard and salt and pepper to taste.

Rinse the cucumber shells in cold water and wipe dry with kitchen paper towels. Fill each half with the tuna fish mixture and place the halves together again. Wrap in foil and chill for at least 2 hours before the picnic.

To serve, slice crosswise on a slant into 2.5cm/1in thick slices.
Serves 4-6

Light Dishes

Jellied grape and cheese salad

juice of 2 lemons
15g/½oz gelatine
2 Tbsp hot water
175g/6oz black grapes, halved and seeded
CHEESE JELLY
175g/6oz cream cheese
125g/4oz cottage cheese, sieved
150ml/5floz soured cream
15g/½oz gelatine
2 Tbsp hot water
2 tsp grated orange rind
4 Tbsp orange juice
4 Tbsp white wine
1 tsp sugar

Add enough water to the lemon juice to make it up to 550ml/18floz. Dissolve the gelatine in the hot water and strain into the lemon juice mixture. Pour about a 6mm/¼in layer of the lemon juice mixture into a greased 1.8l/3 pint mould. Chill until set, then arrange the grape halves, cut sides up, on the lemon jelly. Pour over another 6mm/¼in layer and chill uhtil set. (This will hold the grape halves in position.) Cover with the remaining lemon mixture and chill until set.

Meanwhile, mix together the cream cheese, cottage cheese and soured cream. Dissolve the gelatine in the hot water and strain into the cheese mixture. Add the orange rind, orange juice, wine and sugar. Mix well and chill until on the point of setting.

Spoon the cheese jelly on top of the lemon jelly in the mould and return to the refrigerator. Chill for a further 2 hours or until completely set.

To unmould, dip the bottom of the mould quickly in hot water. Turn the salad out onto a serving dish.
Serves 6

Baked potatoes stuffed with blue cheese

4 large potatoes
150ml/5floz soured cream
125g/4oz blue cheese, crumbled
2 Tbsp chives, freshly chopped
pinch cayenne pepper
salt and black pepper

Bake the potatoes in a fairly hot oven (190°C/375°F or Gas Mark 5) for 1½ hours or until they are tender. Remove from the oven and allow to cool slightly, then cut off a thin slice from the top of each one. Scoop

out the cooked potato to within 6mm/¼in of the skin, being careful not to break the skin.

Mash together the cooked potato, soured cream, cheese, chives, cayenne and salt and pepper to taste. Stuff the potato skins with the potato and cheese mixture, piling it up on top.

Place the filled potatoes on a baking sheet and return to the oven. Bake for 10 to 15 minutes or until the filling is lightly browned. Serve hot.
Serves 4

Lobster Newburg

2x1kg/2lb cooked lobsters, shells split,
claws cracked and grey sac removed
40g/1½oz butter
125ml/4floz sherry
¼ tsp grated nutmeg
salt and black pepper
3 egg yolks
250ml/8floz double cream
8 hot slices of buttered toast

Remove the lobster meat from the shells and claws and dice it. Melt the butter in a frying pan. Add the lobster meat and fry for 4 minutes, stirring frequently. Pour over the sherry and simmer for 3 minutes. Stir in the nutmeg and salt and pepper to taste.

Beat the egg yolks and cream together in a small bowl. Gradually stir into the lobster mixture and cook for 3 to 4 minutes or until the mixture is thick. Do not boil or the mixture will curdle.

Spoon over the hot toast and serve.
Serves 4

The fruit and cheese in this Jellied Grape and Cheese Salad make a light and refreshing main course for a springtime luncheon or buffet table.

Shrimp chow mein

oil for deep frying
250g/8oz thin egg noodles, cooked and drained
10 dried Chinese mushrooms, soaked in hot water for 20 minutes
2 Tbsp vegetable oil
2 carrots, scraped and thinly sliced on the diagonal
250g/8oz bean sprouts
250g/8oz can water chestnuts, drained and sliced
125ml/4floz chicken stock
1 Tbsp sake or dry sherry
1 Tbsp soy sauce
375g/12oz prawns or shrimps (shelled weight), deveined

Heat the oil in a deep-frying pan until it reaches 185°C/360°F on a deep fat thermometer, or until a cube of stale bread dropped into the oil turns golden in 50 seconds.

Lower the noodles into the oil and fry for 3 to 4 minutes or until they are golden brown. Drain on kitchen paper towels and arrange on a warmed serving dish. Keep hot.

Drain the mushrooms and slice into strips. Heat the oil in a frying pan. Add the mushrooms, carrots, bean sprouts and water chestnuts. Fry for 5 minutes, stirring constantly. The vegetables should be tender but still crisp.

Stir in the stock and sake or sherry and bring to the boil. Stir in the soy sauce and prawns or shrimps. Cover and simmer for 3 to 5 minutes or until the fish are heated through.

Make a well in the centre of the noodles and spoon in the fish mixture.

Serve hot.

Serves 2-3

Cheese and ham soufflé

125g/4oz butter
2 Tbsp fine dry white breadcrumbs
75g/3oz flour
500ml/16floz milk, scalded
125g/4oz Cheddar cheese, grated
75g/3oz cooked ham, finely chopped
6 eggs, separated
salt
½ tsp paprika
pinch cayenne pepper

Place a double piece of greaseproof paper around the outside of a 1.2l/2 pint soufflé dish and tie on with string. The paper should come 5cm/2in above the rim of the dish. Use 25g/1oz of the butter to grease the inside of the paper collar and the dish.

Place the breadcrumbs in the dish and swirl round so that all sides are coated. Tip out excess.

Melt the remaining butter in a saucepan. Stir in the flour and cook, stirring, for 1 minute. Remove from the heat and gradually stir in the milk. Return to the heat and cook, stirring until the mixture is thickened and smooth. Remove from the heat and add the cheese and ham. Stir until the cheese has melted.

Lightly beat the egg yolks in a small bowl. Add to the cheese mixture. Season with salt, the paprika and cayenne.

Beat the egg whites until they will hold a stiff peak. Fold into the cheese and ham mixture and spoon into the soufflé dish. Bake in a fairly hot oven (190°C/375°F or Gas Mark 5) for 35 minutes or until the top is puffed up and lightly browned.

Remove the paper collar and serve immediately.

Serves 4

Ricotta cheese omelet with tomato sauce

1½ Tbsp olive oil
1 small onion, finely chopped
250g/8oz tomatoes, peeled and chopped
50g/2oz tomato purée
1 tsp oregano, freshly chopped
salt and black pepper
½ tsp sugar
250g/8oz ricotta cheese
4 Tbsp Parmesan cheese, grated
4 large eggs
15g/½oz butter

Heat the oil in a frying pan. Add the onion and fry until it is soft but not brown. Stir in the tomatoes, tomato purée, oregano, sugar and salt and pepper to taste and simmer gently for 20 minutes, stirring occasionally.

Meanwhile, mix together the ricotta cheese, 3 tablespoons of the Parmesan cheese and salt and pepper to taste in a mixing bowl.

Beat the eggs with the remaining Parmesan cheese and salt and pepper to taste in another bowl.

Melt the butter in a frying pan or omelet pan. Pour in the egg mixture and cook the omelet for about 5 minutes, lifting the set edges to allow the liquid egg mixture to run onto the pan. Spoon the cheese mixture onto half of the omelet and fold over the other half. Continue cooking for about 3 minutes.

Slide the omelet onto a warmed serving dish and pour over the tomato sauce. Serve hot.

Serves 2

Shrimp Chow Mein is something slightly different – and delicious – for a special occasion.

Desserts

Golden gooseberry bake

1kg/2lb gooseberries, topped and tailed
125g/4oz sugar
4 Tbsp water
50g/2oz cornflakes
50g/2oz rolled oats
75g/3oz butter
2 Tbsp golden syrup
1 Tbsp brown sugar

Put the sugar and water in a saucepan and boil for 4 minutes to make a syrup. Add the gooseberries and poach gently for 15 minutes or until the fruit is just softening. Remove from the heat and pour the gooseberries into a baking dish.

Put the cornflakes in a mixing bowl and crush them lightly with your hand. Stir in the rolled oats.

Melt the butter with the golden syrup in a saucepan. Stir into the cornflake mixture and spoon on top of the gooseberries. Sprinkle with the brown sugar and bake in a moderate oven (180°C/350°F or Gas Mark 4) for 20 minutes or until the top is lightly browned. Serve hot, with cream.
Serves 4-6

Green melon mousse

1 medium honeydew melon
300ml/10floz double cream
4 Tbsp Grand Marnier
finely grated rind of 1 lemon
pinch ground ginger
4 eggs, separated
125g/4oz brown sugar
25g/1oz gelatine
4 Tbsp warm water

Halve the melon and discard the seeds. Scoop out the flesh and purée it in a blender or foodmill, or push it through a nylon sieve. Stir in the cream, Grand Marnier, lemon rind and ginger.

Beat the egg yolks and brown sugar together in the top of a double saucepan or in a heatproof bowl placed over a saucepan of hot water. Beat until the mixture is thick and pale and will make a ribbon trail on itself when the beater is lifted.

Stir the egg yolk mixture into the melon mixture. Dissolve the gelatine in the warm water and strain into the melon mixture. Mix well.

Beat the egg whites until they will hold a stiff peak. Fold them into the melon mixture. Spoon into a serving dish and chill for at least 3 hours or until completely set.
Serves 8

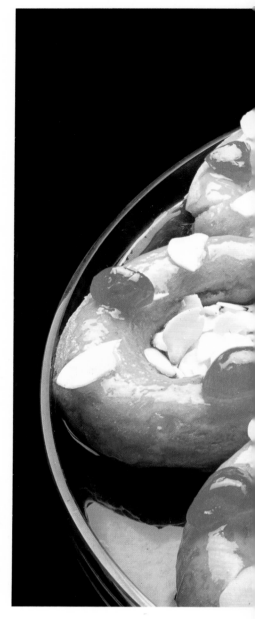

Rum babas

25g/1oz fresh yeast
1 Tbsp lukewarm milk
250g/8oz flour
pinch salt
2 Tbsp sugar
2 eggs
50g/2oz butter, melted
SAUCE
175g/6oz sugar
375ml/12floz water
150ml/5floz rum
12 glacé cherries, halved
50g/2oz slivered almonds

Mash the yeast and milk together to make a smooth paste. Leave in a warm draught-free place for 15 minutes or until frothy. Sift the flour into a mixing bowl and add the salt and sugar. Make a well in the

centre and add the yeast mixture, eggs and melted butter. Mix together well, then beat the dough with your hand, lifting and slapping it vigorously. The dough should be quite sticky, but if it is too difficult to handle, add a little flour.

When the dough begins to lose its stickiness, turn it out onto a lightly floured surface and continue kneading until it is elastic. Roll the dough into a ball and place in a greased bowl. Cover and let rise in a warm place for 1½ to 2 hours or until almost doubled in bulk.

Knock back and knead the dough for 2 minutes. Divide the dough into 12 portions. Gently press each portion into a greased baba mould, filling it only two-thirds full. Leave in a warm place to rise for 35 to 45 minutes or until the dough has risen to the tops of the moulds.

Bake in a fairly hot oven (190°C/375°F or Gas Mark 5) for 15 minutes or until lightly browned and cooked. Test by inserting a skewer: it should come out clean. Unmould the babas onto a wire rack and allow to cool slightly.

Meanwhile, make the sauce. Dissolve the sugar in the water in a small saucepan. Bring to the boil and boil for 5 minutes. Remove from the heat and allow to cool slightly.

Stir most of the rum into the syrup. Arrange the babas, in one layer, in a shallow dish. Pour over the rum syrup and leave to soak for 30 to 40 minutes, basting occasionally.

Carefully transfer the babas to a wire rack and allow to drain. Place the babas on a serving dish and sprinkle with the remaining rum. Decorate with the glacé cherries and almonds.

Makes 12

Rich and light-textured, Rum Babas are soaked in a rum-flavoured syrup and glazed with apricot jam. Although strictly pastries, they make mouth-watering desserts.

Steamed banana pudding

125g/4oz butter
125g/4oz castor sugar
180g/6oz flour
¼ tsp salt
1 tsp baking powder
2 eggs
3 large bananas, mashed
2 Tbsp milk
grated rind of 1 orange

Cream the butter and sugar together until the mixture is light and fluffy. Sift the flour, salt and baking powder into a mixing bowl. Add the eggs to the butter mixture, one at a time, adding a tablespoonful of the flour mixture with each one. Beat well. Fold in the remaining flour mixture, then mix in the mashed bananas, milk and orange rind.

Spoon into a greased 1.2l/2 pint pudding basin and cover with a piece of greased greaseproof paper and aluminium foil. Make a pleat in the centre of the paper and foil top to allow the pudding to expand. Tie securely under the rim of the basin.

Steam for 1½ hours, adding more water as necessary.

Turn the pudding out of the basin onto a warmed serving dish. Serve hot with custard sauce.

Serves 4-6

Steamed Banana Pudding is a warm, homely dessert for one of those chillier spring days.

Honey and cream cheese pie

250g/8oz cream cheese
25g/1oz sugar
3 Tbsp clear honey, warmed
2 eggs, lightly beaten
1 tsp ground cinnamon
PASTRY
180g/6oz flour
pinch salt
90g/3oz butter
2-3 Tbsp iced water

First make the pastry. Sift the flour and salt into a mixing bowl. Add the butter and cut into small pieces with a knife. Then rub the butter into the flour until the mixture resembles breadcrumbs. Stir in enough water to bind the mixture together and knead to a dough. Chill for 30 minutes.

Roll out the dough and use to line a 20cm/8in flan dish. Bake blind for 5 minutes in an oven preheated to fairly hot (190°C/375°F or Gas Mark 5).

Beat the cream cheese, sugar and honey together with a wooden spoon. Add the eggs and mix well. Pour into the pastry case and return to the oven. Bake for 30 to 35 minutes or until lightly browned.

Sprinkle over the cinnamon and leave to cool before serving.

Makes one 20cm/8in pie

Coffee soufflé

6 sponge finger biscuits, broken into small
pieces
75ml/3floz coffee-flavoured liqueur
40g/1½oz butter
25g/1oz icing sugar
25g/1oz flour
175ml/6floz hot milk
4 Tbsp strong black coffee
1 Tbsp sugar
5 egg yolks
6 egg whites
125g/4oz walnuts, chopped

Put the sponge finger biscuits in a shallow
dish and sprinkle over half the liqueur.
Leave to soak for 30 minutes, then mash
with a fork. Grease a 1.5l/2½ pint soufflé
dish with 15g/½oz of the butter. Sprinkle
in the icing sugar and tip the dish to coat
the sides and bottom completely.

Melt the remaining butter in a saucepan.
Remove from the heat and stir in the flour.
Gradually stir in the milk. Return to the
heat and cook, stirring, until the mixture
is thickened and smooth. Stir in the
remaining liqueur, the black coffee and
the mashed biscuits. Leave to cool to
lukewarm.

Beat the sugar into the egg yolks, then
add the coffee mixture and beat well
together. Beat the egg whites until they
will form a stiff peak. Fold into the coffee
mixture. Spoon the mixture into the
soufflé dish and sprinkle the walnuts on
top.

Bake in a moderate oven (180°C/350°F
or Gas Mark 4) for 30 to 45 minutes or
until well risen and lightly browned.

Serve immediately.

Serves 4-6

Rhubarb and banana cream

1kg/2lb rhubarb, cut into 2.5cm/1in pieces
250g/8oz sugar
4 Tbsp water
2 bananas, mashed
250ml/8floz double cream
2 egg whites

Put the rhubarb, sugar and water in a
saucepan and cook the rhubarb for 15
minutes or until it is soft. Remove from the
heat and drain the rhubarb. Put it in a
mixing bowl and allow to cool.

Stir the mashed bananas and cream into
the rhubarb. Beat the egg whites until they
will hold a stiff peak, then fold them
into the rhubarb mixture. Spoon into a
serving dish and chill for at least 4 hours
before serving.

Serves 6

Orange rice mould

250g/8oz round-grain rice, soaked in cold
water for 30 minutes and drained
500ml/16floz milk
juice and grated rind of 1 orange
3 oranges, peel and pith removed,
segmented and chopped
2 Tbsp sugar
250ml/8floz double cream, stiffly
whipped

Put the rice and milk in a saucepan and
bring to the boil. Cover and cook gently
for 15 minutes or until the rice is tender
and all the milk has been absorbed.

Turn the rice into a mixing bowl and
stir in the orange juice and rind. Leave to
cool for 5 minutes. Stir in half the orange
segments and the sugar, then fold in the
cream. Spoon into a plain or decorative
greased 1l/1½ pint ring mould. Smooth the
top.

Chill for at least 2 hours or until the

*Coffee Soufflé makes a delicate light
dessert for a dinner party.*

Grasshopper Pie – a marvellous combination of biscuits, marshmallows liqueurs and cream go together to make this rich, elegant pie.

mixture into the paper circle to make a layer about 6mm/¼in thick. Using a 2.5cm/1in nozzle, pipe the remaining meringue mixture around the edge of the circle in decorative swirls to form a case.

Bake in a cool oven (150°C/300°F or Gas Mark 2) for 1 hour. Turn off the oven and leave the meringue inside for a further 30 minutes.

Remove from the oven and leave to cool, then carefully peel off the paper. Place the meringue case on a serving plate.

To make the filling, cream the butter until it is soft, then beat in the icing sugar until the mixture is light and fluffy.. Stir in the egg yolks, food colouring, orange rind, liqueur if using and cream. Spoon into the meringue case and arrange the orange slices on top. Serve immediately.
Serves 6–8

Grasshopper pie

36 chocolate cream biscuits, crushed
25g/1oz butter, melted
30 large marshmallows
175ml/6floz milk
4 Tbsp crème de menthe
4 Tbsp crème de cacao (clear)
250ml/8floz double cream, stiffly whipped

Combine the crushed biscuits and melted butter and press into the bottom and sides of a greased 23cm/9in pie dish.

Melt the marshmallows in the milk in a saucepan, stirring frequently. Remove from the heat and stir in the liqueurs. Allow the mixture to cool, then fold in the whipped cream. Spoon into the crumb shell and chill for at least 4 hours before serving.
Makes one 23cm/9in pie

Oriental fruit salad

125ml/4floz clear honey
75ml/3floz Kirsch
10 dried figs, coarsely chopped
20 dried or fresh dates, halved and stoned
50g/2oz whole unblanched hazelnuts
50g/2oz whole unblanched almonds
1 medium honeydew melon

Mix together the honey and kirsch in a shallow dish. Add the figs, dates and nuts and stir well. Leave to soak for 4 hours, stirring occasionally.

Halve the melon and scoop out the seeds. Cut away the rind and cut the flesh into cubes. Stir the melon cubes into the nut mixture and pour into a serving dish. Chill for at least 1 hour before serving.
Serves 6

mixture feels firm. Turn out on to a serving plate and fill the centre with the remaining orange segments.
Serves 4

Lemon and orange meringue cake

5 egg whites
300g/10oz caster sugar
2 tsp grated lemon rind
½ tsp lemon essence
FILLING
75g/3oz unsalted butter, softened
375g/12oz icing sugar
2 egg yolks
2 drops orange food colouring
grated rind of ½ orange
1 Tbsp orange-flavoured liqueur (optional)
2 Tbsp double cream
4 oranges, peel and pith removed and sliced

Draw a 23cm/9in circle on a piece of non-stick silicone paper. Put the paper on a baking sheet.

Beat the egg whites until they will hold a stiff peak. Beat in 50g/2oz of the sugar, a teaspoon at a time, and continue beating for 1 minute or until the mixture is very stiff and glossy. Carefully fold in the remaining sugar, the grated lemon rind and lemon essence.

Spoon or pipe one-third of the meringue

Home Baking

Quick bread

15g/½oz fresh yeast
300ml/10floz lukewarm water
375g/12oz flour
125g/4oz wholemeal flour
1 tsp salt
1 Tbsp cracked wheat

Mash the yeast and 1 tablespoon of the water together to make a smooth paste. Leave in a warm, draught-free place for 15 minutes or until frothy. Sift the flour into a mixing bowl and add the wholemeal flour and salt. Make a well in the centre and add the yeast mixture and remaining water. Gradually draw the flour into the liquid, mixing to a dough.

Turn the dough out of the bowl and knead for 3 minutes. Shape into a loaf and place in a greased 500g/1lb loaf tin. Cover the tin and leave to rise in a warm, draught-free place for 1 to 1½ hours or until risen to the top of the tin.

Sprinkle the top of the loaf with the cracked wheat and bake in a very hot oven (220°C/425°F or Gas Mark 7) for 15 minutes. Reduce the oven temperature to hot (190°C/375°F or Gas Mark 5) and bake for a further 25 to 30 minutes.

To test if the loaf is cooked, tip it out of the tin and rap the bottom with your knuckles. It should sound hollow.
Makes one 500g/1lb loaf

Wholewheat bread

25g/1oz fresh yeast
900ml/1½ pints lukewarm water
1.5kg/3lb stone-ground wholewheat flour
1 Tbsp salt
2 Tbsp honey
1 Tbsp vegetable oil

Mash the yeast and 1½ tablespoons of the water together to make a smooth paste. Leave in a warm, draught-free place for 15 minutes or until frothy. Put the flour and salt into a mixing bowl and make a well in the centre. Add the yeast mixture, honey, remaining lukewarm water and oil. Gradually draw the flour into the liquid, mixing to a dough.

Turn the dough out of the bowl and knead for 10 minutes or until elastic and smooth. Return to the bowl and sprinkle the dough with a little flour. Cover and let rise in a warm, draught-free place for 1 to 1½ hours or until almost doubled in bulk.

Knock back and knead the dough again for about 10 minutes. Cut it into four pieces and shape each piece into a loaf. Put into four greased 500g/1lb loaf tins. Alternatively, put the dough into well-greased,

Quick Bread can be made when you are short of time since it requires only one rising and little kneading.

clay flower pots for an unusual shape. Cover and let rise in a warm place for 30 to 45 minutes or until risen to the tops of the tins.

Bake in a very hot oven (240°C/475°F or Gas Mark 9) for 15 minutes. Reduce the oven temperature to hot (220°C/425°F or Gas Mark 7) and bake for a further 25 to 30 minutes. To test if the loaves are cooked, tip them out of the tins and rap the bottoms with your knuckles. They should sound hollow.

Cool on a wire rack.

Makes four 500g/1lb loaves

Streusel kuchen

15g/½oz fresh yeast
1 Tbsp lukewarm water
250g/8oz flour
½ tsp salt
¼ tsp ground ginger
½ tsp grated lemon rind
2 Tbsp sugar
150ml/5floz lukewarm milk
50g/2oz butter, melted
1 egg, lightly beaten
TOPPING
50g/2oz digestive biscuits, crushed
2 Tbsp sugar
1 tsp ground cinnamon
50g/2oz butter, softened

Streusel-Kuchen, a yeast cake from Germany, is ideal buttered, for a mid-morning or tea-time snack.

Mash the yeast and water together to make a smooth paste. Leave in a warm, draught-free place for 15 minutes or until frothy. Sift the flour into a mixing bowl with the salt and ginger. Add the lemon rind and sugar and make a well in the centre. Pour in the yeast mixture, the milk, melted butter and egg. Gradually draw the flour into the liquid, mixing to a dough.

Turn the dough out of the bowl and knead for 3 minutes or until it is smooth and elastic. Return to the bowl, cover and let rise in a warm place for 1 to 1½ hours or until almost doubled in bulk.

Knock back and knead the dough again for about 3 minutes. Let it rest for 10 minutes, then roll it out to a square about 2.5cm/1in thick. With your hands, shape the dough into a rectangle about 5cm/2in thick. Place it in a greased 1kg/2lb loaf tin.

Mix together all the ingredients for the topping, using your fingers. Sprinkle the topping over the dough and let rise in a warm place for about 30 minutes or until the dough has risen to the top of the tin.

Bake in a moderate oven (180°C/350°F or Gas Mark 4) for 40 to 45 minutes or until the kuchen is risen and the topping is golden brown.

Remove from the tin and cool on a wire rack.

Makes one 1kg/2lb loaf

Orange yeast buns

15g/½oz fresh yeast
2 Tbsp lukewarm water
125ml/4floz milk
150g/5oz butter
500g/1lb flour
1 tsp salt
125g/4oz sugar
2 eggs, lightly beaten
25g/1oz butter, melted
75g/3oz currants
grated rind of 2 large oranges
1 Tbsp chopped mixed peel
¼ tsp ground cinnamon
ICING
250g/8oz icing sugar
2 Tbsp orange juice

Mash the yeast and water together to make a smooth paste. Leave in a warm, draught-free place for 15 minutes or until frothy.

Meanwhile, scald the milk in a saucepan. Remove from the heat and add the butter. When the butter has melted, leave to cool to lukewarm.

Sift the flour, salt and half the sugar into a mixing bowl. Make a well in the centre and add the yeast mixture, the milk and butter mixture and the eggs. Gradually draw the flour into the liquid, mixing to a dough.

Turn the dough out of the bowl and knead for about 10 minutes or until elastic and smooth. Return to the bowl, cover and let rise in a warm place for 1 to 1½ hours or until doubled in bulk.

Knock back and knead the dough again for about 2 minutes. Roll out the dough into a square. Brush with the melted butter, then sprinkle over the remaining sugar, the currants, orange rind, mixed peel and cinnamon. Roll up like a Swiss roll. Cut the roll into 4cm/1½in thick slices and place these on a greased baking sheet. Leave a little space between the slices to allow for expansion. Let rise in a warm place for 20 minutes or until the slices are touching each other.

Bake in a fairly hot oven (190°C/375°F or Gas Mark 5) for 30 to 35 minutes or until the buns are golden brown.

Remove the buns from the oven and leave to cool slightly.

Meanwhile, mix together the icing sugar and orange juice. Brush over the warm buns, then, when they are cool enough to handle, transfer them to a wire rack to cool completely.

Makes 10-15 buns

Orange Yeast Rolls may be cut in half and spread with butter and jam. Serve with freshly percolated coffee for a real treat.

Summer

The irony of summer is that when food is at its most
abundant, we don't always feel like cooking, or eating for
that matter! So we've included a large selection of cold
soups, ice-creams and salads for crisp, cool meals that are
quick to prepare and tempting to eat, plus some long, cool
drinks to refresh you while you're making them. Eating
outdoors, however, is such a popular pastime that even the
most undomesticated of guests will be volunteering to
cook food on a barbecue; and the aroma and flavour of meat
cooked over charcoal is enough to tempt the most jaded
palate. Summer is not only the time for making hay—but
also jam—while the sun shines, and capturing the flavour of
fresh fruits in delicious home-made preserves. With these
recipes and some for those inevitably not-so-warm evenings,
you can make the most of what summer has to offer and
have time to enjoy it.

What's best in season

Fruit:

Apples	Figs	Melons	Pineapples
Apricots	Gooseberries	Nectarines	Plums
Bananas	Grapes	Oranges	Raspberries
Bilberries	Grapefruit	Passionfruit	Redcurrants
Blackberries	Lemons	Papayas	Rhubarb
Blackcurrants	Limes	Pawpaws	Strawberries
Blueberries	Loganberries	Peaches	Whitecurrants
Cherries	Mangoes	Pears	

Vegetables:

Asparagus	Celery	Marrows	Runner beans
Aubergines	Courgettes	Mushrooms	Spinach
Avocados	Cucumbers	Onions	Sweetcorn
Beetroot	Fennel	Peas	Swiss chard
Broad beans	French beans	Peppers	Tomatoes
Cabbages	Globe artichokes	Potatoes	Watercress
Calabrese	Kohlrabi	Pumpkin	
Carrots	Lettuces	Radishes	

Herbs:

Basil	Coriander	Marjoram	Sage
Bay	Dill	Mint	Summer savory
Chervil	Fennel	Parsley	Tarragon
Chives	Lemon balm	Rosemary	Thyme

Nuts:

Almonds

Fish:

Bass	Haddock	Perch	Shrimps
Bream	Hake	Pike	Sole
Brill	Halibut	Plaice	Trout
Carp	Herring	Prawns	Turbot
Crab	Lobster	Salmon	Whitebait
Crayfish	Mackerel	Salmon trout	Whiting
Eel	Mullet	Sardine	

Poultry:

Available fresh or frozen
all year round

Game:

Grouse	Pigeon	Rabbit	Venison
Hare	Quail	Snipe	

Meat and offal:

Available fresh or frozen
all year round

Appetizers

Spinach salad

250g/8oz spinach, coarsely chopped
8 lean bacon rashers, grilled until crisp
and crumbled
2 large avocados, peeled, halved, stoned
and chopped
DRESSING
6 Tbsp olive oil
salt and black pepper
½ tsp dry mustard
1 garlic clove, crushed
2 Tbsp white wine vinegar
1 Tbsp lemon juice

Put all the dressing ingredients in a screw-top jar and shake well.

Mix together the spinach, bacon and avocados in a salad bowl. Add the dressing and toss well until the salad ingredients are coated with the dressing. Serve immediately.

Serves 4

Mackerel fillets with mustard sauce

2 large mackerel, cleaned
1 Tbsp lemon juice
75g/3oz butter
1½ Tbsp French mustard
2 egg yolks
1 Tbsp cider vinegar
salt and black pepper
2 Tbsp mixed herbs, freshly chopped

Lay each mackerel on a piece of greased aluminium foil. Sprinkle with the lemon juice and wrap the fish loosely, envelope-style, so they are completely enclosed. Place the parcels on a baking sheet and bake in a moderate oven (180°C/350°F or Gas Mark 4) for 20 minutes or until the mackerel is cooked.

Meanwhile, prepare the sauce. Cream the butter until it is soft and fluffy. Beat together the mustard, egg yolks, vinegar and salt and pepper to taste. Gradually beat the mustard mixture into the butter. Mix in the herbs. Spoon the sauce into a serving bowl and chill.

When the mackerel is cooked, remove it from the oven and open the parcels. Pour any cooking juices into a bowl and reserve. Gently scrape off the skin and cut each fish into four fillets, removing the bones. Arrange the fillets in a shallow serving dish and strain over the reserved cooking juices. Allow to cool, then chill for at least 2 hours before serving with the sauce.

Serves 4

Eggs in tomato shells

6 large tomatoes, peeled
salt and black pepper
2 Tbsp olive oil
1 small onion, finely chopped
2 tsp basil, freshly chopped
1 Tbsp tomato purée
6 eggs, hard-boiled
4 Tbsp mayonnaise
watercress

Cut a circle from the stalk end of each tomato so there is a hole big enough to insert an egg. Scoop out the pulp and seeds, reserving them with the lids. Season the insides of the tomato shells with salt and pepper.

Heat the oil in a saucepan. Add the onion and fry until it is soft but not brown. Add the reserved tomato pulp and seeds, the tomato lids, basil, tomato purée and salt and pepper to taste. Cover and simmer for 15 to 20 minutes.

Remove from the heat and allow to cool. Strain to extract seeds.

Place a hard-boiled egg in each tomato shell and arrange on a serving dish. Chill for 20 minutes.

Stir the mayonnaise into the tomato mixture. Spoon over the eggs and garnish the dish with watercress. Serve with brown bread and butter.

Serves 6

The rich, distinct flavour of Mackerel Fillets served with Mustard Sauce makes a really tasty first course.

Eels in herb sauce

75g/3oz butter
225g/8oz spinach, chopped
1 tsp tarragon, freshly chopped
3 Tbsp parsley, freshly chopped
1 tsp sage, freshly chopped
2x500g/1lb eels, skinned, cleaned and cut
into 8cm/3in pieces
salt and black pepper
300ml/10floz white wine
3 egg yolks
1 Tbsp lemon juice

Melt the butter in a frying pan. Add the spinach, tarragon, parsley and sage and fry lightly. Add the eel pieces and mix together well. Add salt and pepper to taste with the wine and bring to the boil. Cover and simmer for 10 to 15 minutes or until the eel pieces are tender. Remove from the heat.

Beat the egg yolks until well mixed, then beat in 4 tablespoons of the hot liquid. Stir the egg mixture into the frying pan and add the lemon juice.

Turn into a serving dish and allow to cool. Chill for at least 2 hours before serving.
Serves 6-8

Tomato aspic

350ml/12floz hot chicken stock
350ml/12floz tomato juice
2 Tbsp tomato purée
¼ tsp sugar
1 egg shell, crushed
1 egg white, lightly beaten
salt and white pepper
15g/½oz gelatine
watercress

Line a large sieve with a scalded piece of muslin and place it over a large mixing bowl.

Put 300ml/10floz of the chicken stock and the tomato juice in a saucepan. Stir in the tomato purée, sugar, egg shell, egg white and salt and pepper to taste. Bring to the boil, whisking constantly. Remove from the heat.

Dissolve the gelatine in the remaining chicken stock. Strain it into the mixture in the saucepan and stir well. Pour the mixture through the muslin-lined sieve. If it is not absolutely clear, strain it again into another bowl.

Pour into a decorative mould and allow to cool, then chill for at least 2 hours or until completely set.

Unmould onto a serving dish and garnish with watercress.
Serves 4

Crab and avocado mousse

3 large avocados
2 Tbsp mayonnaise
1 tsp lemon juice
2 eggs, hard-boiled and chopped
salt and white pepper
4 spring onions, chopped
20g/¾oz gelatine
4 Tbsp hot water
125g/4oz crabmeat, flaked
125ml/4floz double cream
½ tsp curry powder
watercress

Halve the avocados and remove the stones. Peel off the skin and cut the flesh into cubes. Place in the goblet of an electric blender with the mayonnaise, lemon juice, eggs, salt and pepper to taste and the spring onions. Blend to a smooth purée.

Dissolve the gelatine in the hot water and strain 3 tablespoons into the avocado mixture. Stir well.

Pour half the avocado mixture into a greased 600ml/1 pint mould and smooth the top. Chill for 15 minutes.

Combine the remaining gelatine with the crabmeat, cream and curry powder. Spoon over the avocado mixture in the mould, and top with the remaining avocado mixture. Smooth the top and chill for 4 hours or until completely set.

Unmould onto a serving dish and garnish with watercress.
Serves 4-6

Guacamole ring

3 large avocados
3 Tbsp mayonnaise
juice of 1 lemon
1 tsp prepared French mustard
2 tsp Worcestershire sauce
2 Tbsp tomato purée
¼ tsp cayenne pepper
salt and black pepper
300ml/10floz double cream, stiffly
whipped
25g/1oz gelatine
4 Tbsp warm water
FILLING
500g/1lb prawns or shrimps (shelled
weight), deveined
1 medium green pepper, pith and seeds
removed and thinly sliced
2 small red peppers, pith and seeds
removed and thinly sliced
2 Tbsp lemon juice
3 Tbsp chives, freshly chopped

Halve the avocados and remove the stones. Scoop out the flesh into a mixing bowl and mash in the mayonnaise, lemon juice,

Crab and Avocado Mousse makes a luxurious fish course for a summer dinner party.

Simple and inexpensive, Marinated Mushrooms may also be served on cocktail sticks.

mustard, Worcestershire sauce, tomato purée, cayenne and salt and pepper to taste. Fold in the cream.

Dissolve the gelatine in the water, then strain into the avocado mixture. Mix well. Turn into a greased 23cm/9in ring mould. Chill for at least 4 hours or until the mixture is firm to the touch.

Mix together the prawns or shrimps, green and red pepper slices and lemon juice with salt and pepper to taste.

Turn out the avocado ring onto a serving dish and fill the centre with the pepper mixture. Arrange the remainder around the ring. Sprinkle with the chives and either serve immediately or put in the refrigerator until required.
Serves 8-10

Marinated mushrooms

500g/1lb small button mushrooms, stalks removed
MARINADE
1 tsp salt
3 black peppercorns, coarsely crushed
2 tsp dill, freshly chopped
4 Tbsp tarragon vinegar
1 Tbsp lemon juice
4 Tbsp olive oil

Mix together the marinade ingredients in a shallow dish. Add the mushrooms and stir well. Cover and leave to marinate for 2 hours, stirring occasionally.

Drain the mushrooms, discarding the marinade, and pile in a serving dish. Serve lightly chilled.
Serves 4

Prawns in tomato sauce

500g/1lb prawns (shelled weight), deveined
salt
¼ tsp ground ginger
1½ tsp cornflour
75ml/3floz vegetable oil
SAUCE
1½ Tbsp butter
3 medium tomatoes, peeled and quartered
2½ Tbsp soy sauce
2 Tbsp tomato purée
2 tsp cornflour
75ml/3floz chicken or beef stock
2 Tbsp sherry
1 tsp sugar

Put the prawns in a shallow dish. Sprinkle with salt, the ginger and cornflour and rub into the shellfish with your fingertips. Heat the oil in a frying pan and add the fish. Fry, stirring constantly, for 2 minutes. Remove from the pan with a slotted spoon. Keep hot.

Pour off the oil from the pan and add the butter. When it has melted add the tomato quarters. Fry for 2 minutes. Stir in the soy sauce and tomato purée and cook, stirring, for a further 30 seconds.

Mix together the cornflour, stock, sherry and sugar and pour into the frying pan. Cook, stirring, until the mixture thickens slightly.

Return the prawns to the pan and stir to coat them with the sauce. Cook for 1 to 2 minutes to heat them through, then serve, with boiled rice.
Serves 4

Soups

Gazpacho

3 slices brown bread, cut into 2.5cm/1in
cubes
300ml/10floz tomato juice
2 garlic cloves, finely chopped
½ cucumber, peeled and finely chopped
1 green pepper, pith and seeds removed
and finely chopped
1 red pepper, pith and seeds removed
and finely chopped
1 large onion, finely chopped
750g/1½lb tomatoes, peeled, seeded
and finely chopped
75ml/3floz olive oil
2 Tbsp red wine vinegar
salt and black pepper
1 tsp marjoram, freshly chopped
1 tsp basil, freshly chopped
ice cubes

Put the bread cubes in a mixing bowl and
pour over the tomato juice. Leave to soak
for 5 minutes, then mash to be sure they
are completely saturated. Put the bread
cubes and some of the tomato juice in a
blender goblet and add the garlic, cucumber, peppers, onion, and tomatoes. Blend
to a smooth purée. Alternatively, purée the
ingredients in a foodmill.

Pour the mixture into the mixing bowl
with the remaining tomato juice and add
the oil, vinegar, salt and pepper to taste
and the herbs. Mix well. The soup should
be the consistency of single cream, so add
more tomato juice if necessary.

Pour into a serving bowl or soup tureen
and chill for at least 1 hour. Just before
serving, stir the soup well and drop in a
few ice cubes. Serve with small bowls of
croutons, chopped hard-boiled egg,
chopped cucumber, onion and olives.
Serves 4

Cucumber and beer soup

125ml/4floz soured cream
350ml/12floz light ale
1 medium cucumber, peeled and
finely chopped
salt
1 garlic clove, crushed
½ tsp sugar
1 tsp paprika

Mix together the soured cream and ale in
a mixing bowl. Add the cucumber, salt to
taste, the garlic and sugar. Mix well. Pour
into a serving bowl and chill for at least 1
hour. Serve sprinkled with paprika.
Serves 6

Iced carrot and orange soup

25g/1oz butter
1 large onion, thinly sliced
3 Tbsp flour
900ml/1½ pints chicken stock
600ml/1 pint fresh orange juice
2 Tbsp chives, freshly chopped
salt and black pepper
pinch grated nutmeg
pinch ground allspice
500g/1lb carrots, scraped and cut into
2.5cm/1in pieces

Melt the butter in a saucepan. Add the
onion and fry until it is soft but not brown.
Remove from the heat and stir in the flour.
Gradually stir in the stock, then the orange
juice. Return to the heat and simmer, stirring, until thickened and smooth. Stir in
the chives, salt and pepper to taste, the
nutmeg, allspice and carrots.

Cover and simmer for 1 hour, stirring
occasionally. Allow to cool.

Purée the soup in an electric blender or
foodmill, or push through a sieve. Chill
for at least 2 hours before serving.
Serves 6

Cucumber and Beer Soup is a refreshing summer soup with an unusual flavour.

Lobster bisque

2 x 700g/1½lb lobsters, body shell split and
claws cracked
90g/3½oz unsalted butter
2 celery stalks, finely chopped
1 carrot, scraped and finely chopped
½ onion, finely chopped
1 tsp thyme, freshly chopped
pinch cayenne pepper
salt and white pepper
3 Tbsp brandy
250ml/8floz dry white wine
600ml/1 pint fish stock
1 Tbsp sherry
600ml/1 pint milk
50g/2oz flour
4 Tbsp double cream

Discard the small sac at the back of the
lobsters' heads, inside the shells. If there
is any coral (red roe), reserve it. Remove
the meat from the body shells and claws
and cut it into very small pieces. Reserve
the shells.

Melt 40g/1½oz of the butter in a saucepan. Add the celery, carrot, onion, thyme,
cayenne and salt and pepper to taste. Cook
until the vegetables are soft but not brown.

Heat 2 tablespoons of the brandy in a
ladle and set alight. Pour into the saucepan.
When the flames have died away, add the
wine and stock. Bring to the boil, then
cover and simmer for 20 minutes.

Purée the vegetable and wine mixture
by pushing it through a sieve or using an
electric blender or foodmill. Return to the
saucepan. Crush the lobster shells using a
pestle and mortar or an electric blender.
Add to the saucepan and simmer for 25
minutes.

Meanwhile, mix the lobster meat with
the coral, if any, and the sherry.

Melt the remaining butter in a saucepan.
Add the flour and mix to a smooth paste.
Remove from the heat and gradually stir
in the milk. Return to the heat and cook,
stirring, until the mixture is thickened and
smooth. Strain the wine and lobster shell
mixture and add the strained liquid to the
milk mixture. Stir well, cover and simmer
for 30 minutes.

Stir in the lobster and sherry mixture
and remaining brandy. Taste and adjust
the seasoning if necessary. Reheat gently
and stir in the cream. Pour into a warm
tureen and serve hot.
Serves 4-6

*Rich and creamy, Lobster Bisque is a
perfect hors d'oeuvre for a formal
dinner party.*

Main Dishes

Plaice fillets in asparagus and mushroom sauce

8 plaice fillets, skinned
salt and black pepper
300ml/10floz dry white wine
100g/4oz flour
2 eggs, lightly beaten
75g/3oz dry white breadcrumbs
50g/2oz butter
Parsley sprigs and lemon wedges to serve,
SAUCE
125g/4oz mushrooms, thinly sliced
1 Tbsp water
1 Tbsp lemon juice
25g/1oz butter
1½ Tbsp flour
250ml/8floz single cream
salt and white pepper
15 thin asparagus tips, cooked

Fold four of the fish fillets in half and place in a greased shallow baking dish. Sprinkle with salt and pepper and pour over the wine. Cover the dish and poach in a moderate oven (180°C/350°F or Gas Mark 4) for 25 to 30 minutes. Test with a fork: the flesh should flake easily.

Meanwhile, cut the remaining fillets into three, lengthways. Coat the pieces with the flour, then with egg and then with breadcrumbs. Melt the butter in a frying pan. Place the fillets in the pan and fry for 2 to 3 minutes on each side or until golden brown. Remove from the heat and keep warm.

Remove the dish from the oven. Strain off the liquid and reserve it. Arrange the poached fillets in the centre of a warmed serving dish. Surround with the fried fillets. Keep hot.

To make the sauce, put the mushrooms, water and lemon juice in a saucepan. Simmer for 4 to 5 minutes. Remove the mushrooms from the pan with a slotted spoon. Discard the cooking liquid. Melt the butter in the saucepan and stir in the flour. Cook, stirring, for 1 minute. Remove from the heat and gradually stir in the reserved poaching liquid and cream. Return to the heat and cook, stirring, until the sauce is thickened and smooth. Add salt and pepper to taste with the asparagus tips and mushrooms. Cook gently until the asparagus is heated through, then pour the sauce over the fish. Garnish with the parsley sprigs and lemon wedges and serve.

Serves 4-6

Bream with bananas

1 x 1kg/2lb bream, cleaned and gutted
2 Tbsp olive oil
salt and black pepper
1 tsp ground ginger
300ml/10floz dry white wine
juice of 1 lemon
1 large bay leaf
1 small onion, finely chopped
50g/2oz butter
5 large bananas
2 Tbsp flour
Chervil sprigs and lemon wedges, to serve

Rub the fish with the oil and sprinkle with salt and pepper and the ginger. Place it in a greased baking dish and leave in a cool place for 20 minutes.

Mix together the wine, lemon juice, bay leaf and onion. Pour this over the fish. Bake in a moderate oven (180°C/350°F or Gas Mark 4) for 30 to 40 minutes. Test with a fork: the flesh should flake easily.

Ten minutes before the fish is cooked, melt 25g/1oz of the butter in a frying pan. Add the bananas and fry for 6 minutes, turning frequently to brown evenly. Drain on kitchen paper towels and keep hot.

Transfer the fish to a warmed serving dish and surround with the bananas. Keep hot.

Strain the fish cooking liquid into a saucepan. Blend the remaining butter and the flour to make a smooth paste (beurre manié). Add this in small pieces to the cooking liquid and simmer, stirring, until the sauce is thickened and smooth. Pour the sauce over the fish and garnish with the chervil sprigs and lemon wedges.

Serves 4

Herrings in butter sauce

75g/3oz flour
salt and black pepper
6 herrings, filleted
75g/3oz butter
2 tsp lemon juice
1 Tbsp parsley freshly chopped

Mix together the flour with salt and pepper on a plate. Dip the herrings in this seasoned flour to coat on both sides.

Melt the butter in a frying pan. Add the herrings, in batches, and fry for 3 minutes on each side or until lightly browned and cooked. Test with a fork: the flesh should flake easily.

Transfer the herrings to a warmed serving dish. Spoon over the lemon juice and then the pan juices. Sprinkle with the parsley and serve.

Serves 4

Fresh asparagus, served either on its own or incorporated with other foods, is one of the delights of summer.

Lobster with whisky and cream

2 x 1kg/2lb cooked lobsters, shells split,
claws cracked and grey sac removed
50g/2oz butter
1 small onion, finely chopped
salt and black pepper
4 Tbsp whisky
125ml/4floz double cream
1 Tbsp parsley, freshly chopped

Remove the lobster meat from the shells
and cut it into 2.5cm/1in pieces. Reserve
the shells.

Melt the butter in a frying pan. Add the
onion and fry until it is soft but not brown.
Stir in the lobster meat with salt and
pepper to taste.

Warm the whisky in a small pan. Remove
from the heat and pour into the frying pan.
Ignite. When the flames have died, cover
the pan and cook gently for 5 minutes.

Stir in the cream and heat through
gently. Spoon the lobster mixture into the
reserved shells and sprinkle over the
parsley. Serve immediately.

Serves 4

Salmon with sauce verte

1 x 4kg/8lb salmon, cleaned
salt and black pepper
4 Tbsp olive oil
1 Tbsp grated lemon rind
2 bay leaves, crumbled
1 Tbsp parsley, freshly chopped
2 tsp thyme, freshly chopped
4 Tbsp dry white wine
SAUCE
2 Tbsp watercress, freshly chopped
4 Tbsp spinach, freshly chopped
2 Tbsp parsley, freshly chopped
450ml/15floz mayonnaise
4 Tbsp double cream
1 Tbsp lemon juice
salt and black pepper

Rub the inside of the salmon with salt and
pepper. Grease a sheet of aluminium foil
large enough to enclose the salmon with
2 tablespoons of the oil. Place the salmon
on the greased foil and sprinkle over the
lemon rind, bay leaves, parsley and thyme.
Fold up the two ends of the foil and pour
the remaining oil and the wine over the
fish. Fold the foil over the top so that the
fish is securely enclosed. Place on a baking
sheet and bake in a warm oven (170°C/
325°F or Gas Mark 3) for 1¼ to 1½ hours or
until cooked. Test with a fork: the flesh
should flake easily.

Unwrap the salmon and carefully transfer it to a flat working surface. Discard the
foil and cooking juices. Gently skin the
salmon, being careful not to break up the
flesh. Leave to cool completely, then place
on a serving platter.

Meanwhile, make the sauce. Wash the
watercress, spinach and parsley and place
in a saucepan. Cook in the water clinging
to the leaves, and stirring, for 6 minutes.
Place in the goblet of a blender. Blend to
a purée and cool.

Mix together the mayonnaise, cream,
lemon juice and salt and pepper to taste.
Add the puréed green mixture and mix
well. Pour the sauce into a sauceboat and
serve with the salmon.

Serves 12

Ocean rolls

4 white fish fillets, skinned
1 Tbsp lemon juice
2 Tbsp butter
1 spring onion, finely chopped
125g/4oz shrimps or prawns (shelled
weight), deveined
125g/4oz crabmeat, flaked
4 Tbsp sweetcorn kernels
1 tsp dill, freshly chopped
salt and black pepper
4 Tbsp double cream
350ml/12floz dry white wine
1 bay leaf
1 small onion, sliced
1 Tbsp flour

Lay the fillets on a flat working surface
and sprinkle with the lemon juice. Melt
half the butter in a frying pan. Add the
spring onion and fry for 2 minutes. Stir in
the shrimps or prawns, crabmeat, sweetcorn, dill, salt and pepper to taste and the
cream. Cook gently, stirring constantly,
for 3 minutes.

Remove from the heat. Spoon equal
amounts of the shrimp mixture onto each
fish fillet, pressing it on with your fingertips. Roll up each fillet like a Swiss roll
and tie with string.

Bring the wine to the boil in a saucepan.
Add the bay leaf and onion, then place the
fish rolls in the liquid, in one layer. Simmer
for 10 minutes. Turn the rolls over carefully and simmer for a further 10 minutes.

Transfer the rolls to a warmed serving
dish and remove the string. Keep hot.

Strain the cooking liquid and return to
the pan. Boil until reduced to one-third of
the original quantity. Blend the remaining
butter and the flour to a smooth paste
(beurre manié) and add in small pieces to
the cooking liquid, stirring constantly.
Simmer, stirring, until thickened and
smooth. Pour over the fish and serve.

Serves 4

Sole Veronique

500g/1lb Dover sole fillets, skinned and
halved
salt and black pepper
1 large onion, thinly sliced
1 bay leaf, crumbled
250ml/8floz dry white wine
4 Tbsp water
25g/1oz butter
25g/1oz flour
125ml/4floz milk
4 Tbsp double cream
250g/8oz green grapes, peeled, halved
and seeded

Rub the fish pieces with salt and pepper
and arrange in a greased baking dish.
Sprinkle over the onion and bay leaf and
pour over the wine and water. Bake in a
moderate oven (180°C/350°F or Gas Mark
4) for 15 to 20 minutes or until cooked.
Test with a fork: the flesh should flake
easily.

Transfer the fish to a warmed serving dish.
Keep hot while you make the sauce. Strain
the cooking liquid and reserve 125ml/4floz.

Melt the butter in a saucepan. Add the
flour and cook, stirring, for 1 minute.
Remove from the heat and gradually stir in
the milk and reserved cooking liquid.
Return to the heat and simmer, stirring,
until thickened and smooth. Stir in the
cream and heat through gently.

Pour the sauce over the fish and arrange
the grapes around the edge of the dish.
Serve immediately.
Serves 4

*Salmon with Sauce Verte – an
extravagant but splendid main course
for a summer day.*

Red mullet with tomato sauce

4 Tbsp olive oil
1kg/2lb tomatoes, peeled, seeded and coarsely chopped
2 garlic cloves, crushed
1 Tbsp thyme, freshly chopped
1 bay leaf
salt and black pepper
250g/8oz black olives, stoned
2 lemons, cut into 12 slices
12 small red mullet, cleaned and scaled with heads left on

Heat the oil in a large frying pan. Add the tomatoes, garlic, thyme, bay leaf, and salt and pepper to taste.

Simmer for 15 to 20 minutes or until the mixture is very thick.

Stir in the olives and lemon slices. Spoon half the sauce into another large frying pan. Place six fish in each pan and turn them over in the sauce until they are well coated.

Cover the pans and cook, turning the fish occasionally, for 15 to 20 minutes or until cooked. Test with a fork: the flesh should flake easily.

Discard the bay leaf and serve hot on a bed of boiled rice.
Serves 6

Turbot with orange

4 turbot steaks
salt and black pepper
grated rind and juice of 2 oranges
grated rind and juice of 1 lemon
50g/2oz butter
1 orange, thinly sliced

Put the turbot steaks, in one layer, in a shallow flameproof dish. Sprinkle over salt and pepper, the orange rind and juice and the lemon rind and juice. Leave to marinate for 1 hour.

Cut the butter into small pieces and dot over the fish. Grill for 5 to 8 minutes on each side or until cooked. Test with a fork: the flesh should flake easily.

Transfer the turbot steaks to a warmed serving dish and pour over the juices in the dish. Garnish with the orange slices and serve.
Serves 4

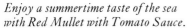

Enjoy a summertime taste of the sea with Red Mullet with Tomato Sauce.

Provençale beef stew

1.5kg/3lb lean chuck steak, cut into
5cm/2in cubes
250g/8oz streaky bacon, cut into
2.5cm/1in strips
100g/4oz flour
250g/8oz mushrooms, sliced
700g/1½lb tomatoes, peeled, seeded
and chopped
1 garlic clove, crushed
1 tsp grated orange rind
1 Tbsp parsley, finely chopped
1 bouquet garni
175ml/6floz beef stock
10 black olives, stoned and halved
MARINADE
300ml/10floz dry white wine
4 Tbsp brandy
salt
6 black peppercorns
1 tsp thyme, freshly chopped
1 bay leaf
1 garlic clove, crushed
4 medium onions, thinly sliced
4 medium carrots, scraped and sliced

Mix together the marinade ingredients in a large bowl. Add the beef cubes and baste them thoroughly. Cover and marinate in the refrigerator for at least 12 hours, basting occasionally.

Blanch the bacon strips in boiling water for 10 minutes. Drain well and pat dry with kitchen paper towels.

Remove the beef cubes from the marinade and pat dry with kitchen paper towels. Strain the marinade, reserving the vegetables but discarding the peppercorns and bay leaf.

Put the flour in a polythene bag and add the beef cubes. Shake so they are all coated with flour. Put two or three bacon strips on the bottom of a flameproof casserole. Spoon in some of the marinated vegetables, mushrooms and tomatoes. Cover with a layer of beef and sprinkle with the garlic, orange rind and parsley. Add the bouquet garni. Continue making layers of bacon, vegetables and beef cubes, ending with a layer of bacon. Pour in the reserved marinating liquid and stock and scatter over the olives.

Bring to the boil on top of the stove, then transfer to a warm oven (170°C/325°F or Gas Mark 3). Cook for 4 hours or until the meat is very tender.

Remove from the oven and skim any fat from the surface. Taste and adjust the seasoning. Discard the bouquet garni and serve hot.

Serves 6-8

Provençal Beef Stew needs only to be accompanied by a crisp, green salad for a light but sustaining meal.

Veal Escalopes with Lemon Sauce is a light summer dish originating from Italy.

Veal escalopes with lemon sauce

4 veal escalopes, pounded thin
4 Tbsp lemon juice
salt and black pepper
65g/2½oz butter
175ml/6floz dry white wine or chicken stock
1 Tbsp flour
1 large lemon, thinly sliced

Put the escalopes in a shallow dish and sprinkle with 2 tablespoons of the lemon juice. Leave to marinate for 30 minutes, then pat dry with kitchen paper towels. Rub the escalopes with salt and pepper.

Melt 50g/2oz of the butter in a frying pan. Add the escalopes and fry for 3 to 4 minutes on each side or until lightly browned. Remove the escalopes from the pan.

Add the remaining lemon juice to the pan with the wine or stock and bring to the boil. Boil for 5 minutes. Return the escalopes to the pan and cook for 1 minute. Blend the remaining butter with the flour to make a smooth paste. Add this in small pieces to the pan, stirring constantly, and simmer until the sauce is thickened and smooth.

Transfer the veal and sauce to a warmed serving dish and garnish with the lemon slices. Serve hot.
Serves 4

Sukiyaki

1kg/2lb fillet steak, cut across the grain into very thin slices
250g/8oz can Shirataki noodles, drained
125g/4oz small spinach leaves, blanched
500g/1lb flat mushrooms, stalks removed and halved
1 large carrot, scraped and cut into 5cm/2in strips
12 spring onions, cut into 5cm/2in pieces
1 canned bamboo shoot, drained, halved and thinly sliced
250ml/8floz dashi or chicken stock
125ml/4floz sake or dry sherry
4 eggs
25g/1oz beef suet or chilled vegetable fat
175ml/6floz soy sauce
50g/2oz soft brown sugar

Arrange the steak, noodles, spinach, mushrooms, carrot, spring onions and bamboo shoot on a serving dish.

Pour the stock and sake or sherry into a small bowl. Break an egg into each of four individual serving bowls and beat lightly with a fork.

Heat a chafing dish or fondue pot over a spirit burner at the table. When the dish or pot is hot, rub the bottom with the suet or fat until lightly coated. Discard any extra fat.

Place about one-quarter of the meat and vegetables in the dish or pot and add about one-quarter of the stock and sake mixture and soy sauce. Sprinkle over one-quarter of the sugar. Fry for 5 to 6 minutes, stirring and turning constantly, until the meat and vegetables are tender.

Transfer the meat and vegetables to individual warmed serving dishes and serve with the egg, while the remaining meat and vegetables are cooked in the same way. The food must be served in batches because it would be overcooked if kept warm while the remainder is being cooked.

The liquid in the pan should always be simmering, and the flavour will become more concentrated as each subsequent batch of meat and vegetables is cooked. You may wish to reduce the quantities of soy sauce and sugar towards the end.
Serves 4

Stuffed veal rolls

8 veal escalopes, pounded thin
8 slices Proscuitto
4 Tbsp parsley, freshly chopped
2 Tbsp slivered almonds
2 Tbsp sultanas or raisins
3 Tbsp grated Parmesan cheese
salt and black pepper
50g/2oz butter
175ml/6floz Marsala

Place the escalopes flat on a working surface. Put a slice of proscuitto on each escalope.

Mix together the parsley, almonds, sultanas or raisins, cheese and salt and pepper to taste in a mixing bowl. Divide this mixture between the escalopes. Roll up the escalopes and tie with string.

Melt the butter in a frying pan. Add the veal rolls and brown on all sides. Pour in the Marsala and bring to the boil. Cover and simmer for 20 minutes or until the veal is tender.

Remove the veal rolls from the pan and discard the string. Place the rolls on a serving dish and pour over the wine sauce in the pan.

Serve hot, with rice.
Serves 4

Vitello tonnato

1.5kg/3lb leg of loin or veal (boned weight)
1 garlic clove, cut into slivers
salt and pepper
4 Tbsp olive oil
SAUCE
200g/7oz can tuna fish, drained and flaked
125ml/4floz mayonnaise
1 Tbsp lemon juice
GARNISH
2 tsp capers
2 Tbsp parsley, freshly chopped

Make incisions in the veal and insert the slivers of garlic. Tie into shape if necessary and rub with salt and pepper. Place in a roasting tin and pour over the oil. Roast in a fairly hot oven (200°C/400°F or Gas Mark 6) for 20 minutes, then reduce the temperature to warm (170°C/325°F or Gas Mark 3). Continue roasting for a further 1 hour 40 minutes or until cooked.

Remove from the roasting tin and allow to cool. Skim the fat off the surface of the cooking juices and strain into a bowl.

When the veal is cold, slice it thinly and arrange the slices in a large shallow dish. Mash the tuna fish, mayonnaise and lemon juice together to make a smooth sauce. Thin to a pouring consistency with some of the veal cooking juices and adjust the seasoning. Pour the sauce over the veal slices and cover the dish. Leave to marinate in a cool place for 4-6 hours.

Sprinkle over the capers and parsley and serve.
Serves 6-8

Planter's pork chops

25g/1oz butter
1 Tbsp vegetable oil
1 garlic clove, crushed
4 pork chops
4 Tbsp lemon juice
2 tsp soft brown sugar
salt and black pepper
150ml/5floz dry white wine
1 banana
4 pineapple rings
4 orange slices
4 watercress sprigs

Melt the butter with the oil in a frying pan. Add the garlic and fry for 1 minute. Add the chops and fry for 4 minutes on each side or until evenly browned. Transfer the chops to a baking dish, arranging them in one layer.

Pour off the cooking liquid from the pan. Add 3 tablespoons of the lemon juice, the sugar, salt and pepper to taste and the wine. Bring to the boil, then pour over the chops.

Used here in the recipe for Sukiyaki, spring onions are equally delicious chopped over summer salads.

Right : A superb dish, Orange and Pork Casserole is flavoured with vermouth and makes a splendid dinner party main course.
Above : Pork has an affinity to fruit, and the succulent, summer plum is no exception.

Bake in a moderate oven (180°C/350°F or Gas Mark 4) for 25 minutes.

Meanwhile, cut the banana in half lengthways, then across to make four pieces. Sprinkle with the remaining lemon juice to prevent discoloration.

Place a pineapple ring, orange slice and piece of banana on each chop. Continue baking for 5 minutes or until the chops are cooked.

Transfer the chops and fruit to individual warmed dishes and garnish with the watercress. Serve hot.
Serves 4

Pork chops with plums

500g/1lb plums, halved and stoned
50g/2oz sugar
¼ tsp ground cinnamon
250ml/8floz red wine
4 thick pork chops, trimmed of excess fat
salt and black pepper

Put the plums, sugar, cinnamon and wine in a saucepan and cook for 10 to 15 minutes or until the plums are very soft.

Meanwhile, rub the chops with salt and pepper. Grill for 3 minutes on each side or until lightly browned. Transfer the chops to a baking dish, arranging them in one layer. Pour over the plum mixture and bake in a moderate oven (180°C/350°F or Gas Mark 4) for 1 hour.

Serve hot.
Serves 4

Orange pork casserole

1.5kg/3lb loin of pork (boned weight),
trimmed of excess fat
1 garlic clove, halved
salt and black pepper
½ tsp ground allspice
grated rind of 1 small orange
1 Tbsp rosemary, freshly chopped
4 large juicy oranges
25g/1oz butter
300ml/10floz sweet vermouth
1 Tbsp cornflour
1 Tbsp orange juice

Rub the pork all over with the garlic halves, then discard the garlic. Rub with

salt and pepper. Lay the pork on a flat working surface and sprinkle over the allspice, orange rind and rosemary. Roll up the meat and tie with string at 2.5cm/1in intervals.

Peel the oranges, removing all the pith, and slice the flesh thinly.

Melt the butter in a flameproof casserole. Put the pork in the pot and brown on all sides. Add the vermouth and bring to the boil. Cover the meat with the orange slices, cover the pot and simmer for 2½ hours or until the pork is cooked through and tender.

Transfer the meat to a warmed serving dish. Remove and discard the string. Arrange the orange slices around the meat. Keep hot.

Skim the fat off the surface of the cooking liquid and strain into a saucepan. Dissolve the cornflour in the orange juice. Stir in a little of the hot liquid. Add to the strained cooking liquid. Simmer, stirring, until the sauce is thickened and smooth. Pour the sauce into a sauceboat and serve with the meat.
Serves 6

Meatballs with hot Mexican sauce

MEATBALLS
1kg/2lb minced pork
1 large onion, finely grated
2 garlic cloves, crushed
50g/2oz ground almonds
50g/2oz fresh breadcrumbs
1 egg, lightly beaten
1 Tbsp parsley, freshly chopped
½ tsp ground cinnamon
salt and black pepper
3 Tbsp medium dry sherry
1 Tbsp butter
2 Tbsp olive oil
SAUCE
1 large onion, finely chopped
1 garlic clove, crushed
½ Tbsp soft brown sugar
6 medium tomatoes, peeled, seeded and chopped
1 medium green pepper, pith and seeds removed and thinly sliced
1 medium red pepper, pith and seeds removed and thinly sliced
1 green chilli, finely chopped
¼ tsp cayenne pepper
1 tsp paprika
1 Tbsp parsley, freshly chopped
150ml/5floz beef stock
salt and black pepper
2 tsp cornflour
4 Tbsp medium dry sherry

Mix together all the ingredients for the meat balls except the butter and oil, adding salt and pepper to taste. Knead well with your hands, then form the mixture into about 36 walnut-sized balls and set aside.

Melt the butter with the oil in a frying pan. Add the meatballs, in batches, and fry for 6 to 8 minutes or until they are evenly browned.

Remove the meatballs from the pan and keep warm while you make the sauce. Add the onion, garlic and brown sugar to the frying pan and fry until the onion is soft and golden brown. Stir in the tomatoes, peppers, chilli, cayenne, paprika and parsley and simmer for a further 3 minutes, stirring occasionally.

Add the stock with salt and pepper to taste and bring to the boil. Dissolve the cornflour in the sherry. Stir a little of the hot sauce into the mixture, then stir into the sauce. Add the meatballs, cover the pan and simmer for 20 to 25 minutes or until the meatballs are cooked through.

Transfer the meatballs and sauce to a warmed serving dish and serve immediately, with noodles or rice.
Serves 4-6

Fresh red and green peppers add flavour and texture to Meatballs with Hot Mexican Sauce.

Canary Island Chicken – even its name suggests a taste of sunshine and colour.

sprinkle with salt and pepper. Fry until the cubes are lightly browned and tender. Transfer to a warmed serving dish, using a slotted spoon. Keep hot.

Melt the remaining butter in another pan. Add the tomatoes and fry gently for 5 minutes. Remove the tomatoes from the pan with a slotted spoon and arrange around the lamb cubes. Keep hot.

Stir the flour into the fat remaining in the pan in which the lamb was cooked. Cook, stirring, until the flour is lightly browned. Gradually stir in the wine and stock with the garlic and simmer, stirring, until the liquid has reduced to half the original quantity. Pour this sauce over the lamb and sprinkle with the parsley. Serve hot.
Serves 4

Canary Island chicken

75g/3oz flour
salt and black pepper
1 x 2kg/4lb chicken, cut into eight serving pieces
75g/3oz butter
4 Tbsp olive oil
2 garlic cloves, crushed
2 medium onions, chopped
300ml/10floz dry white wine
300ml/10floz chicken stock
1 bouquet garni
1 tsp saffron powder
1 Tbsp hot water
50g/2oz slivered almonds
2 eggs, hard-boiled and finely chopped
1 Tbsp parsley, freshly chopped

Mix 50g/2oz of the flour with salt and pepper on a plate. Coat the chicken pieces in this seasoned flour. Melt 50g/2oz of the butter with the oil in a flameproof casserole. Add the garlic and onions and fry until the onions are soft but not brown. Add the chicken pieces and brown lightly on all sides.

Pour in the wine and chicken stock and add the bouquet garni. Bring to the boil, then cover and simmer for 45 minutes.

Dissolve the saffron in the hot water. Add to the casserole with the almonds. Simmer, uncovered, for a further 15 minutes.

Transfer the chicken pieces to a warmed serving dish. Discard the bouquet garni from the casserole. Blend the remaining butter and remaining flour to a paste and add in small pieces to the liquid in the casserole. Simmer, stirring, until thickened and smooth.

Pour the sauce over the chicken and garnish with the egg and parsley. Serve hot.
Serves 4

Grilled lamb chops with rosemary

4 Tbsp olive oil
2 Tbsp lemon juice
salt and black pepper
2 Tbsp rosemary, freshly chopped
1 garlic clove, crushed
8 thick lamb chops

Mix together the oil, lemon juice, salt and pepper to taste, the rosemary and garlic in a shallow dish. Add the chops and turn to coat them on all sides. Leave to marinate for 2 hours.

Grill the chops for 8 to 10 minutes on each side, basting with the marinade frequently. Transfer to a warmed serving dish and spoon over any remaining marinade. Serve hot.
Serves 4

Lamb with tomatoes

50g/2oz butter
2 Tbsp vegetable oil
1kg/2lb shoulder of lamb (boned weight), cut into 4cm/1½in cubes
salt and black pepper
500g/1lb small tomatoes, peeled, halved and seeded
1 Tbsp flour
100ml/4floz white wine
250ml/8floz veal or chicken stock
1 garlic clove, crushed
2 Tbsp parsley, freshly chopped

Melt 25g/1oz of the butter with the oil in a frying pan. Add the lamb cubes and

Chicken with peach sauce

salt and black pepper
1 x 2kg/4lb chicken, skinned and cut
into six serving pieces
4 Tbsp vegetable oil
1 small onion, finely chopped
1 garlic clove, crushed
¼ tsp red pepper flakes
¼ tsp ground ginger
250ml/8floz chicken stock
4 Tbsp lime juice
4 Tbsp lemon juice
25g/1oz butter
4 peaches, peeled, halved, stoned and
sliced

Rub salt and pepper into the chicken pieces. Heat the oil in a frying pan. Add the chicken pieces, in batches, and brown on all sides. Remove from the pan and place in a baking dish.

Add the onion and garlic to the frying pan and fry until the onion is soft but not brown. Stir in the red pepper flakes, ginger and stock and bring to the boil. Remove from the heat and stir in the lime and lemon juices. Pour over the chicken pieces.

Melt the butter in a clean frying pan. Add the peach slices and fry for 6 minutes or until they are beginning to pulp. Add to the baking dish with the chicken. Cover and bake in a moderate oven (180°C/350°F or Gas Mark 4) for 1 hour or until the chicken is tender.

Serve the chicken and peach sauce on a bed of boiled rice.
Serves 4

Chicken Florentine

125g/4oz Parmesan cheese, grated
125g/4oz dry white breadcrumbs
3 Tbsp flour
salt and black pepper
1 egg
1 Tbsp water
6 chicken breasts, boned and skinned
175g/6oz butter
2.5kg/5lb spinach
1½ Tbsp lemon juice
700g/1½lb mushrooms, sliced
1 lemon, sliced

Mix together the cheese and breadcrumbs. Season the flour well with salt and pepper. Beat the egg and water together until well mixed. Dip the chicken breasts first in the seasoned flour, then in the beaten egg and finally in the cheese mixture, coating well with each. Chill for 1 hour.

Melt 125g/4oz of the butter in a frying pan. Add the chicken breasts and brown on all sides. Cover and cook gently for about 25 to 30 minutes or until tender.

Meanwhile, put the spinach in a saucepan. Do not add any water as there should be enough left on the leaves after washing. Cook for about 7 minutes or until tender, then drain well, pressing out all excess moisture. Chop the spinach coarsely and arrange on a warmed serving dish. Sprinkle with the lemon juice and keep hot.

Melt half the remaining butter in a saucepan. Add the mushrooms and fry quickly for 2 to 3 minutes. Using a slotted spoon, transfer the mushrooms to the serving dish, arranging them around the spinach. Place the chicken breasts on top. Keep hot.

Add the remaining butter to the pan in which the mushrooms were cooked. Melt it and cook until it is brown. Pour over the chicken and garnish with the lemon slices. Serve immediately.
Serves 6

Andalusian chicken

1 x 2kg/4lb chicken
50g/2oz butter
1 Tbsp olive oil
1 large onion, halved
1 bouquet garni
1 Tbsp flour
125ml/4floz white wine
2 Tbsp tomato purée
STUFFING
125g/4oz long grain rice, cooked
125g/4oz cooked ham, diced
2 tsp paprika
salt and black pepper
GARNISH
2 Tbsp oil
1 large onion, sliced in rings
2 large green peppers, pith and seeds
removed and sliced into rings
500g/1lb tomatoes, peeled and chopped
salt and black pepper

Mix together the ingredients for the stuffing, with salt and pepper to taste. Use to stuff the chicken and close with a skewer or trussing thread.

Melt the butter with the oil in a flameproof casserole. Add the chicken and brown on all sides. Add the onion and bouquet garni, cover and cook gently for about 1½ hours or until tender.

Meanwhile, make the garnish. Heat the oil in a frying pan. Add the onion and fry until it is soft but not brown. Add the peppers and tomatoes with salt and pepper to taste and continue to cook until the vegetables are just tender. Remove from the heat and keep hot.

Transfer the chicken to a warmed serving dish. Remove the skewer or

Don't reserve summer peaches exclusively for desserts ; in Chicken with Peach Sauce they add flavour and colour.

trussing thread. Surround the chicken with the garnish. Keep hot.

Discard the onion and bouquet garni from the casserole and sprinkle in the flour. Stir well, then stir in the wine and tomato purée. Bring to the boil and simmer, stirring, until thickened and smooth. Pour this sauce over the chicken and serve.

Serves 4

Mango chicken

1 x 2kg/4lb chicken, cut into serving pieces
salt and black pepper
25g/1oz butter
2 Tbsp vegetable oil
1 large onion, thinly sliced
1 mango, peeled, stoned and sliced
1 tsp grated lemon rind
¼ tsp ground coriander
¼ tsp ground cinnamon
250ml/8floz chicken stock
250ml/8floz single cream
2 tsp flour
1 Tbsp lemon juice
1 Tbsp water
2 lemons, thinly sliced

Rub the chicken pieces with salt and pepper. Melt the butter with the oil in a frying pan. Add the chicken pieces and brown on all sides. Transfer to a flame-proof casserole.

Add the onion to the pan and fry until it is soft but not brown. Transfer the onion to the casserole, using a slotted spoon.

Add the mango slices to the pan and fry, turning once, for 4 minutes. Stir in the lemon rind, coriander, cinnamon and chicken stock and bring to the boil. Pour into the casserole.

Cover the casserole and bake in a fairly hot oven (190°C/375°F or Gas Mark 5) for 1¼ hours or until the chicken is tender.

Transfer the chicken pieces to a warmed serving dish. Keep hot. Bring the liquid in the casserole to the boil on top of the stove. Reduce the heat to low and stir in the cream. Mix together the flour, lemon juice and water. Add a little of the hot liquid then stir into the casserole. Heat, stirring, until well mixed and thickened. Pour the sauce over the chicken and garnish with the lemon slices. Serve hot.

Serves 4

Luscious mangoes cooked with chicken, cream and spices, Mango Chicken may be garnished with lemon slices.

Barbecue Food

Hamburgers

1.5kg/3lb lean minced beef
50g/2oz fresh breadcrumbs
salt and black pepper
1½ tsp thyme, freshly chopped
1 egg, lightly beaten
ACCOMPANIMENTS
3 medium tomatoes, thinly sliced
1 large onion, thinly sliced and pushed out
into rings
6 large lettuce leaves
6 hamburger buns or baps
relishes, tomato ketchup, mustard, etc.

Mix together the beef, breadcrumbs, salt and pepper to taste, the thyme and egg. Knead and then form into six patties.

Arrange the tomatoes, onion rings and lettuce on a serving dish. Halve the buns or baps.

Barbecue the hamburgers for about 5 to 7 minutes on each side. This will produce rare hamburgers. If you prefer them well done, increase the cooking time accordingly. When the hamburgers are nearly ready, place the buns or baps on the grid to heat through.

Place a hamburger on each bun or bap bottom and add the tops. Serve hot, with the accompaniments.
Serves 6

Barbecued spiced duck

1 Tbsp ground coriander
2 tsp ground fenugreek
2 tsp ground cumin
1 tsp ground turmeric
1 tsp ground cinnamon
½ tsp ground cardamom
¼ tsp ground cloves
¼ tsp grated nutmeg
1 tsp mild chilli powder
salt and black pepper
1cm/½in piece root ginger, peeled and
finely chopped
juice of 1 lemon
2 small onions, minced
2 garlic cloves, crushed
125g/4oz desiccated coconut
175ml/6floz boiling water
1 x 2.5kg/5lb duck, split open through the
breastbone, ribs broken at the backbone

Mix together the spices, salt and pepper to taste, the ginger, lemon juice, onions and garlic. Soak the coconut in the water for 5 minutes, then add to the spice mixture. Stir well to form a thick paste.

Tie the wings and legs of the duck together so that the cavity is spread open. Cover the duck with some of the spice paste. Place it, cavity side up, on the barbecue grid and cook for about 20 minutes. Turn the duck over and cook for a further 20 minutes. Baste with the spice paste from time to time. Continue cooking and turning until the duck is cooked through and the juices run clear when the thigh is pierced. Serve hot.
Serves 4

Lamb kebabs marinated in yogurt

1kg/2lb leg of lamb (boned weight), cut
into 2.5cm/1in cubes
150ml/5floz plain yogurt
1 Tbsp ground coriander
1 tsp ground turmeric
½ tsp chilli powder
1 tsp salt
2 garlic cloves, crushed
2.5cm/1in piece fresh ginger, grated or
finely chopped
1 Tbsp coriander leaves, freshly chopped
2 lemons, cut into wedges

Put the lamb cubes in a bowl. Mix together the yogurt, coriander, turmeric, chilli powder, salt, garlic and ginger. Pour over the lamb cubes and mix well to coat each cube. Cover and leave to marinate for at least 6 hours or overnight.

Stir the meat and marinade well, then thread the meat cubes onto skewers. Barbecue for about 8 minutes, turning frequently and basting with any remaining marinade.

Slide the lamb cubes onto a warmed serving dish and sprinkle with the coriander leaves. Garnish with the lemon and serve.
Serves 4

Frankfurter and bacon kebabs

8 Frankfurters, each cut into 4 pieces
1 large pineapple, peeled, cored and cut
into chunks
8 bacon rashers, rolled
8 small onions
2 green peppers, pith and seeds
removed and cut into pieces
50g/2oz butter, melted

Thread the frankfurter pieces onto eight skewers, alternating with pineapple chunks, bacon slice rolls, onions and pieces of green pepper. Brush with melted butter and barbecue for about 15 minutes, turning frequently and basting with the melted butter. Serve hot.
Serves 4

Chicken with Orange and Figs makes an elegant kebab dish for a summer barbecue.

Prawn, pepper and mushroom kebabs

16 Dublin Bay prawns, shelled and deveined
2 small green peppers, pith and seeds removed and cut into 16 pieces
16 medium mushrooms, stalks removed
16 sage leaves
2 lemons, quartered and each quarter cut across in half
MARINADE
4 Tbsp olive oil
2 Tbsp lemon juice
3 garlic cloves, crushed
salt and black pepper

Mix together the marinade ingredients, with salt and pepper to taste, in a shallow dish. Add the prawns and stir to coat them with the marinade. Leave to marinate for 1 hour, turning occasionally.

Remove the prawns from the marinade and pat dry with kitchen paper towels. Reserve the marinade.

Thread a prawn onto a skewer, then add a piece of pepper, a mushroom, a sage leaf and a piece of lemon. Continue filling the skewer in this order, allowing four of each ingredient to each of four skewers.

Barbecue the kebabs for about 10 minutes, turning and basting with the reserved marinade. Serve hot.
Serves 4

Chicken with orange and figs

16 chicken portions
50g/2oz butter, melted
salt and black pepper
3 large oranges, each cut into 6 portions
16 figs, fresh or dried

Brush the chicken portions with the butter and sprinkle with salt and pepper. Barbecue for about 8 minutes on each side. Remove the chicken portions from the barbecue and thread onto skewers with the orange portions and figs. (The chicken may be put on skewers from the beginning of the cooking, if wished, but it will not be evenly browned.) Brush with the butter again and continue to barbecue for a further 10 to 15 minutes. Baste with the butter and turn frequently.

Serve hot.
Serves 8

Vegetables

Tomatoes baked with basil

50g/2oz butter
2 large onions, thinly sliced and pushed
out into rings
2 large tomatoes, skinned and thinly
sliced
2 Tbsp basil, freshly chopped
salt and black pepper
1 tsp sugar
75g/3oz fresh breadcrumbs

Melt half the butter in a frying pan. Add the onions and fry until they are soft but not brown. Remove from the heat and place half the onion rings in a greased baking dish. Cover with half the tomato slices and sprinkle with half the basil, salt and pepper and a little sugar. Make another layer of onion rings and tomato slices and sprinkle with the remaining basil, salt and pepper and sugar.

Cover the top with the breadcrumbs. Cut the remaining butter into small pieces and dot over the top. Bake in a fairly hot oven (190°C/375°F or Gas Mark 5) for 30 minutes. Serve hot.
Serves 4

Asparagus with orange sauce

500g/1lb asparagus
125g/4oz butter
juice of 1 orange
1 tsp finely grated orange rind

Scrape and trim the asparagus stalks and tie in a bundle. Place in a pan of boiling salted water, keeping the tips above the water level, and cover partially. Cook for 15 to 20 minutes or until tender. Drain well and arrange on a warmed serving dish. Keep hot.

Melt the butter in a saucepan. Stir in the orange juice and rind and cook for 2 minutes or until the sauce is hot. Pour over the asparagus and serve immediately.
Serves 4

Broad beans with mushrooms

700g/1½lb broad beans (podded weight)
50g/2oz butter
250g/8oz button mushrooms
2 Tbsp flour
225ml/7floz chicken stock
250ml/8floz single cream
salt and black pepper
2 Tbsp Parmesan cheese, grated

Cook the broad beans in boiling salted water for 8 to 10 minutes or until they are just tender. Drain well, then refresh under cold running water. Drain again.

Melt half the butter in a frying pan. Add the mushrooms and fry for 4 minutes. Remove from the heat and set aside.

Melt the remaining butter in a saucepan. Stir in the flour and cook, stirring, for 1 minute. Remove the pan from the heat and gradually stir in the chicken stock. Return to the heat and simmer, stirring, until thickened and smooth.

Stir in the cream, salt and pepper to taste and the Parmesan, then fold in the mushrooms and broad beans. Cook gently for 3 to 4 minutes, or until the vegetables are heated through. Serve hot.
Serves 4

Basil Baked Tomatoes is an unusual and fragrant accompaniment to pork, lamb or chicken.

Courgettes with lemon and parsley

700g/1½lb courgettes, cut into 1cm/½in
thick slices
75g/3oz butter
2 Tbsp olive oil
2 Tbsp lemon juice
salt and black pepper
3 Tbsp parsley, freshly chopped

Blanch the courgette slices in boiling water for 3 minutes. Drain well and dry thoroughly on paper towels.

Melt two-thirds of the butter with the oil in a frying pan. Add the courgette slices and fry for 8-10 minutes. Sprinkle over the lemon juice with salt and pepper to taste, then add the remaining butter and the parsley. When the butter has completely melted, turn over the slices to coat well and serve hot.

Serves 4

Corn fritters

250g/8oz sweetcorn kernels
50g/2oz flour
2 Tbsp sugar
salt and black pepper
2 eggs, lightly beaten
2 Tbsp grated Parmesan cheese
vegetable oil for deep-frying

Mix together the corn, flour, sugar, salt and pepper to taste, the eggs and cheese. Heat the oil until it reaches 185°C/360°F or until a small cube of stale bread dropped into the oil turns golden in 50 seconds.

Drop a few tablespoonsful of the corn mixture into the oil. Fry for 3 to 4 minutes or until the fritters are golden brown. Remove from the pan with a slotted spoon and drain on kitchen paper towels. Keep hot while you fry the remaining fritters in the same way. Serve hot.

Serves 4

Corn Fritters – the Spanish way to cook and serve corn.

Side Salads

Apricot salad

1kg/2lb apricots
4 Tbsp soured cream
3 Tbsp tarragon vinegar
1 Tbsp sugar
salt and black pepper
2 Tbsp tarragon, freshly chopped

Blanch and peel the apricots, then halve and remove the stones. Arrange the apricots in a glass serving dish. Crack the stones and remove the kernels. Chop the kernels.

Mix together the soured cream, vinegar, sugar and salt and pepper to taste. Spoon this dressing over the apricots and sprinkle with the tarragon and chopped apricot kernels.
Serves 4

Fennel and cucumber salad

1 cucumber, peeled and thinly sliced
1 head Florence fennel, cut into thin strips
4 radishes, thinly sliced
3 spring onions, finely chopped
3 Tbsp olive oil
1 Tbsp lemon juice
1 garlic clove, crushed
salt and black pepper
2 tsp parsley, freshly chopped

Put the cucumber, fennel, radishes and spring onions in a serving dish. Put the remaining ingredients except parsley, with salt and pepper to taste, in a screwtop jar and shake well to mix. Pour this dressing over the salad ingredients and toss well to coat. Chill for at least 30 minutes. Sprinkle with parsley just before serving.
Serves 4

Green bean and bacon salad

6 streaky bacon rashers
500g/1lb green beans
6 medium tomatoes, peeled, seeded and chopped
1 egg, hard-boiled and finely chopped
DRESSING
6 Tbsp olive oil
3 Tbsp lemon juice
pinch sugar
salt and black pepper
1 Tbsp basil, freshly chopped
(optional)

Grill the bacon until it is crisp. Meanwhile, cook the beans in boiling salted water for about 10 minutes or until they are just tender but still firm.

Drain the bacon on kitchen paper towels, cool and crumble. Drain the beans and refresh under cold running water. Drain again.

Put all the dressing ingredients, with salt and pepper to taste, in a screwtop jar. Shake well to mix.

Put the bacon, beans and tomatoes in a shallow serving dish. Pour over the dressing and toss well to coat all the ingredients. Chill for 30 minutes. Just before serving, sprinkle the egg on top.
Serves 6

Greek salad

1 cos lettuce, torn into pieces
10 radishes, sliced
250g/8oz Feta cheese, cut into cubes
2 Tbsp marjoram, freshly chopped
4 tomatoes, peeled and sliced
6 anchovies, finely chopped
6 black olives, halved and stoned
1 Tbsp parsley, freshly chopped
DRESSING
4 Tbsp olive oil
1½ Tbsp white wine vinegar
1 tsp chives, freshly chopped
2 tsp lemon thyme, freshly chopped
4 spring onions, finely chopped
1 tsp sugar
salt and black pepper

Arrange the lettuce pieces in a large salad bowl. Scatter over the radishes and pile the cheese cubes in the centre. Sprinkle with the marjoram. Arrange the tomato slices in a ring around the edge, overlapping them, and top with the anchovies and olives.

Put all the dressing ingredients in a screwtop jar, with salt and pepper to taste, and shake well to mix. Pour this dressing over the salad and sprinkle over the parsley. Serve immediately.
Serves 4-6

Yogurt and cucumber salad

600ml/1 pint plain yogurt
½ cucumber, diced
4 spring onions, finely chopped
salt and black pepper
1 green chilli, finely chopped
¼ tsp paprika

Mix together the yogurt, cucumber, spring onions and salt and pepper to taste. Pour into a serving dish, cover and chill for 1 hour.

Sprinkle over the chilli and paprika just before serving.
Serves 4-6

Below : Apricot Salad is a different and colourful accompaniment for hot or cold ham.
Bottom : Fennel, with its delicate, aniseed-like flavour, makes an excellent side salad – especially with fish dishes.

Salads

Lobster and pineapple salad

MARINADE
2 garlic cloves, crushed
salt and black pepper
½ tsp prepared mustard
¼ tsp sugar
1 Tbsp red wine vinegar
3 Tbsp olive oil
SALAD
1 x 1kg/2lb lobster, cooked
2 Tbsp mayonnaise
½ tsp soy sauce
½ tsp cayenne pepper
salt and black pepper
½ pineapple, peeled, cored and diced
2 celery stalks, chopped
6 lettuce leaves
1 lemon, thinly sliced

Mix together the marinade ingredients, with salt and pepper to taste, in a shallow dish.

Cut the soft undershell from the lobster body with scissors. Remove the meat and cut it into thin slices. Reserve the body shell. Crack the claws and remove the meat. Slice it thinly. Add the lobster meat to the marinade and toss well to coat. Cover and marinate in the refrigerator for 45 minutes.

Drain the lobster meat, discarding any remaining marinade. Beat together the mayonnaise, soy sauce, cayenne and salt and pepper to taste in a mixing bowl. Add the lobster meat, pineapple and celery and mix well. Pile into the reserved lobster shell.

Arrange the lettuce leaves on a serving plate. Place the filled lobster on the lettuce and garnish with the lemon slices. Serve immediately.
Serves 2

Chicken and avocado salad with Russian dressing

1 x 2kg/4lb chicken, roasted and cooled
2 avocados
10 black olives, halved and stoned
DRESSING
300ml/10floz mayonnaise
pinch cayenne pepper
1 tsp chilli sauce
1 egg, hard-boiled and finely chopped
1 spring onion, finely chopped
1 tsp parsley, freshly chopped
salt and black pepper

First make the dressing. Mix all the ingredients together well and adjust the seasoning if necessary. Chill for 15 minutes.

Skin the chicken and remove the meat from the bones. Cut the meat into bite-size pieces and place in a serving dish. Halve the avocados and remove the stones, then peel and dice the flesh. Add to the chicken with the olives.

Pour the dressing over the salad ingredients and toss well to coat. Serve immediately.
Serves 4-6

Lobster and Pineapple Salad – an exotic summer dish which may be served as part of a cold buffet or as a starter.

Crab Louis

1 cos lettuce, separated into leaves
500g/1lb crabmeat, flaked
2 tomatoes, thinly sliced
½ cucumber, thinly sliced
4 eggs, hard-boiled and thinly sliced
1 Tbsp capers
DRESSING
250ml/8floz mayonnaise
3 Tbsp olive oil
1 Tbsp lemon juice
2 Tbsp tomato ketchup
1 tsp Worcestershire sauce
1 Tbsp chives, freshly chopped
1 Tbsp parsley, freshly chopped
salt and black pepper
75ml/3floz double cream

First make the dressing. Mix all the ingredients together, with salt and pepper to taste, in a mixing bowl. Chill for 30 minutes.

Line a salad bowl or serving dish with the lettuce leaves. Pile the crabmeat in the centre and spoon over the dressing. Arrange the tomato, cucumber and egg slices around the crabmeat and garnish with the capers. Serve immediately.
Serves 4

Florida salad

125g/4oz cream cheese
4 Tbsp single cream
2 Tbsp lemon juice
pinch cayenne pepper
salt and black pepper
1 medium green pepper, pith and seeds removed and shredded
1 large eating apple, cored and diced
1 small pineapple, peeled, cored and diced
3 large celery stalks, sliced
1 large orange, peeled and thinly sliced
1 banana, sliced
6 large lettuce leaves
4 radishes, thinly sliced
1 Tbsp chives, freshly chopped

Beat together the cream cheese, cream, lemon juice, cayenne and salt and pepper to taste. Put the green pepper, apple, pineapple, celery, orange and banana in a mixing bowl and pour over the cream cheese mixture. Toss well to coat all the fruit and vegetables. Chill for at least 30 minutes.

Line a glass salad bowl with the lettuce leaves and pile the fruit and vegetable mixture on top. Arrange the radish slices around the edge and sprinkle over the chives. Serve immediately.
Serves 4

Simple to prepare, superb to eat, Crab Louis is ideal for a very special occasion.

Pineapple cheese salad

½ pineapple, peeled, cored and chopped
175g/6oz Caerphilly or Cheshire cheese, cut into 6mm/¼in dice
1 pear, peeled, cored and chopped
12 small radishes
2 celery stalks, cut into 6mm/¼in thick slices
1 head chicory, cut into 1cm/½in thick slices
8 watercress sprigs
DRESSING
4 Tbsp olive oil
salt and black pepper
½ tsp sugar
2 Tbsp single cream
1½ Tbsp lemon juice
1 Tbsp tarragon, freshly chopped

Mix together the pineapple, cheese, pear, radishes, celery and chicory in a mixing bowl. Put all the dressing ingredients, with salt and pepper to taste, in a screwtop jar and shake well to mix. Pour this dressing over the salad ingredients and toss well. Pile into a serving dish or individual dishes and garnish with the watercress sprigs. Serve immediately.
Serves 4

Crisp, crunchy sweetcorn is delicious added to summer salads or on its own.

Light Dishes

Seafood pancakes

BATTER
250g/8oz flour
½ tsp salt
2 eggs
25g/1oz butter, melted
475ml/16floz milk
2 Tbsp vegetable oil
FILLING
75g/3oz butter
2 Tbsp vegetable oil
2 Tbsp bean sprouts
4 small spring onions, finely chopped
75ml/3floz dry white wine
2 Tbsp parsley, freshly chopped
1 Tbsp chervil, freshly chopped
175g/6oz clams (shucked weight if fresh) or canned and drained
175g/6oz crabmeat, flaked
175g/6oz prawns or shrimps (shelled weight), deveined
salt and white pepper
2 Tbsp flour
300ml/½ pint milk

Sift the flour and salt into a mixing bowl. Make a well in the centre and add the eggs, melted butter and gradually add half the milk. Mix to a smooth cream, gradually drawing the flour into the the liquids. Beat in the rest of the milk. Alternatively, make the batter in an electric blender.

Lightly grease a frying pan or crepe pan with a little of the oil. Heat the pan, then pour about 4 tablespoons of the batter into the centre. Tip the pan so it is coated with the batter. Cook for just over 1 minute, then turn the pancake over and cook the other side for about 30 seconds.

Slide the pancake out of the pan. Keep hot on a plate over a pan of hot water while you cook the remaining pancakes in the same way. Stack them up, interleaving with greaseproof paper. Keep hot while you make the filling.

Melt two-thirds of the butter with the oil in a saucepan. Add the bean sprouts and spring onions and fry for 1 minute, stirring constantly. Stir in the wine and bring to the boil. Boil to reduce by half.

Remove the pan from the heat. Add half the parsley, the chervil, clams, crabmeat, prawns or shrimps and salt and pepper to taste. Return to a gentle heat and warm the mixture.

Melt the remaining butter in another saucepan. Stir in the flour and cook, stirring, for 1 minute. Remove from the heat and gradually stir in the milk. Return to the heat and simmer, stirring, until thickened and smooth. Stir in the seafood mixture.

Lay the pancakes out flat and put about 2 tablespoons of the filling in the centre of each. Roll up the pancakes and place on a hot serving dish. Sprinkle with the remaining parsley and serve.
Serves 4-6

Corn and prawn savoury

50g/2oz butter
500g/1lb sweetcorn kernels
1 green pepper, pith and seeds removed and finely chopped
375g/12oz prawns (shelled weight), deveined
125ml/4floz double cream
salt and black pepper
6 slices hot buttered toast
pinch cayenne pepper

Melt the butter in a frying pan. Add the corn and green pepper and cook for 5 minutes. Stir in the prawns and cream and cook gently for a further 4 minutes or until heated through. Add salt and pepper to taste.

Arrange the toast on individual warmed serving plates and spoon over the corn mixture. Sprinkle with cayenne and serve.
Serves 3-6

Omelette niçoise

1 Tbsp olive oil
1 small onion, thinly sliced
1 garlic clove, crushed
2 large tomatoes, peeled, seeded and chopped
3 anchovy fillets, chopped
8 black olives, stoned and chopped
6 eggs
salt and black pepper
2 Tbsp cold water
1 Tbsp butter

Heat the oil in a frying pan. Add the onion and garlic and fry until the onion is soft but not brown. Stir in the tomatoes, anchovies, and olives and cook for a further 3 minutes or until the tomatoes are tender but still firm. Remove from the heat and keep hot.

Beat together the eggs, salt and pepper to taste and the water. Melt the butter in a frying pan or omelet pan. Pour in the egg mixture and cook until set, lifting the set edges to let the uncooked egg mixture run onto the pan. Spoon over the anchovy mixture. Fold over the omelet and slide onto a warmed serving dish. Cut into two or three and serve.
Serves 2-3

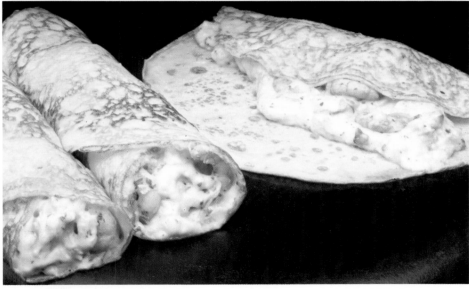

Above : Corn and Prawn Savoury, served on toast, makes an easily prepared lunch or supper snack.
Left : Filled with a tempting assortment of seafood, Seafood Crêpes make an excellent supper dish.

Courgette risotto

125g/4oz butter
2 garlic cloves, crushed
500g/1lb courgettes, thinly sliced
salt and black pepper
500g/1lb tomatoes, peeled and chopped
150ml/5floz dry white wine
500g/1lb Italian rice, such as Avorio
900ml/1½ pints chicken stock, boiling
50g/2oz Parmesan cheese, grated

Melt three-quarters of the butter in a saucepan. Add the garlic and fry for 1 minute. Add the courgette slices and fry for 10 to 12 minutes or until lightly browned. Stir in salt and pepper to taste, the tomatoes and wine. Bring to the boil.

Add the rice and simmer for 5 minutes. Stir in about one-third of the stock. Regulate the heat so that the rice is bubbling all the time. When the rice swells and the liquid is absorbed, add another third of the stock. Add the final third when that has been absorbed.

Stir in the remaining butter and the Parmesan and simmer for a further 1 minute. Transfer to a warmed serving dish and serve immediately.

Serves 4-6

Stuffed green peppers with yogurt and tomato sauce

4 large green peppers
150ml/5floz plain yogurt
4 tsp parsley, freshly chopped
FILLING
2 Tbsp oil
2 onions, finely chopped
2 celery stalks, finely chopped
175g/6oz long-grain rice, cooked
2 Tbsp parsley, freshly chopped
1 tsp basil, freshly chopped
2 tsp marjoram, freshly chopped
salt and black pepper
1 egg, lightly beaten
SAUCE
40g/1½oz butter
1 onion, finely chopped
1 Tbsp flour
250ml/8floz chicken stock
375g/12oz tomatoes, peeled and chopped
salt and black pepper
½ tsp sugar
1 Tbsp tomato purée

Cut the tops off the peppers and scoop out the seeds and white pith.

Heat the oil for the filling in a saucepan. Add the onions and celery and fry until the onions are soft but not brown. Stir in the rice, parsley ,basil, marjoram and salt and pepper to taste. Remove from the heat and cool slightly, then beat in the egg. Stuff the peppers with this mixture, pressing it down well.

To make the sauce, melt the butter in a flameproof casserole. Add the onion and fry until it is soft but not brown. Stir in the flour and cook, stirring, for 1 minute. Remove from the heat and gradually stir in the stock. Return to the heat and simmer, stirring, until thickened. Stir in the tomatoes, salt and pepper to taste, the sugar and tomato purée.

Place the stuffed peppers in the sauce, upright. Cover and transfer to a moderate oven (180°C/350°F or Gas Mark 4). Bake for 35 to 40 minutes or until the peppers are tender.

Remove the lid and spoon the yogurt on top of each pepper. Sprinkle with the parsley and serve, from the casserole.
Serves 4

Stuffed Green Peppers with Yogurt and Tomato Sauce – a taste of the Mediterranean that is ideal for a light summer meal.

Desserts

Summer pudding

1kg/2lb raspberries, or other berries
125g/4oz castor sugar
125ml/4floz milk
8 slices stale white bread, crusts removed
300ml/10floz double cream

Put the raspberries in a mixing bowl and sprinkle over the sugar. Sprinkle the milk over the bread slices to moisten them. Line a greased deep pie dish or pudding basin with the bread slices, reserving two slices for the top. Pour the raspberries into the dish and place the reserved bread slices over them.

Cover the dish with a sheet of grease-proof paper and place a plate and heavy weight on top of the bread. Chill for at least 8 hours or overnight.

Whip the cream until it is thick. Pile into a serving dish. Turn out the pudding onto a plate and serve with the cream.
Serves 4-6

Damson soufflé

500g/1lb damsons, stoned and chopped
450ml/15floz plus 1 Tbsp water
250g/8oz plus 1 tsp sugar
1 Tbsp cornflour
25g/1oz butter
4 eggs, separated

Put the damsons in a saucepan with all but 1 tablespoon of the water. Simmer gently, covered, for 15 to 20 minutes or until the fruit is soft. Remove from the heat and cool slightly, then purée in an electric blender or foodmill. Alternatively, push the fruit mixture through a sieve.

Return the damson purée to the saucepan and stir in all but 1 teaspoon of the sugar. Stir over a gentle heat to dissolve the sugar, then remove from the heat.

Dissolve the cornflour in the remaining water. Add to the damson mixture and stir well. Return to the heat and cook, stirring, until thickened and smooth. Stir in the butter. When it has melted, remove from the heat. Allow to cool.

Lightly beat the egg yolks using a whisk. Stir into the damson mixture. Beat the egg whites until they will hold a stiff peak. Fold into the damson mixture. Spoon into a greased soufflé dish and sprinkle over the remaining sugar. Bake in a fairly hot oven (200°C/400°F or Gas Mark 6) for 30 to 35 minutes or until well risen and lightly browned and serve.
Serves 6

Raspberry bombe with melba sauce

250g/8oz macaroons
300ml/10floz double cream
3 Tbsp brandy
2 Tbsp castor sugar
2 egg whites
500g/1lb raspberries
1 Tbsp icing sugar

Crumble the macaroons into a mixing bowl. Whip the cream until it is thick. Add the brandy and 1 tablespoon of the sugar and continue whipping until stiff. Beat the egg whites until they will hold a stiff peak. Fold the egg whites into the whipped cream. Taste and add more sugar if necessary. Fold in the macaroons.

Spoon into a chilled 1.5l/3 pint mould. Cover the top with foil and freeze for at least 2 hours.

Meanwhile, prepare the sauce. Sieve the raspberries into a mixing bowl and stir in the icing sugar. Taste and add more sugar if necessary. Chill the sauce.

Unmould the bombe onto a serving dish. Pour over the melba sauce and serve.
Serves 10-12

Hazelnut biscuit cake

150g/5oz flour
50g/2oz sugar
75g/3oz hazelnuts, chopped and toasted
125g/4oz butter, softened
1 egg yolk
250ml/8floz double cream
250g/8oz strawberries, hulled
1 Tbsp icing sugar

Sift the flour and sugar into a mixing bowl. Stir in the hazelnuts. Make a well in the centre and add the butter and egg yolk. Work the butter and egg yolk together, then slowly incorporate the flour and sugar to make a soft dough. Chill for 30 minutes.

Divide the dough into three and roll each portion into a ball. Roll out each ball to a 20cm/8in circle. Place the circles on three greased baking sheets and bake in a moderate oven (180°C/350°F or Gas Mark 4) for 15 minutes or until the undersides are pale golden brown. Do not let the tops of the biscuits colour. Cool on the baking sheets for 5 minutes, then carefully transfer to wire racks. Allow to cool completely.

Whip the cream until it is thick. Thinly slice the fruit.

Sandwich together the three biscuits with the cream and fruit. Sift the icing sugar over the top. Serve immediately.
Serves 6-8

Top : Soft white bread enclosing fresh juicy raspberries, Summer Pudding is a traditional British favourite.
Above : Fresh damsons turn a sweet soufflé into a special treat.

Redcurrant Cheesecake – a midsummer dream – tastes just as good as it looks!

Redcurrant cheesecake

250g/8oz digestive biscuits, crushed
125g/4oz butter, melted
1 tsp ground cinnamon
500g/1lb cream cheese
50g/2oz castor sugar
125ml/4floz single cream
625g/1¼lb redcurrants
15g/½oz gelatine
2 Tbsp water
450ml/15floz double cream
1 egg white

Mix together the crushed biscuits, melted butter and cinnamon. Press into the bottom of a greased loose-bottomed 23cm/9in cake tin. Smooth the surface.

Beat the cream cheese and sugar together until well mixed. Stir in the single cream and 500g/1lb of the redcurrants. Dissolve the gelatine in the water and strain into the redcurrant mixture. Stir well and spoon into the cake tin. Chill for at least 30 minutes or until set.

Meanwhile, whip the double cream until it is thick. Beat the egg white until it will hold a stiff peak, Fold the egg white into the whipped cream.

Remove the sides from the cake tin and slide the cheesecake onto a serving plate. Spoon over the cream mixture and top with the remaining redcurrants and serve.
Serves 6

Figs and peaches with soured cream

8 figs, sliced
4 large peaches, peeled, stoned and sliced
300ml/10floz soured cream
2 Tbsp soft brown sugar

Put the fig and peach slices in a shallow serving dish. Stir in the soured cream. Sprinkle the brown sugar over the top. Chill for at least 30 minutes before serving.
Serves 4

Fruit salad with Madeira sauce

250g/8oz raspberries
1 eating apple, peeled, cored and diced
125g/4oz purple grapes, havled and pipped
2 Tbsp chopped walnuts
1 pear, peeled, cored and sliced
125g/4oz cherries, stoned
1 banana, thinly sliced
SAUCE
2 eggs
3 egg yolks
50g/2oz castor sugar
2 Tbsp Madeira

Put the fruit and nuts in a serving dish and chill for 1 hour.

Mix together the eggs, egg yolks, sugar and Madeira in a heatproof mixing bowl. Place over a pan of simmering water and whisk until the mixture is thick and pale and will make a ribbon trail on itself when the whisk is lifted. Do not let the bowl become too hot or the mixture will curdle. Remove from the heat and pour the sauce over the fruit. Serve immediately.
Serves 4

Brandy meringue frozen pudding

MERINGUE
2 egg whites
125g/4oz castor sugar
PUDDING
3 eggs, separated
¼ tsp vanilla essence
75ml/3floz brandy
250ml/8floz double cream
75g/3oz castor sugar

Line a baking sheet with non-stick paper. Beat the egg whites until they will form a stiff peak. Add 2 teaspoons of the sugar and continue beating for 1 minute. Fold in the remaining sugar. Drop tablespoonsful of the meringue mixture onto the baking

A cool summer treat, Fruit Salad with Madeira Sauce is deliciously refreshing.

sheet. Bake in a cool oven (150°C/300°F or Gas Mark 2) for 2½ hours or until they are pale golden brown and crisp. Remove from the oven and allow to cool.

Meanwhile, beat the egg yolks, vanilla and brandy together. Whip the cream until it is thick. Beat the egg whites until they will hold a stiff peak. Add 2 teaspoons of the sugar and continue beating for 1 minute. Fold in the remaining sugar. Fold the cream into the egg yolk and brandy mixture, then fold in the egg white mixture. Spoon into a 1.5l/2 pint pudding basin. Freeze for 1 hour.

Crumble the meringues. Fold into the pudding mixture and return to the freezer. Freeze for a further 1 hour or until hard and set. To serve, unmould onto a serving dish.

Serves 6

Lemon and lime chiffon

4 eggs, separated
125g/4oz castor sugar
1 tsp grated lemon rind
5 Tbsp lemon juice
15g/½oz gelatine
2 Tbsp lime juice, warmed
4 Tbsp double cream

Put the egg yolks and sugar in a heatproof mixing bowl. Place the bowl over a pan of hot water and whisk until the mixture is pale and thick and leaves a ribbon trail when the whisk is lifted. Alternatively, use an electric mixer without heat.

Remove from the heat and beat in the lemon rind and juice. Dissolve the gelatine in the lime juice and strain into the lemon mixture. Stir well. Allow to cool.

Whip the cream until it is thick, then beat into the lemon and lime mixture. Beat the egg whites until they will hold a stiff peak. Fold into the lemon and lime mixture. Spoon into a serving bowl or individual dishes and chill for at least 3 hours or until set.

Serves 4

Pistachio ice-cream

250ml/8floz single cream
125g/4oz pistachio nuts (shelled weight), blanched and chopped
250ml/8floz double cream
½ tsp almond essence
3 eggs, separated
50g/2oz sugar
75ml/3floz water

Put the single cream and nuts in the goblet of an electric blender and blend to a purée. Pour into a saucepan and stir in the double cream. Heat gently, then cover and remove from the heat. Allow to cool.

Pour the pistachio mixture into a mixing bowl and stir in the almond essence. Beat the egg yolks until well mixed. Put the sugar and water in a saucepan and dissolve the sugar over gentle heat. Bring to the boil and boil until the syrup reaches 110°C/220°F on a sugar thermometer. Remove from the heat and allow to cool for 1 minute.

Pour the syrup onto the egg yolks in a steady stream, whisking constantly. Continue whisking until the mixture is thick and fluffy. Stir in the pistachio mixture. Beat the egg whites until they will hold a stiff peak and fold into the pistachio mixture.

Pour the mixture into an ice-cream container equipped with paddles (a sorbetière) or into a hand-propelled ice-cream churn, and freeze. Alternatively, freeze, remove from the freezer, beat and freeze again.

Serve as required.

Makes 600ml/1 pint

Apricot mousse with blackberries

500g/1lb apricots
4 Tbsp water
1 tsp lemon juice
50g/2oz sugar
4 egg whites
250g/8oz blackberries
4 Tbsp icing sugar

Halve and stone the apricots. Put them in a saucepan with the water, lemon juice and sugar and poach until they are very soft. If necessary, add a little more water to the pan if the mixture becomes too dry. Remove from the heat and allow to cool.

Purée the apricots in an electric blender or food mill. Alternatively, push them through a sieve. Return the purée to the saucepan and stir in the sugar. Stir over gentle heat to dissolve the sugar. Remove from the heat and cool.

Beat the egg whites until they will hold a stiff peak. Fold them into the apricot purée. Spoon into a serving dish or individual dishes and chill for at least 2 hours.

Mix together the blackberries and icing sugar.

Just before serving, top each portion of mousse with a spoonful of blackberries.

Serves 6

Note: this may also be made successfully with dried apricots. Use 350g/12oz and simmer them in enough water to cover for 10 to 15 minutes or until very tender. Continue as above.

Rich but deliciously flavoured, serve Nectarine Cream Mould as a summertime treat.

Peach flan

FLAN CASE
175g/6oz flour
pinch salt
40g/1½oz butter
40g/1½oz vegetable fat
2-3 Tbsp iced water
FILLING
4 large peaches, peeled, stoned and sliced
1 Tbsp peach brandy (optional)
TOPPING
2 Tbsp ground almonds
1 Tbsp chopped almonds
1 Tbsp chopped walnuts
3 Tbsp soft brown sugar
1 tsp grated orange rind
1 Tbsp butter, cut into small pieces

To make the flan case, sift the flour and salt into a mixing bowl. Add the butter and fat and cut into small pieces. Rub the fat into the flour until the mixture resembles breadcrumbs. Stir in enough water to bind the mixture and knead to a dough. Chill for 30 minutes.

Roll out the dough and use to line a 23cm/9in flan case. Bake blind in a fairly hot oven (200°C/400°F or Gas Mark 6) for 15 minutes. Allow to cool.

Arrange the peach slices in the flan case and sprinkle with the peach brandy, if using. Mix together the ground and chopped almonds, walnuts, sugar and orange rind. Sprinkle over the peaches and dot the butter over the top. Grill until the topping is crisp and bubbling.

Serve hot or cold, with cream.
Serves 4-6

Nectarine cream mould

6 medium nectarines, peeled, stoned
and finely chopped
pinch ground allspice
75g/3oz icing sugar
2 Tbsp brandy
15g/½oz gelatine
4 Tbsp hot water
300ml/10floz double cream

Mix together the nectarines, allspice, icing sugar and brandy. Dissolve the gelatine in the hot water and strain into the nectarine mixture. Stir well. Whip the cream until it is thick and fold into the nectarine mixture. Spoon into a greased 1.2l/2 pint mould. Chill for at least 2 hours or until set. To serve, unmould onto a dish.
Serves 4

Drinks

Badminton cup

½ cucumber, peeled and sliced
125g/4oz icing sugar
juice of 1 lemon
pinch grated nutmeg
5 Tbsp orange-flavoured liqueur
1 bottle claret or other dry red wine
175ml/6floz soda water, chilled
2 borage sprigs (optional)

Put the cucumber, sugar, lemon juice, nutmeg, liqueur and wine in a punch bowl. Stir to dissolve the sugar. Stir in the soda water and add some ice cubes. Float the borage sprigs on top, if using. Serve immediately.
Makes about 1 litre/1¾ pints.

Tea punch

2 Tbsp tea leaves
1.2 litres/2 pints boiling water
finely pared rind of 1 large lemon
175g/6oz soft brown sugar
250ml/8floz dark rum
250ml/8floz brandy
600ml/1 pint soda water (optional)

Place the tea leaves in a teapot or jug and pour over the boiling water. Cover and leave to infuse for 5 minutes.
Put the lemon rind and sugar in a mixing bowl and crush them together with a wooden spoon or pestle to release the zest from the rind. Pour the tea onto the sugar mixture and stir to dissolve the sugar. Allow to cool.
Strain the tea mixture into a punch bowl. Discard the lemon rind and tea leaves. Stir the rum and brandy into the strained tea. Serve chilled, adding the soda water, if used, just before serving.
Makes about 1.8 litres/3 pints

Vermouth punch

1 bottle dry vermouth, chilled
125ml/4floz orange-flavoured liqueur
125ml/4floz brandy
3 drops orange bitters
400ml/14floz soda water, chilled
1 orange, thinly sliced
1 lemon, thinly sliced

Put some crushed ice in a chilled punch bowl. Pour over the vermouth, liqueur, brandy, orange bitters and soda water and stir well. Float the oranges and lemon slices on the surface and serve.
Makes about 1.5 litres/2½ pints

Ginger beer

1 lemon
250g/8oz sugar
50g/2oz root ginger, bruised
1 Tbsp cream of tartar
3l/5 pints boiling water
7g/¼oz fresh yeast

Peel the lemon and set the rind aside. Squeeze the juice into a small jug or bowl and reserve.
Mix together the lemon rind, sugar, root ginger, cream of tartar and boiling water in a bowl. Stir well to dissolve the sugar. Set aside in a cool place and allow to cool to lukewarm.
Mash the yeast and 2 tablespoons of the ginger liquid to a paste. Add to the remaining ginger liquid and stir well. Leave in a warm, draught-free place for 1 to 2 days or until the yeast has stopped frothing.
Strain the mixture into a large jug or crock, discarding the lemon rind and ginger. Stir in the lemon juice. Pour the ginger beer into bottles and cover. Serve cold.
Makes about 3.6 litres/6 pints

Lemonade

grated rind and juice of 6 lemons
250g/8oz sugar
1.2 litres/2 pints boiling water

Put the lemon rind and sugar in a tall jug. Pour in the boiling water and stir to dissolve the sugar. Allow to cool, then chill for 2 hours.
Stir in the lemon juice and strain the lemonade into another jug.
Serve chilled.
Makes 1.5 litres/2 pints

Mint ale

6 large mint sprigs, roughly chopped
250g/8oz icing sugar
3 Tbsp water
juice of 12 lemons, chilled
900ml/1½ pints dry ginger ale, chilled
3 mint sprigs (optional)

Mix together the chopped mint, sugar and water in a mixing bowl. Pound with a wooden spoon or pestle until the sugar has dissolved. Set aside for 2 hours to allow the full flavour to be extracted.
Strain the mint mixture into a jug. Stir in the lemon juice and ginger ale. Garnish with the mint sprigs if you are using them and serve.
Makes about 1.2 litres/2 pints

Don't reserve mint for sauce alone. Mint Ale is a deliciously refreshing drink.

Lemonade and Ginger Beer – two fresh thirstquenchers for those long summer days.

Preserves

Jam

Jam-making is one of the best ways of preserving the lush fruits of summer. The bright colour and fresh taste of home-made jam will recapture the warmth of the summer sun when skies threaten rain or snow.

The equipment for making jam is basic and reasonably cheap. You will need a preserving pan, jam jars, jam covers, a heat-proof jug, a large bowl, a square of muslin or cheesecloth, a sugar thermometer and some labels.

Fruit for jam-making should be dry, fresh, in good condition and just ripe. Those which make an easily set jam or jelly, being rich in pectin, are black and redcurrants, gooseberries, damsons, crab-apples, apples, cranberries, quinces and some plums. Fruit with a moderate setting quality are apricots, gage plums, black-berries, loganberries and raspberries. Finally, those which will not produce a good set without some help are cherries, strawberries, pears, figs and pineapple.

To add pectin, the natural jellying substance present in most unripe fruit, to pectin-poor fruit, mix it with fruit rich in pectin. A popular combination is black-berry and apple. Alternatively, the pectin-rich fruit can be added in the form of juice (called pectin stock). Try redcurrant, apple or gooseberry. Or use a commercial liquid or powder pectin.

The first stage in jam making is to soften the fruit by cooking it with a little water if it is not sufficiently juicy. This cooking releases the pectin. If the fruit is deficient in acid, lemon juice, tartaric or citric acid, redcurrant or gooseberry juice may be added. Next, the sugar is stirred in until dissolved.

The jam is brought to the boil and boiled until setting point is reached. The simplest test for setting point is to spoon a little of the jam onto a saucer. When it has cooled, push it with your finger: it should set and crinkle. If you prefer, use a sugar thermometer which should register 105°C/220°F if the jam is ready.

Before bottling jam containing whole fruit, allow it to cool until a skin forms on top. Spoon the jam into clean, dry jars, filling right to the top. Cover with a well-fitting lid of waxed paper, pressing it down to exclude any air. Cover the jars with cellophane or plastic covers and secure with rubber bands.

When the jam is cold, label the jars and store in a cool, dark place.

Preserve the warmth and colour of summer fruits to cheer you in the colder seasons.

Strawberry jam

2.5kg/5lb strawberries, hulled
125ml/4floz lemon juice
2kg/4lb sugar

Put the strawberries and lemon juice in an aluminium or stainless steel pan. Simmer, stirring frequently, until the fruit is very soft. Stir in the sugar and continue stirring until it has dissolved.

Bring to the boil and boil rapidly until setting point is reached. Remove from the heat and allow to cool for 10 minutes before bottling.
Makes about 3.25kg/7lb

Peach jam

1 medium cooking apple, chopped
thinly pared rind of 2 lemons
2 whole cloves
1.5kg/3lb peaches, skinned, stoned and sliced
300ml/10floz water
1 tsp ground allspice
1.5kg/3lb sugar

Tie the apple, lemon rind and cloves in a piece of muslin. Put the peaches, water and muslin bag in an aluminium or stainless steel pan. Bring to the boil, stirring constantly, then simmer until the peaches are soft.

Remove the muslin bag, pressing it against the side of the pan to extract all the liquid. Stir the allspice and sugar into the peaches and continue stirring until the sugar has dissolved. Bring to the boil and boil rapidly until setting point is reached.

Remove from the heat and allow to cool for 10 minutes before bottling.
Makes about 2.25kg/5lb

Plum and apple jam

700g/1½lb plums, halved and stoned
700g/1½lb cooking apples, peeled, cored and sliced
1 Tbsp lemon juice
300ml/10floz water
1.5kg/3lb sugar

Put the plums, apples, lemon juice and water in an aluminium or stainless steel pan. Bring to the boil, stirring constantly, then simmer until the fruit is soft.

Stir in the sugar and continue sitrring until the sugar has dissolved. Bring to the boil and boil rapidly until setting point is reached.

Remove from the heat and bottle according to the information supplied.
Makes about 2.25kg/5lb

Autumn

As the leaves turn to gold and the evenings draw in, so our appetites tend to increase. Fortunately this coincides with the maturing of the fruits on trees and hedgerows heralded by the spring blossom, and the opening of the game season. Use the fresh root vegetables to help fill out warming casseroles, and the tree fruits to make chutneys and relishes to add bite to cold meats. Satisfy the family's hunger with tea breads, buttered crumpets and scones spread with jam made in the summer. Autumn is the time for gathering field mushrooms, eating parkin by a bonfire, baking cakes and meats and sitting down to enjoy freshly harvested and prepared food.

What's best in season

Fruit:				
	Apples	Figs	Pawpaws	Quinces
	Bananas	Grapes	Peaches	Satsumas
	Blackberries	Grapefruit	Pears	Strawberries
	Blueberries	Lemons	Persimmons	Tangerines
	Crabapples	Limes	Pineapples	Uglifruit
	Cranberries	Melons	Plums	
	Damsons	Oranges	Pomegranates	
	Dates	Papayas	Pumpkin	

Vegetables:				
	Aubergines	Celery	Leeks	Runner beans
	Avocados	Chicory	Lettuces	Salsify
	Beetroot	Courgettes	Marrows	Shallots
	Broccoli	Cucumbers	Mushrooms	Spinach
	Brussels sprouts	Endive	Onions	Swede
	Cabbages	Fennel	Parsnips	Sweetcorn
	Calabrese	French beans	Peppers	Swiss chard
	Carrots	Jerusalem artichokes	Potatoes	Tomatoes
	Cauliflowers	Kale	Pumpkin	Turnips
	Celeriac	Kohlrabi	Radishes	Watercress

Herbs:				
	Bay	Fennel	Parsley	Tarragon
	Chives	Lemon balm	Rosemary	Thyme
	Coriander	Marjoram	Sage	
	Dill	Mint	Summer and winter savory	

Nuts:				
	Almonds	Brazil nuts	Chestnuts	Hazelnuts

Fish:				
	Bream	Haddock	Pike	Trout
	Brill	Halibut	Plaice	Turbot
	Carp	Herring	Prawns	Whelk
	Clam	Mackerel	Scallop	Whiting
	Cockles	Mullet	Shrimps	Winkles
	Cod	Mussels	Skate	
	Crab	Oysters	Sole	
	Eel	Perch	Sprat	

Poultry: Available fresh or frozen all year round

Game:				
	Grouse	Partridge	Quail	Teal
	Hare	Pheasant	Rabbit	Woodcock
	Mallard	Pigeon	Snipe	Venison

Meat and offal: Available fresh or frozen all year round

Appetizers

Ham custard moulds

50g/2oz butter
125g/4oz button mushrooms, sliced
1 medium onion, finely chopped
25g/1oz fresh breadcrumbs
1 Tbsp milk
250g/8oz cooked ham, finely chopped or minced
250ml/8floz white or béchamel sauce
50g/2oz Cheddar cheese, grated
1 Tbsp tomato purée
1 Tbsp parsley, freshly chopped
¼ tsp Worcestershire sauce
1 tsp marjoram, freshly chopped
3 eggs, separated

Melt 15g/½oz of the butter in a frying pan. Add the mushrooms and cook until they are just tender. Remove the mushrooms from the pan with a slotted spoon and chop them very finely.

Add the remaining butter to the pan and when it has melted add the onion. Fry until it is soft but not brown. Meanwhile, sprinkle the breadcrumbs with the milk and press to moisten them.

Add the onions to the mushrooms with the breadcrumbs, ham, sauce, cheese, tomato purée, parsley, Worcestershire sauce, marjoram and egg yolks. Mix together well.

Beat the egg whites until they will hold a stiff peak. Fold them into the ham mixture. Spoon into eight small greased moulds and place the moulds in a roasting tin. Add enough boiling water to the tin to come halfway up the sides of the moulds. Bake in a warm oven (170°C/325°F or Gas Mark 3) for 40 minutes or until lightly set.

Turn the individual custards out of the moulds and serve hot.
Serves 8

Courgettes stuffed with almonds

4 large or 8 small courgettes
3 Tbsp olive oil
1 medium onion, finely chopped
75g/3oz ground almonds
125ml/4floz double cream
75g/3oz dry breadcrumbs
75g/3oz Gruyére cheese, grated
salt and pepper
1 tsp marjoram, freshly chopped
1 tsp chervil, freshly chopped
1 egg, lightly beaten
50g/2oz butter, melted

Blanch the courgettes in boiling salted water for 5 minutes. Drain and refresh under cold running water, then drain again. Cut the courgettes in half lengthways and carefully hollow out the flesh, leaving boat-shaped shells of skin. Chop the flesh. Press it with a wooden spoon to extract as much liquid as possible and drain away the liquid.

Heat the oil in a frying pan. Add the onion and fry until soft but not brown. Stir in the courgette flesh and cook for a further 5 minutes. Turn into a mixing bowl and stir in the almonds, cream and half of the breadcrumbs. Add two-thirds of the cheese, salt and pepper to taste, the herbs and egg and mix well. If the mixture is not thick and firm, add more breadcrumbs.

Arrange the courgette shells in a greased baking dish and fill with the almond-cheese mixture. Mix together the remaining cheese and breadcrumbs and sprinkle over the tops. Sprinkle with the melted butter. Bake in a fairly hot oven (200°C/400°F or Gas Mark 6) for 15 to 20 minutes or until bubbling and brown. Serve hot.
Serves 4

These moulded Ham Custards make unusual and attractive savoury appetizers.

Below: Moules Marinières – an impressive yet simple dish to prepare which originated from France's Atlantic coast.
Bottom: Mussels must be purchased fresh. Discard any with open shells.

Moules marinières

4 dozen mussels
50g/2oz butter
1 small onion, finely chopped
1 garlic clove, crushed
1 celery stalk, finely chopped
1 bouquet garni
500ml/16floz dry white wine
salt and black pepper
2 Tbsp parsley, freshly chopped

Scrub the mussels and scrape off the beards. Discard any mussels that are not tightly shut or any that seem too heavy as they may be full of sand. Leave to soak in cold water for 2 hours, then wash and drain again. Discard any that float or have broken shells.

Melt the butter in a saucepan. Add the onion and garlic and fry until the onion is soft but not brown. Add the celery, bouquet garni, wine and salt and pepper to taste and bring to the boil. Add the mussels to the pan and cook gently, shaking the pan occasionally, for 5 to 10 minutes or until the mussels open.

Transfer the mussels to a warmed serving dish with a slotted spoon. Discard the empty shell halves. Keep hot. Reserve the cooking liquid.

Strain the cooking liquid and return to the heat. Bring to the boil and boil for 2 minutes. Pour over the mussels and sprinkle with the parsley.

Serve hot.
Serves 4

Aubergine slices

1 large aubergine, peeled and cut into
1cm/½in thick slices
salt
40g/1½oz butter, melted
40g/1½oz dry breadcrumbs
1 Tbsp oregano, freshly chopped
50g/2oz Parmesan cheese, grated
TOMATO SAUCE
2 Tbsp olive oil
1 small onion, finely chopped
1 garlic clove, crushed
500g/1lb tomatoes, peeled and chopped
salt and black pepper
1 Tbsp oregano, freshly chopped

First make the tomato sauce. Heat the oil in a saucepan. Add the onion and garlic and fry until the onion is soft but not brown. Stir in the tomatoes with salt and pepper to taste and the oregano and simmer gently for 20 minutes or until the sauce is very thick.

Meanwhile, place the aubergine slices in a colander, sprinkle with salt and leave for 20 minutes. Rinse and pat dry with kitchen paper towels.

Dip each aubergine slice in the melted butter and then in the breadcrumbs to coat well. Place on a greased baking sheet. Bake in a very hot oven (230°C/450°F or Gas Mark 8) for 15 minutes or until the slices are tender and lightly browned.

Top each slice with a spoonful of tomato sauce and sprinkle with the oregano and cheese. Return to the oven and bake for a further 10 minutes or until the topping is lightly browned. Serve hot.
Serves 6-8

Cold marinated oysters

16 oysters, removed from the shells
MARINADE
175ml/6floz dry white wine
4 Tbsp olive oil
4 Tbsp lemon juice
salt and black pepper
1 tsp thyme, freshly chopped
1 tsp chervil, freshly chopped
1 tsp parsley, freshly chopped
1 garlic clove, crushed

Mix together all the marinade ingredients,

with salt and pepper to taste, in a saucepan. Leave for 15 minutes.

Add the oysters to the saucepan and bring to the boil. Remove from the heat and pour the oysters and marinade into a shallow serving dish. Allow to cool, then chill well. Serve cold.

Serves 4

Pears stuffed with blue cheese

2 large dessert pears, peeled, halved and cored
1 tsp lemon juice
40g/1½oz unsalted butter, softened
75g/3oz blue cheese, such as Roquefort, crumbled
4 large lettuce leaves

Brush the pears all over with the lemon juice to prevent discoloration.

Mix together the butter and blue cheese, mashing with a fork. Form into four balls.

Place a lettuce leaf on each of four small plates. Place a pear half on each, cut side up, and top with a cheese ball. Chill for 30 minutes before serving.

Serves 4

Mushroom and bacon pots

250g/8oz streaky bacon, rinds removed and coarsely chopped
25g/1oz butter
500g/1lb button mushrooms
salt and black pepper
2 Tbsp brandy
4 Tbsp double cream
4 Tbsp Gruyére cheese, grated
4 parsley sprigs

Fry the bacon in a frying pan until it is crisp and has rendered most of its fat. Add the butter and when it has melted add the mushrooms with salt and pepper to taste. Cook for 3 to 4 minutes or until the mushrooms are just tender.

Warm the brandy in a ladle. Pour over the mushroom mixture and set alight. When the flames have died down, stir in the cream. Remove from the heat and spoon into four individual flameproof dishes. Sprinkle a tablespoon of cheese over each.

Grill for 4 minutes or until the cheese has melted and is lightly browned. Garnish with the parsley sprigs and serve.

Serves 4

A delectable combination of oysters, white wine and herbs, Marinated Oysters make an exquisite first course.

Soups

Pumpkin soup

25g/1oz butter
2 small onions, thinly sliced and
pushed out into rings
500g/1lb pumpkin flesh, chopped
1.2l/2 pints chicken stock
salt
1 celery stalk, chopped
1 large potato, peeled and chopped
1 Tbsp lemon juice
few drops Tabasco sauce
1 tsp paprika
250ml/8floz double cream
croutons, to serve

Melt the butter in a saucepan. Add the onions and pumpkin and fry until the onions are soft but not brown. Stir in the stock, salt to taste, the celery, potato, lemon juice, Tabasco and paprika. Bring to the boil, then cover and simmer for 30 to 35 minutes or until the vegetables are tender.

Purée the soup in an electric blender, then strain it back into the saucepan.

Alternatively, push the soup through a sieve. Stir the cream into the puréed soup and reheat gently without boiling.

Serve hot, garnished with croûtons.
Serves 4-6

Game soup

25g/1oz butter
1 Tbsp vegetable oil
1 pheasant or partridge carcass,
broken into several pieces
250g/8oz cooked game meat, cut into small
cubes
1 large onion, sliced
1 large carrot, scraped and sliced
1 small turnip, peeled and chopped
1 Tbsp flour
900ml/1¼ pints beef stock
50g/2oz cooked ham, chopped
1 bouquet garni
salt and black pepper
150ml/5floz Madeira

Melt the butter with the oil in a saucepan. Add the carcass, meat, onion, carrot and turnip and fry until the vegetables are lightly browned. Sprinkle over the flour and cook, sitrring, for 1 minute. Remove

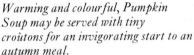

Warming and colourful, Pumpkin Soup may be served with tiny croûtons for an invigorating start to an autumn meal.

from the heat and gradually stir in the stock.

Return to the heat and bring to the boil. Simmer, stirring, until the liquid has thickened. Add the ham, bouquet garni and salt and pepper to taste. Cover and simmer gently for 2 hours.

Remove and discard the carcass pieces and bouquet garni. Stir in the Madeira. Simmer, uncovered, for a further 10 minutes and serve.

Serves 4-6

Corn chowder

25g/1oz butter
1 medium onion, finely chopped
1 Tbsp flour
250ml/8floz chicken stock
300ml/10floz milk
2 medium potatoes, parboiled for 10
minutes, drained and finely chopped
500g/1lb sweetcorn kernels
salt and pepper
250ml/8floz double cream
2 Tbsp chopped pimiento

Melt the butter in a saucepan. Add the onion and fry until it is soft but not brown. Sprinkle over the flour and cook, stirring, for 1 minute. Remove from the heat and gradually stir in the stock and milk. Return to the heat and bring to the boil. Simmer, stirring, until thickened and smooth.

Stir in the potatoes, corn and salt and pepper to taste, cover and cook gently for 20 minutes.

Stir in the cream and heat through gently without boiling. Stir in the pimiento and serve.

Serves 4-6

Donegal mussel soup

3 dozen mussels
40g/1½oz butter
2 shallots, finely chopped
1 Tbsp parsley, freshly chopped
1 tsp thyme, freshly chopped
1 bay leaf
salt and black pepper
175ml/6floz cider
1 large leek, thinly sliced
1 celery stalk, chopped
4 Tbsp flour
600ml/1 pint milk, scalded
600ml/1 pint fish stock, warmed
3 fennel sprigs, freshly chopped
½ tsp grated nutmeg
150ml/5floz double cream

Scrub the mussels and scrape off the beards. Discard any mussels that are not tightly shut or any that seem too heavy as they may be full of sand. Leave to soak in cold water for 2 hours, then wash and drain again.

Grease a large saucepan with 15g/½oz of the butter. Sprinkle the shallots over the bottom and add the parsley, thyme and bay leaf. Arrange the mussels on top and season with pepper. Pour in the cider. Bring to the boil, cover and cook for 10 minutes, shaking the pan occasionally.

Remove from the heat. Take the mussels out of the pan, discarding any which are still closed. Remove the meat from the shells, discarding the shells. Strain the cooking liquid and reserve.

Melt the remaining butter in the cleaned-out saucepan. Add the leek and celery and fry until lightly browned. Sprinkle over the flour and cook, stirring, for 1 minute. Remove from the heat and stir in the milk and fish stock. Return to the heat and simmer, stirring, until thickened. Simmer for 15 minutes.

Remove from the heat and strain the liquid into another saucepan. Stir in the reserved mussel cooking liquid, the fennel, nutmeg and salt and pepper to taste. Add the mussels and cream and stir well. Heat through gently without boiling. Serve hot.

Serves 4

Cucumber, potato and dill soup

25g/1oz butter
2 shallots, finely chopped
2 small potatoes, peeled and diced
1 Tbsp flour
1l/1¾ pints chicken stock
1 Tbsp lemon juice
salt and black pepper
1 bay leaf
1 Tbsp dill, freshly chopped
2 medium cucumbers, peeled and
thickly sliced
250ml/8floz soured cream

Melt the butter in a saucepan. Add the shallots and fry until they are soft but not brown. Add the potatoes and fry for a further 4 minutes. Sprinkle over the flour and stir well. Gradually stir in the stock, then stir in the lemon juice, salt and pepper to taste, the bay leaf, dill and cucumbers. Bring to the boil, stirring, then cover and simmer for 30 minutes.

Remove from the heat. Discard the bay leaf and purée the soup in an electric blender or by pushing it through a sieve. Return the puréed soup to the saucepan and stir in the soured cream. Heat through gently without boiling. Serve hot.

Serves 6

Delicately flavoured with fennel and nutmeg, Donegal Mussel Soup makes a rich, creamy first course.

Main Dishes

Grey mullet Martigues

4 small grey mullets, cleaned
salt and black pepper
2 medium onions, thinly sliced
3 tomatoes, peeled and sliced
1 carrot, scraped and cut into strips
4 Tbsp olive oil
250ml/8floz dry white wine
1 tsp oregano, freshly chopped
1 tsp marjoram, freshly chopped
1 lemon, thinly sliced

Sprinkle the fish with salt. Make three parallel diagonal cuts across each fish. Place half the onions in a greased shallow baking dish. Top with the tomato slices and carrot strips, then the remaining onions. Place the fish on top, in one layer, and pour over the olive oil and wine. Sprinkle with salt and pepper, the oregano and marjoram and top with the lemon slices.

Cover the dish with foil and bake in a moderate oven (180°C/350°F or Gas Mark 4) for 35 minutes. Remove the foil and continue baking for 15 minutes or until the fish are cooked. Test with a fork: the flesh should flake easily.

Serve hot.

Serves 4

Bream with fennel and white wine

1 x 1kg/2lb bream, cleaned
2 fennel sprigs
2 sprigs thyme
25g/1oz butter
salt and black pepper
150ml/5floz dry white wine
1 Tbsp olive oil
1 bulb Florence fennel, sliced
2 tomatoes, sliced
1 lemon, thinly sliced

Make two deep incisions along the back of the fish. Insert the fennel sprigs in the incisions. Place the thyme sprigs and butter inside the fish and sprinkle with salt and pepper. Place the fish on a rack in a roasting tin. Pour over the wine and olive oil and arrange the fennel, tomato and lemon slices over the top.

Bake in a moderate oven (180°C/350°F or Gas Mark 4) for 30 minutes or until the fish is cooked. Test with a fork: the flesh should flake easily.

Transfer the fish to a warmed serving dish and serve hot.

Serves 4

Haddock with cider

250ml/8floz cider
2 medium onions, thinly sliced
1 green pepper, pith and seeds removed and chopped
700g/1½lb haddock fillets, skinned
3 tomatoes, peeled and chopped
1 tsp marjoram, freshly chopped
pinch cayenne pepper
salt and white pepper
3 Tbsp fresh white breadcrumbs
25g/1oz Parmesan cheese, grated

Bring the cider to the boil in a saucepan. Add the onions and green pepper and simmer for 5 minutes or until the cider has reduced by about one-quarter. Remove the heat.

Cut the fish into 10cm/4in pieces and put them into a flameproof casserole. Add the cider mixture and tomatoes and mix well. Stir in the marjoram, cayenne and salt and pepper to taste. Cover the casserole and bake in a warm oven (170°C/325°F or Gas Mark 3) for 30 minutes or until the fish is cooked. Test with a fork: the flesh should flake easily.

Mix together the breadcrumbs and cheese. Uncover the casserole and sprinkle the breadcrumb and cheese mixture over the top. Grill until the topping is lightly browned. Serve hot.

Serves 4

Cod provençale

4 Tbsp olive oil
1 small onion, thinly sliced
1 garlic clove, chopped
1 green pepper, pith and seeds removed and thinly sliced
50g/2oz can anchovies, drained and chopped
50g/2oz black olives, stoned
pinch fennel seeds, crushed
8 x 125g/4oz cod steaks
3 small tomatoes, thinly sliced
salt and black pepper
3 Tbsp tomato purée
125ml/4floz dry red wine

Heat half the oil in a frying pan. Add the onion, garlic and green pepper and fry until the onion is soft but not brown. Remove from the heat and stir in the anchovies, olives and fennel seeds.

Place four cod steaks in a greased shallow baking dish. Top each with one-quarter of the anchovy mixture. Place the remaining cod steaks on top and arrange the tomato slices over these. Brush the tomatoes with the remaining oil and sprinkle with salt and pepper.

Mix together the tomato purée and wine. Pour into the baking dish around the fish. Bake in a fairly hot oven (200°C/400°F or Gas Mark 6) for 30 minutes. Baste the fish with the cooking liquid in the dish at least twice during baking.

Serve hot.

Serves 4

Seafood casserole

250g/8oz crabmeat, shell and cartilage removed
1 egg, lightly beaten
2 Tbsp parsley, freshly chopped
salt and black pepper
4 sole fillets, skinned and halved
250g/8oz Dublin Bay prawns (shelled weight), deveined
250g/8oz shrimps (shelled weight), deveined
250g/8oz scallops, quartered
125ml/4floz fish stock
125ml/4floz dry white wine
4 Tbsp lemon juice
150ml/5floz double cream
1 lemon, cut into wedges

Mash the crabmeat, egg, parsley and salt and pepper to taste together to make a paste. Spread thickly over one side of each half fillet of sole and roll up like Swiss rolls. Place in a flameproof casserole. Add the prawns, shrimps, scallops, stock, wine and lemon juice. Bring the liquid to the boil, then cover and transfer to a moderate oven (180°C/350°F or Gas Mark 4). Cook for 20 minutes or until the sole is tender.

Transfer the fish rolls and shellfish to a warmed serving dish. Keep hot.

Strain the cooking liquid into a saucepan. Bring to the boil and boil until the liquid has reduced to about half the original quantity. Stir in the cream and heat through gently without boiling. Pour this sauce over the seafood and serve immediately, garnished with the lemon.

Serves 8

Cod Provençal is an attractive dish of cod steaks with anchovies, olives and green peppers in a delicious red wine and tomato sauce.

A simple, unassuming dish of Mackerel in White Wine Sauce makes a pleasant lunch or dinner.

Mackerel in white wine sauce

4 mackerel, cleaned and filleted
salt and black pepper
40g/1½oz butter
175ml/6floz fish stock
175ml/6floz white wine
2 Tbsp dry sherry
½ tsp fennel seed, crushed
1 tsp grated lemon rind

Place the mackerel fillets in a greased shallow baking dish. Sprinkle with salt and pepper and dot with the butter, cut into small pieces.

Bring the stock, wine, sherry, fennel seed and lemon rind to the boil in a saucepan. Boil for 10 minutes or until reduced to half the original quantity. Pour over the fillets and bake in a fairly hot oven (190°C/375°F or Gas Mark 5) for 10 to 15 minutes or until the fish is cooked. Test with a fork: the flesh should flake easily.

Transfer the fish and cooking liquid to a warmed serving dish and serve.
Serves 4

Eel stew

500g/1lb fish heads and trimmings
1.2l/2 pints plus 1 Tbsp water
1 bouquet garni
salt and black pepper
4 peppercorns
1 celery stalk, chopped
1 carrot, scraped and chopped
3 Tbsp olive oil
50g/2oz blanched almonds, chopped
1 large red pepper, pith and seeds removed and sliced
1 large onion, halved and sliced
3 garlic cloves, crushed
1 tsp thyme, freshly chopped
1 tsp paprika
½ tsp cayenne pepper
1kg/2lb eels, skinned and cut into serving pieces
1 tsp cornflour

Put the fish heads and trimmings, all but 1 tablespoon water, the bouquet garni, 1 teaspoon salt, the peppercorns, celery and carrot in a saucepan. Bring to the boil, then cover and simmer for 30 minutes. Strain this court bouillon.

Heat the oil in a flameproof casserole. Add the almonds, red pepper, onion and garlic. Fry until the almonds are golden and the onion soft but not brown. Stir in the thyme, paprika, cayenne and black pepper to taste. Cook for a further 2 minutes. Add the eel pieces and fry, stirring, for 5 minutes.

Stir in the court bouillon and bring to the boil. Cover and simmer for 30 minutes. Dissolve the cornflour in the remaining tablespoon of water and stir in a little of the hot liquid. Stir into the stew. Cook for a further 2 to 3 minutes, stirring, or until the stew has thickened slightly. Serve hot.
Serves 4

Scallops with vermouth sauce

500g/1lb Jerusalem artichokes, peeled
16 scallops, halved
juice of 1 lemon
75g/3oz flour
salt and black pepper
50g/2oz butter
4 shallots, finely chopped
2 garlic cloves, crushed
125g/4oz mushrooms, sliced
1 Tbsp tarragon, freshly chopped
1 Tbsp parsley, freshly chopped
75ml/3floz dry vermouth
250ml/8floz single cream

Cook the artichokes in boiling water, to which you have added a squeeze of lemon juice and salt, for 30 minutes, or until they are tender. Drain well and slice.

Sprinkle the scallops with the lemon juice and leave to marinate for 5 minutes. Mix together the flour with salt and pepper and use to coat the scallops.

Melt the butter in a frying pan. Add the scallops and fry until lightly browned. Add the shallots, garlic, artichoke slices, mushrooms, tarragon, parsley and salt and pepper to taste. Stir well and cook for 5 minutes.

Meanwhile, heat the vermouth in a small saucepan. Ignite it and when the flames die down stir in the cream. Heat through gently without boiling, then stir into the scallop mixture. Transfer to a warmed serving dish and serve immediately.
Serves 4

Carpetbag steak

1kg/2lb rump or fillet steak, in one piece, about 5cm/2in thick
12 oysters, removed from the shells
salt and black pepper
¼ tsp cayenne pepper
15g/½oz butter, melted
watercress, to garnish

Slit the steak lengthways to form a pocket. Fill the pocket with the oysters and sprinkle the oysters with salt and pepper and the cayenne. Sew up the opening with a trussing needle and thread or string.

Brush the steak with the melted butter

A sensational dish for a dinner party, Carpetbag Steak is a famous Australian recipe of rump or fillet steak stuffed with oysters.

and grill for 5 to 6 minutes on each side, using a fierce heat to seal the meat. Reduce the heat, or increase the distance from the heat, and grill for a further 10 minutes on each side, depending on how well done you like your steak.

Remove the string or thread and place the steak on a warmed serving dish. Garnish with the watercress and serve.
Serves 4

Veal stroganoff

6 veal escalopes, pounded thin
50g/2oz butter
2 Tbsp olive oil
2 medium onions, thinly sliced
350g/12oz button mushrooms
350ml/12floz soured cream
1 tsp prepared French mustard
1 Tbsp tomato purée
salt and black pepper
1 Tbsp parsley, freshly chopped

Cut the escalopes into strips 5cm/2in long and 6mm/¼in wide. Melt the butter with the oil in a frying pan. Add the veal strips and fry until they are lightly browned. Remove from the pan and keep hot.

Add the onions to the pan and fry until they are soft but not brown. Add the mushrooms and fry until they are just tender.

Mix together the soured cream, mustard, tomato purée and salt and pepper to taste. Stir into the onion and mushroom mixture and cook, stirring, for 1 minute. Return the veal strips to the pan and cook for a further 2 minutes to reheat.

Transfer the stroganoff to a warmed serving dish and sprinkle with the parsley. Serve hot.
Serves 6

Breast of veal with piquant lemon stuffing

2kg/4lb breast of veal (boned weight)
50g/2oz butter
½ small onion, finely chopped
3 bacon rashers, rinded and chopped
125g/4oz fresh white breadcrumbs
1 Tbsp parsley, freshly chopped
grated rind and juice of ½ lemon
1 small cooking apple, peeled, cored and grated
salt and pepper
1 egg, beaten
1 green eating apple, cored and sliced, to garnish

Melt the butter in a frying pan. Add the onion and bacon and fry until the onion is soft but not brown and the bacon crisp.

Transfer to a mixing bowl with a slotted spoon. Stir in the breadcrumbs, parsley, lemon rind and juice, grated apple, salt and pepper to taste and the beaten egg. Mix well.

Lay the veal flat on a work surface and cover with the stuffing. Roll up like a Swiss roll and tie at 2.5cm (1in) intervals with string.

Wrap the veal roll in foil and place in a roasting tin. Roast in a moderate oven (180°C/350°F or Gas Mark 4) for 2 hours. Remove the foil and roast for a further 30 minutes or until the veal is cooked through. During the final 30 minutes, baste well with the juices collected in the foil.

Transfer the veal roll to a warmed serving dish and remove the string. Garnish with the apple slices and serve hot. Note: This dish may be prepared up to the stage of tying with string the night before and then cooked as required.
Serves 6

Beef with corn and tomatoes

2 Tbsp paprika
25g/1oz flour
1kg/2lb topside of beef, cut into 5cm/2in cubes
50g/2oz butter
2 medium onions, chopped
2 garlic cloves, chopped
250g/8oz tomatoes, peeled and chopped
1 Tbsp thyme, freshly chopped
1 bay leaf
salt and black pepper
2 carrots, scraped and sliced
250ml/8floz dry white wine
500g/1lb sweetcorn kernels
150ml/5floz single cream
75ml/3floz brandy

Mix together the paprika and flour. Place in a polythene bag. Toss the beef cubes in the seasoned flour. Melt the butter in a flameproof casserole. Add the onions and garlic and fry until the onions are soft but not brown. Add the meat cubes, in batches, and brown them on all sides. Stir in the tomatoes, thyme, bay leaf, salt and pepper to taste and the carrots. Cover and cook gently for 20 minutes.

Stir in the wine, re-cover and simmer for a further 45 minutes. Add the sweetcorn, stir well and re-cover. Simmer for a further 20 minutes or until the meat is very tender.

Mix together the cream and brandy. Stir into the casserole and simmer gently, uncovered, for 15 minutes. Serve hot, from the casserole.
Serves 4

Below : Breast of Veal with Piquant Lemon Stuffing makes a meal with a fruity tang.
Opposite : A substantial, autumn-coloured dish, Beef with Corn and Tomatoes is best served straight from the casserole.

Beef Stew with Dumplings served with sour cream is a hearty, satisfying main dish.

Beef stew with dumplings

25g/1oz flour
salt and black pepper
1kg/2lb stewing steak, cut into 2.5cm/1in cubes
25g/1oz butter
1 Tbsp vegetable oil
1 large onion, finely chopped
2 Tbsp brandy, warmed (optional)
1 bay leaf
1.2l/2 pints beef stock, boiling
175g/6oz small mushrooms
150ml/5floz soured cream
DUMPLINGS
250g/8oz fresh breadcrumbs
4 Tbsp water
3 eggs, lightly beaten
salt and black pepper
1½ Tbsp parsley, freshly chopped
1 medium onion, finely chopped
½ tsp ground mace

Mix together the flour with salt and pepper in a polythene bag. Add the beef cubes and shake to coat them all with the flour. Melt the butter with the oil in a frying pan. Add the onion and fry until it is soft but not brown. Transfer the onion to a casserole.

Add the beef cubes to the pan, in batches, and fry until they are browned on all sides. Transfer to the casserole.

If you are using the brandy, set it alight and pour it over the beef cubes in the casserole. When the flames have died down, add the bay leaf and stock. Cover the casserole and bake in a warm oven (170°C/ 325°F or Gas Mark 3) for 2 hours.

Meanwhile, make the dumplings. Put the breadcrumbs in a mixing bowl and sprinkle with the water. Toss lightly with a fork, then mix in the remaining ingredients with salt and pepper to taste. Form the mixture into walnut-sized balls.

Add the dumplings and mushrooms to the casserole, re-cover and continue to cook for 30 minutes.

Spoon the soured cream over the top and serve hot, from the casserole.
Serves 4

Brewer's beef pot roast

2kg/4lb top rump of beef
salt and black pepper
4 Tbsp vegetable oil
4 medium leeks, washed, trimmed and
thinly sliced
6 medium parsnips, peeled and sliced
900ml/1½ pints beef stock
1 bouquet garni
250ml/8floz light beer
1 tsp butter
2 tsp flour
parsley sprigs, to garnish

Rub the meat with salt and pepper. Heat the oil in a flameproof casserole. Put the beef in the pot and brown on all sides. Add half the sliced leeks and parsnips and cook for 8 minutes. Pour in the stock and bring to the boil. Add the bouquet garni. Cover and simmer gently for 2½ to 3 hours or until the meat is very tender.

Transfer the meat to a warmed dish and keep hot.

Skim any fat from the surface of the liquid in the casserole. Strain into a saucepan and add the remaining leeks and parsnips. Bring to the boil and boil for 20 to 25 minutes or until the liquid is reduced to about half the original quantity.

Stir in the beer and bring back to the boil. Blend the butter and flour together to make a smooth paste (beurre manié). Add in small pieces to the beer mixture and simmer, stirring, until thickened. Taste and adjust the seasoning if necessary.

Carve the meat into thick slices and arrange on a warmed serving dish. Pour over the sauce and garnish with parsley sprigs. Serve hot.
Serves 6

Sautéed steak with shallot and wine sauce

1kg/2lb fillet steak
25g/1oz butter
1 Tbsp vegetable oil
SAUCE
25g/1oz flour
50g/2oz butter
1 Tbsp vegetable oil
2 shallots, finely chopped
1 garlic clove, crushed
300ml/10floz red wine
300ml/10floz beef stock
1 bay leaf
1 tsp thyme, freshly chopped
salt and black pepper

Cut the steak into pieces about 5cm/2in square and 1cm/½in thick. Melt the butter with the oil in a frying pan. Add the steak

Brewer's Pot-Roast makes a delicious family meal. Serve it with potatoes baked in their jackets and a glass of beer.

pieces and sauté until the outside is browned but the inside is still pink—about 2 to 3 minutes on each side. Transfer the meat to a warmed serving dish and keep hot while you make the sauce.

Mix together the flour and 25g/1oz of the butter to make a paste (beurre manié). Melt the remaining butter with the oil in the cleaned-out frying pan. Add the shallots and garlic and fry until the shallots are soft but not brown. Stir in the wine, stock, bay leaf, thyme and salt and pepper to taste. Bring to the boil and boil until the liquid has reduced to half the original quantity.

Add the beurre manié in small pieces, stirring, and continue simmering, stirring, until the sauce thickens. Remove the bay leaf and pour the sauce over the steak. Serve immediately.
Serves 6

Danish pork

1kg/2lb boned rolled loin of pork
2 cooking apples, peeled, cored and sliced
salt and black pepper
25g/1oz butter
1 medium onion, chopped
300ml/10floz water
25g/1oz flour
1 tsp prepared mustard
125ml/4floz soured cream

A subtle yet remarkably tasty dish, Danish Pork is surprisingly quick and easy to prepare.

Make about 10 long slits in the pork on both sides. Insert half the apple slices in the slits. Rub the pork with salt and pepper. Melt the butter in a flameproof casserole. Add the pork, onion and remaining apple slices. Brown the pork on all sides.

Pour in the water and cover the casserole. Simmer gently for 1¾ hours.

Transfer the pork to a warmed serving dish. Keep hot.

Mix together the flour and mustard. Add a little water and mix to a paste. Stir in a little hot lqiuid from the casserole and then stir the liquid into the casserole Cook, stirring, for 3 minutes. Remove from the heat and stir in the soured cream. Spoon some of this sauce over the pork and serve the remainder in a sauceboat.
Serves 4

Marinated pork escalopes

1 kg/2lb pork fillets
2 garlic cloves, crushed
1cm/½in piece root ginger, peeled and finely chopped
1 tsp rosemary, freshly chopped
salt and black pepper
6 juniper berries, bruised
1 Tbsp clear honey
2 Tbsp lemon juice
125ml/4floz dry sherry
40g/1½oz butter
250g/8oz button mushrooms, sliced
3 Tbsp tomato purée
2 tsp cornflour
3 Tbsp water

Ask the butcher to partly slit the fillets and bash them to make escalopes. Cut into manageable pieces and lay in a shallow dish.

Mix together the garlic, ginger, rosemary, salt and pepper to taste, the juniper berries, honey, lemon juice and half the sherry. Pour this marinade over the pork. Cover the dish and leave to marinate in the refrigerator for 6 hours, turning the pieces of pork occasionally.

Remove the pork pieces from the marinade and pat dry with kitchen paper towels. Reserve the marinade.

Melt the butter in a frying pan. Add the pork pieces and fry until lightly browned on all sides. Transfer to a shallow baking dish.

Add the mushrooms to the frying pan and fry for 3 minutes. Add to the pork in the baking dish.

Put the reserved marinade in the frying pan and stir in the tomato purée and remaining sherry. Bring to the boil. Pour over the pork in the baking dish and bake in a moderate oven (180°C/350°F or Gas Mark 4) for 30 minutes.

Dissolve the cornflour in the water. Stir in a little of the hot liquid, then stir into the liquid in the casserole and bake for a further 10 minutes. Serve hot, from the baking dish.

Serves 4

Maple spareribs

150ml/5floz maple syrup
¼ tsp cayenne pepper
salt and black pepper
2 garlic cloves, crushed
2 Tbsp tomato purée
1 Tbsp prepared mustard
2 Tbsp lemon juice
2kg/4lb barbecue pork spareribs, cut into
2-rib serving pieces

Mix together the maple syrup, cayenne, salt and pepper to taste, the garlic, tomato purée, mustard and lemon juice.

Put the spareribs in a roasting tin. Roast in a fairly hot oven (200°C/400°F or Gas Mark 6) for 30 minutes.

Remove the spareribs from the tin and pour off the fat. Return the ribs to the tin and pour over the maple syrup mixture. Return to the oven and reduce the temperature to moderate (180°C/350°F or Gas Mark 4). Roast for a further 45 minutes, basting frequently with the maple syrup mixture, or until the ribs are brown and glazed.

Serve hot.

Serves 4

Aromatic Maple Spareribs is an unusual and delicious dish adapted from a New England recipe.

Junipered pork chops

4 large pork chops
2 garlic cloves, halved
salt and black pepper
20 juniper berries, crushed
4 Tbsp olive oil

Rub the chops with the cut sides of the garlic cloves. Discard the garlic. Rub the chops with salt and pepper, then press the juniper berries into the meat. Brush with the oil and grill the chops for about 10 minutes on each side. Serve hot.
Serves 4

Ham braised in white wine with mushroom sauce

90g/3½oz butter
2 Tbsp vegetable oil
1 medium onion, thinly sliced
1 large carrot, scraped and sliced
775ml/1 pint 6floz dry white wine
1 bouquet garni
4.5kg/10lb ham, soaked, boiled, drained, rind and excess fat removed
2 spring onions, thinly sliced
500g/1lb mushrooms, thinly sliced
salt and pepper
2 Tbsp flour
300ml/10floz double cream

Melt 25g/1oz of the butter with the oil in a flameproof casserole. Add the onion and carrot and fry until the onion is soft but not brown. Stir in the wine, then add the bouquet garni. Bring to the boil and simmer for 2 minutes. Remove from the heat.

Place the ham in the casserole and baste it with the pan liquids. Braise in a warm oven (170°C/325°F or Gas Mark 3) for 2 hours. Baste the ham occasionally.

Meanwhile, make the sauce. Melt 50g/2oz of the remaining butter in a sacuepan. Add the spring onions and fry until they are soft. Stir in the mushrooms and cook until they are lightly browned. Remove from the heat.

Transfer the ham to a warmed serving dish or carving board. Keep hot.

Strain the cooking liquid from the casserole into a saucepan. Add the liquid from the pan of mushrooms. Bring to the boil and boil until the liquid has reduced to about half the original quantity.

Blend the remaining butter with the flour to make a smooth paste (beurre manié). Add this in small pieces to the cooking liquid. Simmer, stirring, until thickened and smooth. Stir in the mushroom mixture and the cream. Heat through and serve with the ham.
Serves 16-18

Lamb chops in dried fruit sauce with saffron rice

50g/2oz butter
6 large lamb chops
250ml/8floz water
salt and black pepper
¼ tsp ground cinnamon
½ tsp garam masala
75g/3oz raisins
175g/6oz dried apricots, soaked overnight and drained
RICE
175g/6oz long-grain rice, soaked in cold water for 30 minutes and drained
500ml/16floz water
salt
1 tsp ground saffron
50g/2oz butter, melted

Melt the butter in a frying pan. Add the chops, in batches, and brown on all sides. Pour the fat out of the pan and add the water, salt and pepper to taste, the cinnamon, garam masala, raisins and apricots. Bring to the boil, then cover and simmer for 20 minutes.

Meanwhile, prepare the rice. Put the rice and water in a saucepan. Stir in salt and the saffron. Bring to the boil, then cover and simmer for 15 minutes or until the rice is tender and all the liquid has been absorbed.

Transfer the rice to a warmed serving dish. Sprinkle over the melted butter and toss to coat. Top with the chops and fruit sauce. Serve hot.
Serves 6

Lamb roasted with gin

2kg/4lb leg of lamb
2 garlic cloves, cut into slivers
salt and black pepper
1 tsp ground ginger
50g/2oz butter
250g/8floz beef stock
75ml/3floz gin
3 rosemary sprigs

Make incisions in the meat and insert the garlic slivers in the cuts. Rub the meat with salt, pepper and ginger.

Melt the butter in a roasting tin. Put the meat in the tin and brown it on all sides. Pour over the stock and gin. Lay the rosemary sprigs over the meat.

Transfer the tin to a fairly hot oven (200°C/400°F or Gas Mark 6) and roast for 15 minutes. Reduce the temperature to moderate (180°C/350°F or Gas Mark 4) and continue roasting for a further 1½ hours or until the juices run only faintly pink when pierced with a skewer.

A straightforward roast – with a little difference – Lamb Roasted with Gin.

Transfer the lamb to a warmed serving dish or carving board. Skim any fat from the surface of the cooking juices, then pour them over the meat. Serve immediately.

Serves 4

Spicy lamb and aubergine stew

2 small aubergines, thinly sliced
salt and black pepper
125ml/4floz olive oil
1kg/2lb boned shoulder of lamb, cut into
5cm/2in cubes
1 medium onion, thinly sliced
2 large tomatoes, peeled, seeded and
chopped
2 Tbsp tomato purée
3 Tbsp lemon juice
½ tsp grated nutmeg
½ tsp curry powder
400ml/14floz water

Sprinkle the aubergine slices with salt and leave for 30 minutes. Rinse and pat dry with kitchen paper towels.

Heat 2 tablespoons of the oil in a frying pan. Add the lamb cubes, in batches, and brown on all sides. Remove the meat from the pan and place it in a casserole.

Add the onion to the frying pan and fry until it is soft but not brown. Stir in the tomatoes, tomato purée, lemon juice, nutmeg, curry powder and salt and pepper to taste. Cook, stirring, for 6 minutes. Stir in the water and bring to the boil. Pour over the meat in the casserole.

Heat one-third of the remaining oil in the cleaned-out frying-pan. Add about one-third of the aubergine slices and fry until they are lightly browned on all sides. Drain on kitchen paper towels. Fry the remaining aubergine slices in the same way, then cut them into 1cm/½in strips. Add the aubergine strips to the casserole and mix well.

Place the casserole in a moderate oven (180°C/350°F or Gas Mark 4) and bake for 1 hour or until the lamb cubes are tender. Serve hot, from the casserole.

Serves 4

Moussaka

500g/1lb aubergines, sliced
salt and black pepper
25g/1oz butter
1 medium onion, finely chopped
1 garlic clove, crushed
500g/1lb lean lamb or mutton, minced
4 tomatoes, chopped
2 Tbsp tomato purée
2 tsp thyme, freshly chopped
3 Tbsp flour
125ml/4floz vegetable oil
300ml/10floz white or béchamel sauce
2 egg yolks
25g/1oz Kefalotiri or Parmesan cheese,
grated

Sprinkle the aubergine slices with salt and leave for 30 minutes. Meanwhile, melt the butter in a frying pan. Add the onion and garlic and fry until the onion is soft but not brown. Add the meat and fry until it is evenly browned. Stir in the tomatoes, tomato purée, thyme and salt and pepper to taste. Cook for 4 minutes. Remove from the heat.

Rinse the aubergine slices and dry with kitchen paper towels. Coat the slices with the flour. Heat half the oil in a frying pan. Add half the aubergine slices and fry until lightly browned on each side. Drain on kitchen paper towels and fry the remaining slices in the remaining oil.

Arrange half the aubergine slices in a baking dish. Spoon over the meat and tomato mixture and cover with the remaining aubergine slices. Mix together the sauce and egg yolks. Pour over the

Moussaka – a favourite and filling dish from Greece.

aubergine slices to cover them completely. Sprinkle with the cheese.

Bake in a fairly hot oven (190°C/375°F or Gas Mark 5) for 35 to 40 minutes or until the top is lightly browned. Serve hot, from the baking dish.

Serves 4

Chicken casserole

50g/2oz flour
salt and black pepper
1 Tbsp dill, freshly chopped
2.5kg/5lb chicken, skinned and cut into serving pieces
2 eggs, lightly beaten
50g/2oz butter
2 Tbsp vegetable oil
300ml/10floz chicken stock
1 medium green pepper, pith and seeds removed and cut into rings
2 tomatoes, peeled and sliced
125ml/4floz double cream
50g/2oz Samsoe or Cheddar cheese, grated

Mix together the flour, salt and pepper and dill. Coat the chicken pieces with the beaten egg and then with the dill mixture. Melt the butter with the oil in a flameproof casserole. Add the chicken pieces, in batches, and brown on all sides. Pour in the chicken stock and bring to the boil. Cover and simmer gently for 40 minutes or until the chicken is tender.

Transfer the chicken pieces to a warmed flameproof serving dish. Keep hot.

Add the green pepper to the casserole and simmer for 4 minutes. Stir in the tomatoes and cook for a further 2 minutes. Remove the vegetables from the casserole with a slotted spoon and arrange around the chicken.

Stir the cream into the liquid in the casserole. Heat through gently without boiling, then pour this sauce over the chicken. Sprinkle over the cheese and grill until it has melted and browned. Serve hot.

Serves 4-6

Chicken Casserole, topped with cheese, is a tempting dish ideal for a family supper.

Chicken curry

2 tsp salt
1 Tbsp turmeric
1.5kg/3lb chicken pieces, skinned
4 Tbsp vegetable oil
1 large onion, finely chopped
2 garlic cloves, finely chopped
5cm/2in piece root ginger, peeled and
finely chopped
1 green chilli, finely chopped
1 Tbsp ground coriander
1½ tsp ground cumin
1 Tbsp garam masala
1 tsp chilli powder
500g/1lb tomatoes, peeled and sieved
1cm/½in slice creamed coconut
1 Tbsp coriander leaves, freshly chopped

Combine 1 teaspoon of salt and 2 teaspoons of turmeric and rub the chicken pieces with this mixture.

Heat the oil in a frying pan. Add the chicken pieces, in batches, and fry until lightly browned on all sides. Remove from the pan. Add the onion to the pan and fry until it is golden brown. Add the garlic, ginger and green chilli and fry for a further 4 minutes. Mix together the coriander, cumin, garam masala, chilli powder, remaining teaspoon of turmeric and 2 tablespoons of water. Add this spice paste to the frying pan and fry, stirring, for 8 minutes. If the mixture becomes too dry, add 2 to 3 tablespoons of water.

Stir in the tomatoes and remaining teaspoon of salt. Return the chicken pieces to the pan, cover and simmer for 40 to 45 minutes or until the chicken is tender.

Add the creamed coconut and stir until it has dissolved into the sauce. Simmer for a further 10 minutes, uncovered. Taste and adjust the seasoning if necessary. If you like, add a teaspoon of sugar. Stir in the coriander leaves and serve with boiled rice.
Serves 4

Yogurt chicken

2kg/4lb chicken, skinned
1 tsp salt
juice of ½ lemon
2 green chillis, very finely chopped
250ml/8floz plain yogurt
4 Tbsp coriander leaves, freshly chopped
5cm/2in piece root ginger, peeled and
finely chopped
4 garlic cloves, crushed
50g/2oz butter, melted
lemon and cucumber slices, to garnish

Prick the chicken all over with a fork. Rub with the salt, lemon juice and chillis. Leave to marinate for 30 minutes.

Mix together the yogurt, coriander, ginger and garlic. Rub this mixture over the chicken. Cover and leave to marinate for 8 hours.

Put half the butter in a roasting tin. Put the chicken and marinade in the tin and roast in a fairly hot oven (200°C/400°F or Gas Mark 6) for 20 minutes. Reduce the temperature to moderate (180°C/350°F or Gas Mark 4) and roast for a further 30 minutes or until the chicken is tender. Baste frequently with the marinade in the tin and the remaining butter.

Transfer the chicken to a warmed serving dish. Keep hot. Boil the cooking juices for 3 to 5 minutes to reduce slightly. Pour over the chicken and serve.
Serves 4

Normandy duck

1 x 2½kg/5lb duck
250g/8oz fresh white breadcrumbs
300ml/10floz strong cider
50g/2oz butter
2 Tbsp olive oil
1kg/2lb cooking apples, peeled, cored and
sliced
3 celery stalks, finely chopped
1 tsp ground cinnamon or cloves
salt and black pepper
75ml/3floz Calvados
175ml/6floz double cream

Prick the skin of the duck all over. Put the breadcrumbs in a mixing bowl and pour over 4 tablespoons of the cider. Squeeze with your hand so the breadcrumbs are completely moistened.

Melt the butter with the oil in a saucepan. Add the apples and celery and fry for about 10 minutes or until tender. Stir in the cinnamon or cloves and salt and pepper to taste. Remove from the heat and stir in the breadcrumbs. Spoon this stuffing into the cavity in the duck and truss with string or skewers.

Place the duck on a rack in a roasting tin and roast in a moderate oven (180°C/350°F or Gas Mark 4) for 15 minutes. Pour over the remaining cider and continue roasting for 1¼ hours or until the juices run clear when the thigh is pierced with a fork.

Transfer the duck to a warmed serving dish. Untruss and keep hot.

Skim the fat from the surface of the liquid in the roasting tin. Pour the liquid into a saucepan and bring to the boil. Boil until reduced to half the original quantity. Stir in the Calvados and cream and heat through gently without boiling. Pour this sauce into a sauceboat and serve with the duck.
Serves 4

Cooked in a spicy yogurt sauce, Yogurt Chicken is first marinated then roasted to make a really scrumptious dish.

Duck with braised red cabbage

125g/4oz butter
2 medium onions, finely chopped
1 garlic clove, finely chopped
1 large red cabbage, shredded
2 medium cooking apples, peeled, cored
and coarsely chopped
1 small onion, studded with 4 cloves
1 tsp ground allspice
salt and black pepper
300ml/10floz dry red wine
150ml/5floz beef stock
1 x 2½kg/5lb duck

Melt half the butter in a flameproof casserole. Add the onions and garlic and fry until the onions are soft but not brown. Stir in the cabbage, apples, clove-studded onion, allspice and salt and pepper to taste. Simmer for 5 minutes, stirring occasionally to brown the cabbage evenly. Stir in the wine and stock and bring to the boil. Cover and braise in a warm over (170°C/ 325°F or Gas Mark 3) for 3½ hours.

After the cabbage has been cooking for 1½ hours, prepare the duck. Prick the skin all over and rub the cavity with salt and pepper. Truss the duck. Melt the remaining butter in a frying pan. Put the duck in the pan and brown on all sides. Transfer it to a rack in a roasting tin and place in the oven. Roast for 1¾ to 2 hours, or until the juices run clear when the thigh is pricked with a fork.

Transfer the duck to a warmed serving platter. Arrange the braised cabbage around it and serve.
Serves 4

Pheasant in red wine

2 young pheasants
salt and black pepper
2 medium onions, finely chopped
100g/4oz butter
1 Tbsp vegetable oil
900ml/1½ pints dry red wine
1 bay leaf
125g/4oz mushrooms, thinly sliced
4 streaky bacon rashers, derinded
25g/1oz flour
150ml/5floz double cream

Rub the insides of the pheasants with salt and pepper. Put half the onions into the cavities in the birds. Truss.

Melt 75g/3oz of the butter with the oil in a frying pan. Add the pheasants and

A splendid dish befitting autumn, Pheasant in Red Wine can be served with the season's juicy cranberries.

brown on all sides. Transfer the pheasants to a flameproof casserole. Keep hot.

Add the remaining onions to the frying pan and fry until golden brown. Stir in the wine and bring to the boil. Add salt and pepper to taste with the bay leaf and mushrooms. Simmer for 5 minutes.

Place the bacon rashers over the breasts of the pheasants. Pour the wine mixture around the birds. Cover the casserole and braise on top of the stove for 50 minutes to 1 hour or until the pheasants are tender.

Transfer the pheasants to a warmed serving dish. Dsicard the bacon and keep the birds hot.

Bring the liquid in the casserole back to the boil and boil until it has reduced to half the original quantity. Blend the remaining butter with the flour to make a smooth paste. Add this, in small pieces, to the liquid in the casserole. Simmer, stirring, until thickened and smooth. Stir in the cream and heat through without boiling. Pour this sauce into a sauceboat and serve with the pheasant.

Serves 4

Marinated venison stew

1kg/2lb lean venison, cut into 5cm/2in cubes
50g/2oz butter
salt and black pepper
1 Tbsp rosemary, freshly chopped
3 medium carrots, scraped and quartered
1 small turnip, peeled and chopped
250g/8oz small onions, peeled
3 medium potatoes, peeled and halved
400g/14oz can tomatoes
3 Tbsp tomato purée
MARINADE
350ml/12floz red wine
250ml/8floz beef stock
3 Tbsp olive oil
1 large onion, thinly sliced
8 black peppercorns
3 garlic cloves, crushed
2 Tbsp parsley, freshly chopped
1 Tbsp rosemary, freshly chopped
1 bouquet garni

Mix together all the marinade ingredients in a shallow dish. Add the venison cubes

Full of flavour, Marinated Venison Stew makes a nourishing meal for the hunting season.

Because different varieties can be grown throughout the year, the potato is not a seasonal vegetable. It is used, however, in different ways at different times of the year. In spring, we enjoy the delicate flavour of new potatoes, in summer mayonnaise and potato salads, and in winter and autumn they taste particularly good mashed, baked or used to fill out warming stews and casseroles as in Marinated Venison Stew.

and leave to marinate for 12 hours.

Remove the meat from the marinade and pat dry with kitchen paper towels. Reserve the marinade, discarding the peppercorns. Melt the butter in a flameproof casserole. Add the venison cubes and brown on all sides. Stir in the reserved marinade, salt and pepper to taste and the rosemary. Bring to the boil, then cover and simmer for 1½ hours.

Add the carrots, turnip ,onions, potatoes, tomatoes with the can juice and the tomato purée and stir well. Re-cover the casserole and continue to simmer for a further 1 hour or until the meat is very tender.

Discard the bouquet garni and serve, from the casserole.

Serves 4

Hare casseroled in wine and herb sauce

8 bacon rashers, derinded
salt and black pepper
1 tsp thyme, freshly chopped
75g/3oz flour
2.5kg/5lb hare, skinned and cut into serving pieces
15g/½oz butter
1 medium onion, finely chopped
2 garlic cloves, crushed
250ml/8floz dry red wine
175ml/6floz chicken stock
2 Tbsp dry sherry
1 Tbsp cranberry sauce
1 tsp parsley, freshly chopped
1 tsp marjoram, freshly chopped
½ tsp tarragon, freshly chopped
grated rind of ½ lemon

Grill the bacon until crisp and golden brown. Drain on kitchen paper towels. Reserve the bacon fat in the grill pan.

Mix together salt and pepper, half the thyme and the flour. Coat the hare pieces in this mixture.

Pour the bacon fat into a frying pan and add the butter. Melt it and add the hare pieces. Brown well on all sides. Transfer the hare pieces to a casserole. Add the onion and garlic to the frying pan and fry until the onion is soft but not brown. Transfer to the casserole.

Discard the fat in the frying pan. Put the wine, stock and sherry in the pan and bring to the boil. Stir in the cranberry sauce, parsley, marjoram, tarragon, lemon rind and remaining thyme. Pour over the hare.

Crumble the bacon into the casserole. Cover and braise in a moderate oven (180°C/350°F or Gas Mark 4) for 2½ hours or until the hare pieces are tender. Serve immediately, from the casserole.

Serves 4-6

Pigeon pie

PASTRY
350g/12oz flour
1 tsp salt
150ml/5floz water
125g/4oz vegetable fat
1 egg yolk, lightly beaten
1 egg, lightly beaten
FILLING
8 pigeon breasts, boned and sliced
125g/4oz cooked ham, finely chopped
275g/10oz pork sausagemeat
175g/6oz button mushrooms, quartered
1 egg, hard-boiled and finely chopped
salt and black pepper
1 tsp grated lemon rind
pinch cayenne pepper
125ml/4floz beef stock
4 Tbsp dry red wine

Sift the flour and salt into a mixing bowl. Bring the water and vegetable fat to the boil in a saucepan. When the fat has melted, remove from the heat. Make a well in the centre of the flour and add the egg yolk and fat and water mixture. Gradually draw the flour into the liquid, mixing to a smooth dough. Knead the dough until it is shiny.

Cut off one-third of the dough and set aside in a warm place. Roll out the remaining dough to a circle about 25cm/10in in diameter. Turn a deep 15cm/6in pie mould or cake tin upside-down and grease the outside. Cover the outside of the mould or tin with the dough circle. Place a sheet of greaseproof paper over the mould or tin and turn it right side up. Wrap the paper around the dough-covered tin and tie with string. Chill for 20 minutes.

Mix together the pigeon meat, ham, sausagemeat, mushrooms, egg, salt and pepper to taste, the lemon rind and cayenne.

Gently ease the mould or tin out of the dough case. Place the dough case on a greased baking sheet. Fill with the pigeon mixture. Roll out the remaining piece of dough to a circle just larger than the top of the dough case. Place this lid on top and press the edges together to seal. Brush the pie all over with the beaten egg. Make a 5cm/2in slit in the centre of the dough lid.

Bake in a fairly hot oven (200°C/400°F or Gas Mark 6) for 1 hour. Reduce the temperature to moderate (180°C/350°F or Gas Mark 4). Remove the paper.

Bring the stock and wine to the boil in a saucepan. Pour through the slit in the dough lid. Bake for a further 1 hour or until the meat is tender and the pastry well browned. Serve hot or cold.

Serves 4-6

Vegetables

Aniseed carrots

700g/1½lb carrots, scraped
1 Tbsp soft brown sugar
50g/2oz butter
1½ tsp aniseed
salt and black pepper

Leave small carrots whole; quarter large ones lengthways.

Put the sugar, butter, aniseed and salt and pepper to taste in a saucepan. Heat until the mixture starts to bubble, stirring to dissolve the sugar. Add the carrots, stir well to coat and cover the pan. Simmer for about 15 minutes or until the carrots are tender. Serve hot.
Serves 4

Cauliflower with Italian sauce

25g/1oz butter
1 medium onion, chopped
3 large mushrooms, sliced
2 Tbsp cooked ham, shredded
1 Tbsp flour
75ml/3floz white wine
175ml/6floz beef stock
2 tsp tomato purée
salt and black pepper
1 large cauliflower, broken into flowerets

Melt the butter in a saucepan. Add the onion, mushrooms and ham and fry, stirring, for 10 minutes. Sprinkle over the flour and cook, sitrring, for 1 minute. Gradually stir in the wine and stock with the tomato purée and salt and pepper to taste. Bring to the boil and simmer, stirring, until thickened. Simmer for 20 minutes.

Meanwhile, cook the cauliflower in boiling salted water for 9 to 12 minutes or until the flowerets are just tender. Drain well and transfer to a warmed serving dish. Pour over the sauce and serve hot.
Serves 4

Corn bake

4 eggs
25g/1oz flour
350ml/12floz single cream
50g/2oz butter, melted
salt and black pepper
500g/1lb sweetcorn kernels

Beat the eggs in a mixing bowl until they are frothy. Stir in the flour, cream and melted butter, then the remaining ingredients with salt and pepper to taste. Pour into a greased shallow baking dish. Bake in a moderate oven (180°C/350°F or Gas Mark 4) for 1 to 1½ hours or until the top is golden brown and a skewer inserted in the centre comes out clean. Serve hot.
Serves 4

Brussels sprouts with peppers and tomatoes

40g/1½oz butter
1 large onion, finely chopped
1 garlic clove, crushed
1 green pepper, pith and seeds removed and chopped
500g/1lb tomatoes, skinned and chopped
700g/1½lb Brussels sprouts
salt and black pepper
½ tsp basil

Melt the butter in a saucepan. Add the onion, garlic and green pepper and fry until the onion is soft but not brown. Stir in the tomatoes, sprouts, salt and pepper to taste and the basil. Cover and cook for 15 to 20 minutes or until the sprouts are tender. Serve hot.
Serves 4

Left : Aniseed Carrots is an unusual combination of flavours making a most attractive vegetable dish.
Below : Brussels sprouts, with their delicate, slightly nutty flavour are one of the treats of the colder months.

Red cabbage braised with red wine

25g/1oz butter
1 medium red cabbage, coarsely chopped
250ml/8floz dry red wine
4 Tbsp wine vinegar
2 Tbsp soft brown sugar
salt and black pepper
pinch grated nutmeg

Melt the butter in a flameproof casserole. Add the cabbage and cook for 10 minutes, stirring occasionally. Stir in the remaining ingredients, with salt and pepper to taste, and bring to the boil. Cover the casserole and transfer to a warm oven (170°C/325°F or Gas Mark 3). Braise for 2 to 2½ hours or until the cabbage is tender. Serve hot, from the casserole.
Serves 6

Glazed turnips

25g/1oz butter
1 Tbsp olive oil
700g/1½lb young turnips, peeled and quartered
2 Tbsp soft brown sugar
175ml/6floz chicken stock

Melt the butter with the oil in a saucepan. Add the turnips and cook until they are golden brown. Sprinkle over the sugar and cook, sitrring occasionally, for 5 minutes.

Add the chicken stock and bring to the boil. Cover and simmer gently for 30 minutes or until the turnips are tender but still firm and most of the stock has been absorbed. Serve hot.
Serves 4

Swede and apple purée

5 medium swedes, peeled and diced
3 large tart apples, peeled, cored and chopped
50g/2oz butter, softened
1 tsp lemon juice
½ tsp mixed spice
salt and pepper

Cook the swedes in boiling salted water for 30 minutes or until they are tender. Meanwhile, put a 1cm/½in layer of water in another saucepan and add the apple slices. Cook gently until the apples are very soft. Mash the apples to a purée.

Drain the swedes and put in a mixing bowl. Add the apple purée and butter and mash with a fork or potato masher. Beat in the lemon juice and spice. Spoon into a warmed serving dish and serve.
Serves 6-8

Ratatouille

3 medium aubergines, thinly sliced
25g/1oz butter
4 Tbsp olive oil
2 large onions, thinly sliced
3 garlic cloves, crushed
1 large green pepper, pith and seeds removed and chopped
1 large red pepper, pith and seeds removed and chopped
5 medium courgettes, sliced
500g/1lb tomatoes, skinned and chopped
1 tsp basil
1 Tbsp parsley, freshly chopped
salt and black pepper

Sprinkle the aubergine slices with salt and leave for 30 minutes. Rinse and pat dry.

Melt the butter with the oil in a frying pan. Add the onions and garlic and fry until the onions are soft but not brown. Add the remaining ingredients, with salt and pepper to taste, and cover the pan. Simmer for 40 to 45 minutes or until the vegetables are tender. Serve hot or cold.
Serves 4-6

Breaded pumpkin slices with tomato sauce

1kg/2lb pumpkin, peeled and sliced
2 eggs, lightly beaten
50g/2oz dry breadcrumbs
50g/2oz butter
25g/1oz Parmesan cheese, grated
SAUCE
2 Tbsp olive oil
1 onion, finely chopped
1 garlic clove, crushed
500g/1lb tomatoes, skinned, seeded and chopped
1 Tbsp tomato purée
1 tsp dried basil
1 Tbsp parsley, freshly chopped
1 tsp sugar
salt and black pepper

First make the sauce. Heat the oil in a saucepan. Add the onion and garlic and fry until the onion is soft but not brown. Stir in the remaining ingredients, with salt and pepper to taste, and simmer for 10 minutes.

Coat the pumpkin slices with the eggs, then with the breadcrumbs. Melt the butter in a frying pan. Add the pumpkin slices, in batches, and brown on all sides. Transfer to a greased baking dish.

Pour the tomato sauce over the pumpkin slices and sprinkle with the Parmesan. Bake in a moderate oven·(180°C/350°F or Gas Mark 4) for 30 minutes. Serve hot.
Serves 4

Below : As lettuce becomes scarce and more expensive, try thinly-sliced cabbage as a substitute in salads.
Bottom : Swedes puréed with apples, make an ideal autumn vegetable dish.

Salads

Cabbage and pepper salad

1 red pepper, pith and seeds removed
and thinly sliced
1 green pepper, pith and seeds removed
and thinly sliced
6-8 spring onions, finely chopped
1 cucumber, cut into 1cm/½in dice
500g/1lb tomatoes, thinly sliced
½ white cabbage, thinly sliced
2 Tbsp clear honey
juice of 1 lemon
150ml/5floz oil
4 Tbsp vinegar
salt and black pepper

Mix together the peppers, spring onions, cucumber cubes, tomatoes and cabbage in a large salad bowl. Put the remaining ingredients, with salt and pepper to taste, in a screwtop jar and shake well. Pour this dressing over the salad and toss to coat thoroughly.

Serve soon after dressing the salad.
Serves 8

Chicory and tomato salad

3 heads chicory, thinly sliced
6 tomatoes, sliced
8 black olives, stoned
2 Tbsp red wine or cider vinegar
1 Tbsp clear honey
1 small onion, finely chopped
3 Tbsp olive oil
2 tsp lemon juice
salt and black pepper
½ tsp sugar

Put the chicory, tomatoes and olives in a salad bowl. Mix together the remaining ingredients, with salt and pepper to taste, in a screwtop jar. Shake well, then pour this dressing over the vegetables. Toss to coat and chill for 20 minutes before serving.
Serves 4

Beetroot and dill salad

6 small beetroots, cooked and skinned
salt and black pepper
1 medium onion, thinly sliced and
pushed out into rings
75ml/3floz wine vinegar
3 Tbsp olive oil
1½ tsp sugar
1 Tbsp dill, freshly chopped

Thinly slice the warmed beetroots and

place them in a bowl. Refrigerate the slices until they are chilled.

Sprinkle salt and pepper over the beetroot slices, then add the remaining ingredients. Toss gently to coat and transfer to a serving dish. Chill before serving.
Serves 6

Leek and soured cream salad

1kg/2lb leeks, washed, trimmed and cut
into 2.5cm/1in slices
150ml/5floz soured cream
1 Tbsp lemon juice
1 tsp prepared German mustard
½ tsp sugar
salt and black pepper

Cook the leeks in boiling salted water for 8 to 12 minutes or until they are just tender. Drain well and allow to cool to room temperature.

Put the leeks in a salad bowl. Mix together the remaining ingredients, with salt and pepper to taste, and pour over the leeks. Stir gently to mix.

Chill before serving.
Serves 4-6

Below : Chicory is another salad vegetable which comes into its own in colder weather.
Bottom : A clean tasting, crunchy Cabbage and Pepper Salad makes a pleasant change as an accompaniment to roast meat.

Light Dishes

Courgette eggah

500g/1lb small courgettes, thinly sliced
¼ tsp grated nutmeg
300ml/10floz milk
2 Tbsp olive oil
1 small onion, halved and thinly sliced
1 garlic clove, crushed
8 eggs
salt and black pepper
1 Tbsp chives, freshly chopped
50g/2oz fresh white breadcrumbs
25g/1oz butter

Lay the courgette slices in a shallow dish. Sprinkle with the nutmeg and pour over the milk. Leave to soak for 30 minutes, then drain off the milk, reserving 2 tablespoons.

Heat the oil in a frying pan. Add the courgette slices, onion and garlic and fry until the onion is soft but not brown. Remove from the heat.

Mix together the eggs, reserved milk, salt and pepper to taste and the chives. Stir in the courgette mixture and breadcrumbs.

Melt the butter in the cleaned-out frying pan. Pour in the egg mixture and cook slowly for 30 minutes. Place the pan under the grill and cook until the top is lightly browned. Serve hot, cut into wedges.
Serves 4

Stuffed aubergines

4 aubergines
2 Tbsp olive oil
2 small onions, chopped
2 garlic cloves, crushed
4 large tomatoes, skinned and chopped
12 green olives, stoned
salt and black pepper
50g/2oz Parmesan cheese, grated
25g/1oz dry breadcrumbs
25g/1oz butter, cut into small pieces

Put the aubergines in a saucepan and cover with water. Bring to the boil, then cover and simmer for 15 minutes. Drain well and cut the aubergines in half, lengthways. Scoop out the flesh, leaving shells 6mm/¼in thick. Reserve the shells. Chop the flesh.

Heat the oil in a frying pan. Add the onions and garlic and fry until the onions are soft but not brown. Stir in the tomatoes, olives, aubergine flesh and salt and pepper to taste. Simmer for 10 minutes.

Fill the aubergine shells with the tomato mixture and place in a baking dish. Sprinkle the cheese and breadcrumbs over the tops and dot with the pieces of butter. Bake in a moderate oven (180°C/350°F or Gas Mark 4) for 30 minutes. Serve hot.
Serves 4

Canelloni with spinach and meat

TOMATO SAUCE
2 Tbsp olive oil
1 small onion, finely chopped
400g/14oz can tomatoes
5 Tbsp tomato purée
½ tsp dried basil
1 tsp sugar
salt and black pepper
FILLING
15g/½oz butter
1½ Tbsp olive oil
1 small onion, finely chopped
2 garlic cloves, finely chopped
175g/6oz spinach
250g/8oz lean minced beef
25g/1oz Parmesan cheese, grated
1½ Tbsp double cream
1 egg
1 Tbsp oregano, freshly chopped
salt and black pepper
CREAM SAUCE
25g/1oz butter
25g/1oz flour
150ml/5floz milk
3 Tbsp double cream
salt and white pepper
PASTA
250g/8oz cannelloni rolls or sheets
75g/3oz Parmesan cheese, grated
15g/½oz butter, cut into small pieces

First make the tomato sauce. Heat the oil in a saucepan. Add the onion and fry until it is soft but not brown. Stir in the remaining ingredients, with salt and pepper to taste, and cover the pan. Simmer for 40 minutes.

To make the filling, melt the butter with the oil in a frying pan. Add the onion and garlic and fry until the onion is soft but not brown. Meanwhile, cook the spinach for 5 to 7 minutes or until it is tender. (Do not add any water: there should be enough left on the leaves after washing.) Drain the spinach well and chop finely.

Add the meat to the frying pan and fry until it is evenly browned. Stir in the spinach and cook, stirring, until the moisture has evaporated. Turn the mixture into a mixing bowl. Allow to cool slightly, then mix in the remaining ingredients with salt and pepper to taste.

To make the cream sauce, melt the butter in a saucepan. Remove the pan from the heat and stir in the flour. Gradually stir in the milk and return to the heat.

Canelloni with Spinach and Meat is popular, filling and reasonably economical – the perfect family meal.

Simmer, stirring until thickened and smooth. Remove from the heat and stir in the cream with salt and pepper to taste.

Cook the cannelloni in boiling salted water for 6 to 15 minutes or until it is just *al dente* (tender to the bite). Drain well. Fill the cannelloni rolls with the filling (or place a spoonful of filling on each cannelloni sheet and roll up).

Pour a thin layer of tomato sauce into a large shallow baking dish. Place the cannelloni on top, in one or two layers. Pour over the cream sauce, then the tomato sauce. Sprinkle with the Parmesan cheese and dot with the pieces of butter. Bake in a fairly hot oven (190°C/375°F or Gas Mark 5) for 30 minutes or until the sauce is bubbling and the cheese is lightly browned. Serve hot, from the dish.
Serves 4

Neapolitan pizza

15g/½oz fresh yeast
125ml/4floz plus 1 Tbsp lukewarm water
250g/8oz strong flour
1 tsp salt
FILLING
2 Tbsp tomato purée
4 medium tomatoes, peeled, seeded and chopped
250g/8oz Mozzarella cheese, sliced
8 anchovies, halved
black pepper
2 tsp oregano, freshly chopped
2 tsp olive oil

Mash the yeast and 1 tablespoon of the water together to make a smooth paste. Set aside in a warm, draught-free place until frothy. Sift the flour and salt into a mixing bowl. Make a well in the centre and pour in the yeast mixture and remaining water. Gradually draw the flour into the liquids, mixing to a dough.

Turn the dough out of the bowl and knead for 10 minutes or until elastic and smooth. Return to the bowl, cover and leave in a warm, draught-free place for 45 minutes to 1 hour or until doubled in bulk.

Knock back and knead the dough again for 3 minutes. Cut it in half and roll out each half to a circle about 6mm/¼in thick. Place the dough circles on a greased baking sheet.

Cover the top of each dough circle with tomato purée, then arrange the tomatoes, cheese and anchovies on top. Sprinkle with the pepper and oregano, then with the oil. Bake in a very hot oven (230°C/450°F or Gas Mark 8) for 15 to 20 minutes or until the dough is crisp and the cheese melted. Serve hot.
Serves 2-4

Three cheese quiche

PASTRY
175g/6oz flour
½ tsp salt
40g/1½oz butter
40g/1½oz lard or margarine
2-3 Tbsp iced water
FILLING
75g/3oz blue cheese, crumbled
75g/3oz Camembert cheese, rind removed
75g/3oz cream cheese
15g/½oz butter, softened
1 shallot, finely chopped
4 Tbsp single cream
3 eggs
salt and white pepper

Sift the flour and salt into a mixing bowl. Add the butter and lard or margarine and cut into small pieces. Rub the fat into the flour until the mixture resembles breadcrumbs. Stir in enough of the water to bind the mixture, then knead to a dough. Chill for 20 minutes.

Roll out the dough and use to line a 23cm/9in flan ring. Bake blind in a fairly hot oven (200°C/400°F or Gas Mark 6) for 5 minutes to crisp the pastry.

Mash the cheeses and butter together in a mixing bowl. Beat in the shallot. Mix together the cream, eggs and salt and pepper to taste. Stir this mixture into the cheese mixture. Pour into the flan case and place on a baking sheet. Bake in a fairly hot oven (200°C/400°F or Gas Mark 6) for 30 to 35 minutes or until the filling is set. Serve hot or cold.
Serves 4-6

Traditional Neapolitan Pizzas made with tomatoes, anchovies, Mozarella cheese and oregano should be served sizzling hot, with an Italian wine.

Marrow soufflé

50g/2oz butter
1 small onion, finely minced
50g/2oz flour
salt and black pepper
¼ tsp cayenne pepper
1 Tbsp chives, freshly chopped
300ml/10floz milk
250g/8oz marrow, peeled, seeded and
grated
2 Tbsp soured cream
4 egg yolks
5 egg whites

Melt the butter in a saucepan. Add the onion and fry until it is golden brown. Stir in the flour and cook, stirring, for 1 minute. Remove the pan from the heat and stir in salt and pepper to taste, the cayenne and chives. Gradually stir in the milk. Return to the heat and cook, stirring, until thickened and smooth. Remove from the heat.

Stir in the marrow, soured cream and egg yolks. Allow to cool slightly.

Beat the egg whites until they will hold a stiff peak. Fold them into the marrow mixture. Spoon into a greased 1.5l/3 pint soufflé dish. Bake in a fairly hot oven (190°C/375°F or Gas Mark 5) for 35 to 40 minutes or until well risen and golden brown. Serve at once.
Serves 4

Crab patties

500g/1lb crabmeat
75g/3oz fresh white breadcrumbs
1 egg yolk
2 Tbsp mayonnaise
12 spring onions, finely chopped
1 egg, hard-boiled and finely chopped
½ tsp marjoram, freshly chopped
2 tsp lemon juice
salt and black pepper
pinch cayenne pepper
125ml/4floz vegetable oil
watercress, to garnish

Mix together the crabmeat, breadcrumbs, egg yolk, mayonnaise, spring onions, egg, marjoram, lemon juice, salt and pepper to taste and the cayenne. Form the mixture into 5cm/2in balls and flatten into patties.

Heat the oil in a frying pan. Add the patties, in batches, and fry for 3 to 5 minutes on each side or until deep golden brown. Drain on kitchen paper towels and keep hot while you fry the remaining patties.

Transfer the patties to a warmed serving dish and garnish. Serve hot.
Serves 4-6

Home Baking

Parkin

500g/1lb flour
1 tsp bicarbonate of soda
1 tsp salt
2 tsp ground ginger
500g/1lb rolled oats
250g/8oz butter
250ml/8floz dark treacle
250ml/8floz golden syrup
4 Tbsp clear honey
2 Tbsp soft brown sugar
350ml/12floz milk

Sift the flour, soda, salt and ginger into a mixing bowl. Stir in the rolled oats. Put the butter, treacle, syrup, honey and sugar in a saucepan and heat gently, stirring to dissolve the sugar and melt the butter. Remove from the heat and add to the flour mixture with the milk. Mix well.

Pour the batter into two greased 25cm/10in square cake tins. Bake in a moderate oven (180°C/350°F or Gas Mark 4) for 45 to 50 minutes or until the cakes are firm to the touch.

Cool in the tins for 15 minutes, then turn out onto a wire rack. Store the parkins in an airtight tin for 1 week before eating for an even better flavour.
Makes two 25cm/10in cakes

German spice squares

350g/12oz flour
½ tsp salt
1 tsp baking powder
½ tsp ground ginger
½ tsp ground cinnamon
¼ tsp grated nutmeg
½ tsp ground cloves
2 Tbsp cocoa powder
3 large eggs
125g/4oz soft brown sugar
175ml/6floz clear honey

Sift the flour, salt, baking powder, spices and cocoa powder into a mixing bowl. Beat together the eggs and sugar. Warm the honey and add with the eggs and sugar to the flour mixture. Mix well together until the batter is smooth. Pour into a greased 30cm/12in square baking tray. Smooth the top.

Bake in a moderate oven (180°C/350°F or Gas Mark 4) for 30 minutes or until a skewer inserted into the centre of the cake comes out clean.

Allow to cool in the tin before cutting into squares.
Makes 36 squares

Dundee cake

275g/10oz flour
½ tsp baking powder
½ tsp mixed spice
125g/4oz raisins
125g/4oz currants
125g/4oz sultanas
50g/2oz mixed candied fruit, chopped
50g/2oz glacé cherries
grated rind of 1 small orange
grated rind of 1 small lemon
½ tsp ground cinnamon
250g/8oz butter
250g/8oz caster sugar
5 eggs
50g/2oz blanched almonds, halved

Sift the flour, baking powder, mixed spice and cinnamon into a mixing bowl. Fold in the fruit and rind and stir to coat each piece. Cream the butter and sugar together in another bowl until light and fluffy. Beat in the eggs, one at a time.

Fold the fruit and flour mixture into the creamed mixture.

Grease a deep 20cm/8in round cake tin and line the bottom and sides with grease-proof paper. Grease the paper lining. Spoon in the cake mixture and smooth the top. Arrange the almond halves on top in concentric circles, their pointed ends towards the centre.

Bake in a warm oven (170°C/325°F or Gas Mark 3) for 2 hours or until a skewer inserted in the centre of the cake comes out clean. If the top of the cake is browning too quickly, cover it with brown paper. Turn off the oven and leave the cake inside for 10 to 15 minutes.

Allow to cool in the tin, then remove it from the tin and peel off the paper. The cake will keep for several weeks, stored in an airtight tin.
Makes one 20cm/8in cake

Date cakes

75g/3oz butter
2 Tbsp light brown sugar
4 Tbsp clear honey
2 eggs, lightly beaten
125g/4oz plus 2 Tbsp self-raising flour
1 tsp mixed spice
4-6 Tbsp milk
50g/2oz dates, stoned and finely chopped

Cream the butter and sugar together until the mixture is fluffy. Beat in the honey, then the eggs. Sift in 125g/4oz of the flour and the spice and fold in. Stir in enough of the milk to give the batter a dropping consistency.

A rich, Scottish fruit cake, Dundee cake makes a lovely teatime treat for an autumn afternoon.

Appetizing, home-baked Dried Fruit Scones should be served piping hot with butter and jam.

Coat the date pieces with the remaining flour and add to the batter. Mix well and spoon into 12 greased patty pans. Bake in a fairly hot oven (200°C/400°F or Gas Mark 6) for 15 to 20 minutes or until risen and golden brown.

Remove the cakes from the pans and cool on a wire rack.

Makes 12

Dried fruit scones

250g/8oz self raising flour
1 tsp baking powder
¼ tsp salt
40g/1½oz vegetable fat
50g/2oz castor sugar
50g/2oz raisins
2 Tbsp currants
1 large egg
75ml/3floz milk

Sift the flour, baking powder and salt into a mixing bowl. Rub in the fat until the mixture resembles breadcrumbs. Stir in the sugar, raisins and currants. Mix together the egg and milk and stir gradually into the fruit mixture until it is stiff and glossy. Knead lightly to a dough.

Roll out the dough to approximately 1cm/½in thick. Cut into 5cm/2in circles and place these on a greased baking sheet. Bake in a very hot oven (230°C/450°F or Gas Mark 8) for 10 to 15 minutes or until the scones are golden brown and risen.

Serve hot or cold, with butter and jam.

Makes 12

Banana walnut loaf

150g/5oz sugar
40g/1½oz butter or margarine
3 eggs
4 bananas, mashed
250g/8oz flour
1 tsp baking powder
½ tsp salt
¼ tsp bicarbonate of soda
175g/6oz walnuts, chopped

Cream together the sugar, butter or margarine and eggs. Beat until the mixture is light, then beat in the bananas. Sift the flour, baking powder, salt and soda into the bowl and mix well. Fold in the walnuts.

Pour the batter into a greased 500g/1lb loaf tin. Bake in a moderate oven (180°C/350°F or Gas Mark 4) for 1 hour, or until a skewer inserted into the centre of the loaf comes out clean. Turn out of the tin onto a wire rack and cool before serving.

Makes one 500g/1lb loaf

Desserts

Apple dumplings

PASTRY

350g/12oz flour
½ tsp salt
100g/3oz butter
75g/3oz vegetable fat
4-5 Tbsp cold water

FILLING

6 large tart apples, cored
125g/4oz brown sugar
grated rind of 1 lemon
6 cloves
milk
castor sugar

Sift the flour and salt into a mixing bowl. Add the butter and fat and cut into small pieces. Rub the fat into the flour until the mixture resembles breadcrumbs. Stir in enough water to bind the mixture and knead to a dough. Chill for 20 minutes.

Roll out the dough and cut into six squares large enough to enclose the apples. Reserve some of the dough for decoration. Place one apple on each dough square and fill the centre cavity of the apple with sugar, lemon rind and a clove. Brush the edges of the squares with water or milk and bring the dough up around the apple to enclose it and seal the edges.

Decorate with the reserved dough, cut into leaves. Brush with the milk and sprinkle with the sugar. Bake on a baking sheet in a hot oven (200°C/400°F or Gas Mark 6) for 30 minutes. Serve hot.
Serves 6

Chocolate and rum fondue

250g/8oz dark chocolate, broken into pieces
6 Tbsp double cream
2 Tbsp rum
50g/2oz icing sugar, sifted
fresh fruit (banana, pear and apple slices, berries, etc.) and cubes of cake, to serve

Melt the chocolate in the top of a double saucepan. Stir in the cream. Remove from the heat and stir in the rum and icing sugar. Pour into a fondue pot or chafing dish set over a small spirit lamp. Serve with the fruit and cake.
Serves 6-8

A traditional English pudding, Apple Dumplings make the most of autumn's scrumptious fruit crop.

Steamed orange pudding

125g/4oz butter
125g/4oz sugar
2 large eggs
175g/6oz flour
1 tsp baking powder
1 Tbsp finely grated orange rind
1 orange, peel and pith removed and
segmented
3 Tbsp orange juice

Cream the butter and sugar together until
the mixture is light and fluffy. Beat in the
eggs, one at a time, then sift in the flour
and baking powder. Fold in with the
orange rind, then stir in the orange segments and juice. Spoon into a greased
900ml/1½ pint pudding basin. Cover with
a lid of pleated greased greaseproof paper
and foil and tie on securely with string.

Steam the pudding for 2½ hours,
replenishing the boiling water when
necessary.

Turn the pudding out of the basin onto
a warmed serving dish and serve hot, with
custard sauce.

Serves 4-6

Berry cheesecake

175g/6oz digestive biscuits, crushed
75g/3oz butter, melted
700g/1½lb cream cheese
175g/6oz sugar
4 eggs, lightly beaten
1 Tbsp lemon juice
2 tsp grated lemon rind
2 tsp cornflour
3 Tbsp water
350g/12oz berries (blueberries,
blackberries, loganberries, raspberries)

Mix together the biscuits and melted
butter. Press into the bottom and sides of
a greased, loose-bottomed 20cm/8in round
cake tin.

Beat the cream cheese until it is soft.
Beat in 125g/4oz of the sugar, the eggs
gradually, the lemon juice and half the
lemon rind. Pour into the cake tin and bake
in a moderate oven (180°C/350°F or Gas
Mark 4) for 40 minutes. Allow to cool,
then chill.

Put the remaining sugar in a saucepan
with the berries, remaining lemon rind and
2 tablespoons of the water. Poach for 3

*Cream cheese in a crumb crust topped
with any of autumn's soft fruits,
mouthwatering Berry Cheesecake
makes a lovely rich dessert.*

minutes. Meanwhile, dissolve the corn-flour in the remaining water. Stir in a little of the poaching liquid. Stir the cornflour mixture into the poaching liquid and simmer for 2 to 3 minutes or until the liquid has thickened. Remove from the heat and allow to cool or leave in the refrigerator overnight.

Spoon the berry mixture onto the centre of the cheesecake and serve.
Serves 6

Blackberry and apple pie

PASTRY
175g/6oz flour
2 tsp castor sugar
pinch salt
40g/1½oz butter
40g/1½oz vegetable fat
1-2 Tbsp iced water
FILLING
150ml/5floz water
500g/1lb cooking apples, peeled, cored and
thickly sliced
1kg/2lb blackberries, hulled
250g/8oz plus 1 Tbsp castor sugar

Sift the flour, sugar and salt into a mixing bowl. Add the butter and fat and cut into small pieces. Rub the fat into the flour until the mixture resembles breadcrumbs. Stir in enough water to bind the mixture and knead to a dough. Chill for 20 minutes.

To make the filling, bring the water to the boil in a saucepan. Add the apples, blackberries and all but 1 tablespoon of the sugar. Cover and simmer for 10 minutes, then pour into a deep pie dish.

Roll out the dough. Cut a narrow strip long enough to go around the edge of the pie dish. Brush with water. Cover with the rest of the pastry and press the edges to seal. Trim and knock up with the blade of a knife. Brush with water and sprinkle with the remaining sugar. Bake in a hot oven (220°C/425°F or Gas Mark 7) for 25 to 30 minutes or until the pastry is golden brown.

Serve hot or cold.
Serves 6

Hazelnut cream

125g/4oz hazelnuts, peeled
7g/¼oz gelatine
2 Tbsp cold water
300ml/10floz milk
4 egg yolks
125g/4oz sugar
2 Tbsp coffee essence
300ml/10floz double cream

Coarsely crush the nuts in the grinder attachment of a blender or using a pestle and mortar. Dissolve the gelatine in the water. Scald the milk with the nuts in a saucepan. Remove from the heat.

Beat the egg yolks and sugar together until the mixture is pale and thick. Pour on the milk and nut mixture, beating constantly. Return to the saucepan and cook, stirring constantly, until the mixture thickens. Do not boil or the custard will curdle. Remove from the heat and strain in the gelatine. Mix well. Stir in the coffee essence. Allow to cool.

Whip the cream until it is thick. When the hazelnut mixture is cold, but not yet set, fold in the cream. Pour into a 1.2 litres/2 pint soufflé dish or individual dishes and chill until set.
Serves 4-6

Jam, soured cream and hazelnut pancakes

175g/6oz apricot jam
3 Tbsp brandy
25g/1oz icing sugar, sifted
65g/2½oz hazelnuts, chopped
250ml/8floz soured cream
PANCAKE BATTER
150g/5oz flour
1 Tbsp castor sugar
3 egg yolks
65g/2½oz butter, melted
250ml/8floz milk
2 Tbsp vegetable oil

First make the pancake batter. Sift the flour and sugar into a mixing bowl. Make a well in the centre and add the egg yolks and melted butter. Mix together, then gradually stir in the milk, beating until the batter is smooth.

Grease a crêpe pan or frying pan with a little of the oil. Pour in about 4 tablespoons of the batter and tilt the pan to cover the bottom completely. Cook over high heat for about 1 minute, then turn the pancake over and cook the other side for about 30 seconds. Slide the pancake out of the pan. Keep hot while you cook the remaining pancakes in the same way. Keep them hot, interleaved with greaseproof paper.

Warm the jam and brandy in a saucepan. When the jam has melted remove from the heat and keep hot. Mix together the icing sugar and hazelnuts. Put the soured cream in a serving bowl.

Lay the pancakes on a flat surface and cover each one with the jam mixture. Roll up the pancakes and arrange on a warmed serving dish. Sprinkle with the sugar and nut mixture and serve immediately, with the soured cream.
Serves 4

Whether added to apple pies, or served with cheesecake, blackberries are always popular.

Apple and caramel mould

125g/4oz lump or granulated sugar
4 Tbsp water
1.5kg/3lb cooking apples, peeled, cored
and sliced
½ tsp ground allspice
¼ tsp ground cloves
50g/2oz castor sugar
4 Tbsp Calvados
50g/2oz butter
3 eggs
1 egg white, lightly beaten

Put the lump sugar and water in a saucepan and stir over gentle heat to dissolve the sugar. Bring to the boil and boil until the syrup turns a rich brown. Remove from the heat and pour into a warmed 900ml/1½ pint mould. Tilt the mould so the sides and bottom are evenly coated.

Put the apples, allspice and cloves in a saucepan. Cover and cook gently for 20 to 25 minutes or until the apples are very soft. Remove from the heat and mash the apples to a purée. Return to the heat, uncovered, and cook for a further 10 to 15 minutes or until the purée is stiff and dry. Remove from the heat.

Beat the sugar into the apple purée, then stir in the Calvados, butter and eggs. Fold in the egg white and spoon into the caramel-lined mould. Cover with foil and place in a roasting tin. Pour enough boiling water into the tin to come halfway up the sides of the mould. Bake in a fairly hot oven (190°C/375°F or Gas Mark 5) for 1¼ to 1½ hours or until set.

Remove from the oven and allow to cool for 15 minutes. Then, to serve hot, unmould onto a serving dish.
Serves 4-6

Honey baked pears

4 large pears, peeled, halved and cored
4 Tbsp lemon juice
4 Tbsp brandy
125ml/4floz clear honey
½ tsp ground cinnamon
¼ tsp grated nutmeg
25g/1oz butter, cut into small pieces

Arrange the pear halves, cut sides down, in a greased baking dish. Warm the lemon juice, brandy and honey in a small saucepan. Remove from the heat and stir in the cinnamon and nutmeg. Pour over the pears. Dot with the pieces of butter and bake in a moderate oven (180°C/350°F or Gas Mark 4) for 30 to 35 minutes or until the pears are tender but still firm.

Serve hot or cold, with whipped cream.
Serves 4

Maple and orange mousse

3 large egg yolks
50g/2oz soft brown sugar
15g/½oz gelatine
4 Tbsp dark rum
75ml/3floz maple syrup
finely grated rind of 1 orange
75ml/3floz orange juice
300ml/10floz double cream

Put the egg yolks and sugar in the top of a double saucepan or in a heatproof bowl over a pan of hot water. Beat over gentle heat until the mixture is pale and thick and leaves a ribbon trail on itself when the beater is lifted. Remove from the heat.

Dissolve the gelatine in the rum and strain into the egg yolk mixture. Mix well. Stir in the maple syrup, orange rind and juice. Leave to cool until on the point of setting.

Whip the cream until it is thick. Fold into the maple syrup mixture. Pour into a chilled 900ml/1½ pint mould or dish. Chill for at least 3 hours or until set. Unmould onto a serving dish and serve.
Serves 4

Peach cobbler

10 peaches, peeled, stoned and sliced
50g/2oz sugar
½ tsp ground cinnamon
15g/½oz butter, cut into small pieces
2 Tbsp brandy (optional)
PASTRY TOPPING
175g/6oz flour
1 tsp baking powder
½ tsp salt
40g/1½oz butter
25g/1oz vegetable fat
6 Tbsp milk

Put the peaches in a 20cm/8in square cake tin that is 5cm/2in deep. Sprinkle with the sugar and cinnamon and dot with the pieces of butter.

Sift the flour for the pastry into a mixing bowl with the baking powder and salt. Add the butter and fat and cut into small pieces. Rub the fat into the flour until the mixture resembles breadcrumbs. Stir in the milk and mix to a dough.

Roll out the dough to a 20cm/8in square, about 6mm/¼in thick. Place over the peaches in the tin. Bake in a fairly hot oven (200°C/400°F or Gas Mark 6) for 40 minutes or until the pastry is golden brown. If you are using the brandy, carefully lift up the pastry crust and sprinkle the brandy over the peaches. Replace the crust and serve hot, with cream.
Serves 4-6

Spiced up with cinnamon and nutmeg, Honey Baked Pears make an extremely tasty dessert.

Normandy pear tart

PASTRY

275g/10oz flour
½ tsp salt
75g/3oz butter
50g/2oz vegetable fat
125g/4oz plus 2 Tbsp castor sugar
40g/1½oz walnuts, finely chopped
2 egg yolks, finely beaten
3 Tbsp iced water
1 egg white, lightly beaten

FILLING

50g/2oz sugar
150ml/5floz water
4 large pears, peeled, halved and cored
150ml/5floz double cream
2 Tbsp walnuts, chopped

Sift the flour and salt into a mixing bowl. Add the butter and fat and cut into small pieces. Rub the fat into the flour until the mixture resembles breadcrumbs. Stir in all but 2 tablespoons of the sugar and the walnuts, then the egg yolks and enough of the water to bind the mixture. Knead to a dough. Chill for 30 minutes.

To make the filling, dissolve the sugar in the water in a saucepan over gentle heat. Bring to the boil and boil for 4 minutes. Add the pear halves and poach for 10 to 15 minutes or until they are just tender. Remove from the heat.

Roll out two-thirds of the dough and use to line a 23cm/9in flan ring. Drain the pears and arrange them in a ring in the pastry case, narrow ends towards the middle and cut sides down. Brush the edges with water. Roll out the remaining dough to a circle large enough to cover the top of the tart. Cut an 8cm/3in hole in the centre, using a biscuit cutter, and place the dough ring on top of the tart. Press the edges together to seal. Knock up and crimp. Brush with the egg white and sprinkle over the remaining sugar.

Bake in a fairly hot oven (190°C/375°F or Gas Mark 5) for 30 to 35 minutes or until the pastry is firm to the touch. Remove from the oven and allow to cool.

Carefully remove the flan ring and place the tart on a serving plate. Whip the cream until it is thick and pile in the centre of the tart. Sprinkle with the chopped walnuts and serve.

Serves 4-6

Melting walnut pastry and tender pears combine to make Normandy Pear Tart a delicious dessert. Serve cold with extra cream.

Crab apples can be found growing wild in some parts of the country.

Preserves

Crab apple preserve

1 Tbsp whole cloves
5cm/2in cinnamon stick
1 Tbsp allspice berries
pared rind of 2 lemons
1.2l/2 pints malt vinegar
1kg/2lb light brown sugar
2.5kg/2lb crab apples, peeled

Tie the cloves, cinnamon, allspice berries and lemon rind in a piece of muslin. Put the vinegar and sugar in a saucepan and stir over gentle heat to dissolve the sugar. Add the bag of spices and bring to the boil. Boil for 5 minutes.

Add the crab apples and simmer gently for 1 hour or until the fruit is just tender. Do not overcook or they will be mushy. Discard the bag of spices.

Pack the apples loosely into jam jars, being careful not to squash them.

Boil the liquid in the saucepan for 15 minutes or until it is thick and syrupy. Allow to cool, then pour into the jars. Cover the jars with vinegar-proof covers and secure with rubber bands. Label and store in a cool, dry, dark place.
Makes 2–2.5kg/4–5lb

Piccalilli

1 medium cauliflower, broken into small flowerets
1 cucumber, quartered lengthways and cut into 1cm/½in pieces
250g/8oz pickling onions
1 large Spanish onion, chopped
4 green tomatoes, peeled and chopped
175g/6oz coarse salt
600ml/1 pint malt vinegar
SAUCE
600ml/1 pint malt vinegar
3 Tbsp mustard seed, bruised
5cm/2in piece root ginger, peeled and chopped
4 garlic cloves, halved
1 Tbsp black peppercorns, bruised
1 Tbsp turmeric
1 Tbsp dry mustard
125g/4oz sugar
3 Tbsp flour
4 Tbsp water

Put the vegetables in a large bowl and sprinkle with the salt. Leave for 4 hours, then drain well in a colander and discard the liquid.

Bring the vinegar to the boil in a large saucepan. Add the vegetables and cover the pan. Simmer for 15 minutes or until the vegetables are almost tender. Drain the vegetables and place in a large mixing bowl.

To make the sauce, put the vinegar, mustard seed, ginger, garlic, peppercorns, turmeric, mustard and sugar in a saucepan. Bring to the boil, stirring to dissolve the sugar, and simmer for 15 minutes. Remove from the heat and strain the liquid. Return the strained liquid to the rinsed-out saucepan and bring back to the boil.

Mix together the flour and water to make a smooth paste. Add a little of the hot liquid. Add to the strained liquid and bring to the boil, stirring. Cook, stirring, for 2 minutes or until the sauce is thickened and smooth. Pour the sauce over the vegetables and toss well to coat.

Ladle the piccalilli into warmed jars with screwtop lids lined with vinegar-proof paper. Fill the jars completely. Allow to cool completely, before sealing. Then screw the lids on firmly, label and store in a cool, dry place.
Makes about 1.5kg/3lb

Norfolk fruit chutney

1kg/2lb dried apricots, soaked overnight, drained and chopped
1kg/2lb cooking apples, peeled, cored and chopped
4 medium peaches, peeled, halved, stoned and chopped
2 medium onions, finely chopped
250g/8oz raisins
5cm/2in piece root ginger, peeled and finely diced
¾ tsp grated nutmeg
¾ tsp ground allspice
¾ tsp dry mustard
finely grated rind of 1 large lemon
juice and finely grated rind of 2 oranges
750ml/1¼ pints white wine vinegar
500g/1lb sugar
500g/1lb soft brown sugar

Put the apricots, apples, peaches, onions, raisins, ginger, nutmeg, allspice, mustard, lemon rind, orange juice and rind and 600ml/1 pint of the vinegar in a large saucepan. Bring to the boil, stirring, then simmer gently for 1 to 1½ hours or until the fruit mixture is soft and pulpy.

Stir in the sugars and remaining vinegar and simmer, stirring occasionally, for a further 45 to 50 minutes or until the chutney is very thick.

Ladle into warmed jam jars. Seal with vinegar-proof covers and secure with rubber bands. Label and store in a cool, dry, dark place for at least 6 weeks before serving.
Makes about 3.5kg/8lb

Green tomato chutney

500g/1lb onions, chopped
4 Tbsp water
2.5kg/5lb green tomatoes, sliced
½ tsp salt
1 Tbsp pickling spice
600ml/1 pint malt vinegar
500g/1lb brown sugar

Simmer the onions in the water in a large saucepan until they are soft. Remove from the heat and drain well. Return the onions to the pan and add the tomatoes, salt and pickling spice. Return to the heat and bring to the boil, stirring occasionally and adding just enough vinegar from time to time to prevent the mixture sticking to the pan.

Cook for 1½ hours or until the chutney is thick.

Stir in the remaining vinegar and the sugar. Simmer for a further 20 to 25 minutes, stirring occasionally, or until the chutney is very thick.

Ladle into warmed jam jars. Seal with vinegar-proof covers and secure with rubber bands. Label and store in a cool, dry place.

Makes about 3kg/6lb

A traditional English mustard pickle, Piccalilli adds a special zest to cold meats.

Winter

Fortunately, winter no longer means living on what we managed to harvest
and preserve earlier in the year. Meat, game (furred and feathered) and
vegetables are all freely available. Now is the time for steaming soups
made from cheap, fresh root vegetables, hot, hearty pies topped with crisp
pastry and steamed fruit puddings served with sweet, warm sauces.
Get into the habit of eating a hot breakfast of eggs and bacon, smoked
fish or sweet waffles with maple syrup and you'll feel ready to face the
outside world, whatever the weather.
The seasonal fruits are all citrus, and winter is traditionally the time
for making marmalades. Use lemons and oranges for giving flavour and
colour to warming punches, too, to cheer guests at parties, and—remember
that winter is also a festive season.

What's best in season

Fruit:				
	Apples	Grapes	Melons	Rhubarb
	Apricots	Grapefruit	Oranges (especially	Satsumas
	Bananas	Lemons	Sevilles)	Tangerines
	Clementines	Limes	Passionfruit	Uglifruit
	Cranberries	Lychees	Pears	
	Dates	Mandarins	Persimmons	

Vegetables:				
	Aubergines	Celery	Lettuces	Shallots
	Avocados	Chicory	Mushrooms	Spinach
	Beetroot	Cucumbers	Okra	Swede
	Broccoli	Endive	Onions	Sweet potatoes
	Brussels sprouts	Fennel	Parsnips	Swiss chard
	Cabbages	Jerusalem artichokes	Peppers	Turnips
	Carrots	Kale	Potatoes	Watercress
	Cauliflowers	Kohlrabi	Radishes	
	Celeriac	Leeks	Salsify	

Herbs:				
	Bay	Parsley	Sage	Thyme
	Mint	Rosemary	Winter Savory	

Nuts:				
	Almonds	Brazil nuts	Chestnuts	Walnuts

Fish:				
	Carp	Herring	Prawns	Turbot
	Cod	Mackerel	Scallops	Whelks
	Cockles	Mullet	Shrimps	Whitebait
	Clam	Mussels	Skate	Whiting
	Eel	Oysters	Smelt	Winkles
	Haddock	Perch	Sole	
	Hake	Pike	Sprats	
	Halibut	Plaice	Trout	

Poultry:	
	Available fresh or frozen all year round

Game:				
	Grouse	Partridge	Quail	Teal
	Hare	Pheasant	Rabbit	Woodcock
	Mallard	Pigeon	Snipe	Venison

Meat and offal:	
	Available fresh or frozen all year round

Appetizers

Clams in tomato and garlic sauce

2 eggs, hard-boiled
3 Tbsp olive oil
1 large onion, chopped
2 garlic cloves, crushed
40g/1½oz fresh white breadcrumbs
700g/1½lb tomatoes, peeled and chopped
salt and black pepper
4 dozen clams
450ml/15floz dry white wine
2 Tbsp parsley, freshly chopped
lemon wedges, to serve

Separate the egg whites from the yolks. Finely chop the whites. Sieve the yolks.

Heat the oil in a frying pan. Add the onion and garlic and fry until the onion is soft but not brown. Stir in the breadcrumbs, tomatoes, egg yolks and salt and pepper to taste. Mash the mixture to a purée. Remove from the heat.

Put the clams in a heavy saucepan. Pour over the wine and bring to the boil. Cover and simmer for 10 minutes or until the clams have opened. Discard any that are still closed.

Transfer the clams to a warmed serving dish. Keep hot. Strain the cooking liquid into the tomato mixture and return to the heat. Bring to the boil and pour over the clams. Sprinkle with the parsley and serve with the lemon wedges.
Serves 4

Scallops with garlic and basil

700g/1½lb scallops, cut into 1cm/½in pieces
juice of ½ lemon
salt and white pepper
50g/2oz flour
75ml/3floz vegetable oil
3 shallots, finely chopped
3 garlic cloves, crushed
½ tsp dried basil
25g/1oz butter
1 Tbsp parsley, freshly chopped

Sprinkle the scallops with lemon juice and salt and pepper, then coat with the flour. Heat enough of the oil in a frying pan just to cover the bottom. Add the scallops and fry, stirring, until they are lightly browned.

Stir in the shallots, garlic and basil and cook for a further 2 minutes. Remove from the heat and stir in the butter and parsley. Spoon into four dishes and serve hot.
Serves 4

Gnocchi alla romana

600ml/1 pint milk
1 onion, chopped
1 tsp salt
¼ tsp grated nutmeg
150g/5oz semolina
2 eggs
125g/4oz Parmesan cheese, grated
40g/1½oz butter, melted

Put the milk, onion, salt and nutmeg in a saucepan and bring to the boil. Remove from the heat and leave for 15 minutes. Strain the milk and return to the saucepan. Bring to the boil again and gradually stir in the semolina. Cook, stirring, for 2 minutes or until the mixture is very thick.

Remove from the heat and beat in the eggs and half the cheese. Pour into a greased 20cm/8in square baking dish. Allow to cool, then chill for 30 minutes.

Cut the gnocchi mixture into squares and triangles. Place these in a shallow ovenproof dish and pour over the melted butter. Sprinkle the rest of the cheese on top. Bake in a fairly hot oven (200°C/400°F or Gas Mark 6) for 20 to 25 minutes or until golden brown. Serve hot.
Serves 2-3

Scallops with Garlic and Basil – an exquisite first course for a dinner party accompanied by French bread.

A classic French dish, Snails in Garlic Butter make a sophisticated appetizer for a special occasion.

Potted hare or rabbit

1kg/2lb hare or rabbit meat, cut into
2.5cm/1in pieces
125ml/4floz red wine
1 Tbsp red wine vinegar
250g/8oz unsalted pork fat, diced
600ml/1 pint boiling water
salt and black pepper
½ tsp grated nutmeg
1 tsp thyme, freshly chopped
¼ tsp dried marjoram

Put the meat in a mixing bowl and pour over the wine, vinegar and enough water just to cover the meat. Leave to soak for 2 hours. Drain the meat and pat dry with kitchen paper towels.

Cook the pork fat in a frying pan until it has rendered most of its fat. Add the meat and brown on all sides. Transfer the meat mixture to a baking dish. Stir in the boiling water, salt and pepper to taste, the nutmeg and herbs. Cover the dish and bake in a cool oven (150°C/300°F or Gas Mark 2) for 2½ hours or until the meat is very tender.

Drain the meat in a strainer over a mixing bowl. Chill the liquid in the mixing bowl for 20 minutes. Finely chop the meat and place in a large terrine.

Skim the fat from the liquid in the mixing bowl and place it in a saucepan. Melt the fat and pour over the meat in the terrine. Cover and chill for at least 2 hours before serving.
Serves 10

Stuffed mushrooms

12 large mushrooms, wiped
salt and black pepper
15g/½oz butter, melted
25g/1oz butter
2 shallots, finely chopped
1 Tbsp flour
125ml/4floz single cream
3 Tbsp parsley, freshly chopped
1½ Tbsp Parmesan cheese, grated

Remove the stems from the mushrooms and set aside. Rub the caps with salt and pepper and brush with the melted butter. Arrange in one layer, hollow side up, in a greased, shallow baking dish.

Finely chop the mushroom stems. Melt the butter in a frying pan. Add the mushroom stems and shallots and fry for 4 to 5 minutes. Sprinkle over the flour and cook, stirring, for 1 minute. Remove from the heat and stir in the cream. Return to the heat and simmer, stirring, until thickened. Stir in the parsley and salt and pepper to taste.

Fill the mushroom caps with the cream mixture. Top each with a little grated cheese. Bake in a fairly hot oven (190°C/375°F or Gas Mark 5) for 15 minutes or until the mushrooms are tender and the topping lightly browned. Serve hot.
Serves 4

Snails in garlic butter

175g/6oz butter, softened
2 Tbsp parsley, freshly chopped
2 garlic cloves, crushed
salt and black pepper
2 Tbsp brandy
24 snail shells
24 snails

Mix together the butter, parsley, garlic, salt and pepper to taste and 1 tablespoon of the brandy. Push a little of the butter mixture into each snail shell and follow with a snail. Seal with more butter.

Place the filled shells in a shallow oven-proof dish or *escargotière* and pour over the remaining brandy. Bake in a fairly hot oven (190°C/375°F or Gas Mark 5) for 15 to 20 minutes or until the butter is bubbling and beginning to brown and serve.
Serves 4

Soups

Goulash soup

salt and black pepper
2 Tbsp paprika
500g/1lb lean stewing steak, cut into
2.5cm/1in cubes
50g/2oz butter
2 medium onions, thinly sliced
½ tsp ground cumin
1 garlic clove, crushed
2 Tbsp flour
1.8l/3 pints beef stock
2 large potatoes, cubed
400g/14oz can tomatoes, chopped

Mix together salt and pepper and the paprika and coat the meat cubes with the mixture. Melt the butter in a saucepan. Add the meat cubes, in batches, and brown on all sides. Add the onions and cook for a further 5 minutes. Stir in the cumin, garlic and flour. Cook, stirring, for 1 minute.

Gradually stir in the stock and bring to the boil. Cover and simmer for 2 hours.

Add the potatoes and tomatoes with the can juice. Re-cover and simmer for a further 1 hour or until the meat and potatoes are tender. Serve hot.
Serves 6

Bean and vegetable soup

500g/1lb dried white haricot beans, soaked
overnight and drained
1 small cabbage, shredded
6 medium potatoes, quartered
2 medium onions, thinly sliced
2 carrots, scraped and sliced
2 celery stalks, sliced
2 garlic cloves, crushed
125g/4oz streaky bacon, in one piece
1 bouquet garni
1 tsp salt
1.5l/2½ pints water
2 Tbsp parsley, freshly chopped

Put the beans in a saucepan and cover with water. Bring to the boil and simmer for 1 to 1½ hours or until the beans are tender.

Halfway through the beans' cooking time, put the remaining ingredients in another saucepan. Bring to the boil, then simmer for 30 to 45 minutes or until the bacon and vegetables are cooked and tender. Remove the bacon and chop it finely. Return to the pan. Discard the bouquet garni.

Drain the beans and add to the soup, stirring well. Cook for a further 3 minutes, then transfer the soup to a warmed soup tureen, sprinkle over the parsley and serve immediately.
Serves 4-6

Bean and Vegetable Soup – hearty and satisfying enough to be a meal in itself.

Leeks, parsnips and turnips – three popular winter vegetables.

Kidney bean and frankfurter soup

400g/14oz red kidney beans, soaked
overnight and drained
1.8l/3 pints water
1 medium onion, very finely chopped
1 bay leaf
1 tsp winter savory, freshly chopped
¼ tsp dried basil
salt and black pepper
250g/8oz frankfurters, cut into 6mm/¼in
thick slices
1 Tbsp Worcestershire sauce
1 tsp dry mustard

Cook the beans in boiling salted water for 1½ to 2 hours or until they are tender. Drain well.

Bring the measured water to the boil in a saucepan. Add the beans and onion, then the bay leaf, savory, basil and salt and pepper to taste. Simmer for 20 minutes or until the beans are tender.

Add the remaining ingredients and simmer for a further 10 minutes or until the frankfurters are heated through. Serve hot.
Serves 8

Parsnip and tomato soup

25g/1oz butter
2 medium onions, thinly sliced
1 garlic clove, crushed
500g/1lb parsnips, peeled and chopped
3 Tbsp flour
salt and black pepper
1 tsp thyme, freshly chopped
900ml/1½ pints chicken stock
150ml/5floz milk
1 bay leaf
400g/14oz can tomatoes

Melt the butter in a saucepan. Add the onions and garlic and fry until they are soft but not brown. Add the parsnips and fry for 4 minutes. Sprinkle over the flour, salt and pepper to taste and the thyme and cook, stirring, for 1 minute. Remove from the heat and gradually stir in the stock and milk. Add the bay leaf and tomatoes with the can juice and stir well.

Return to the heat and bring to the boil, stirring. Cover and simmer for 40 minutes or until the parsnips are very tender.

Remove from the heat, discard the bay leaf and allow to cool slightly. Purée the soup in an electric blender or by pushing it through a sieve. Return the puréed soup to the saucepan and reheat gently without boiling.

Serve hot.
Serves 6

Leek and cress soup

4 streaky bacon rashers
15g/½oz butter
500g/1lb leeks, thinly sliced
500g/1lb potatoes, peeled and chopped
2 Tbsp flour
salt and black pepper
¼ tsp cayenne pepper
¼ tsp grated nutmeg
1.2l/2 pints chicken stock
300ml/10floz milk
1 bunch watercress, coarsely chopped
8 Tbsp mustard and cress, chopped
1 bay leaf
150ml/5floz soured cream

Fry the bacon in a saucepan until it is crisp and has rendered most of its fat. Remove the bacon from the pan with a slotted spoon and drain on kitchen paper towels. Crumble the bacon and keep hot.

Add the butter to the saucepan. When it has melted add the leeks and potatoes. Fry the vegetables until they are golden. Sprinkle over the flour, salt and pepper to taste, the cayenne and nutmeg and cook, stirring, for 1 minute.

Remove the pan from the heat and gradually stir in the stock and milk. Add the watercress, mustard and cress and bay leaf and stir well. Return to the heat and bring to the boil, stirring. Cover and simmer for 30 minutes.

Remove from the heat, discard the bay leaf and allow the soup to cool slightly. Purée in an electric blender or push through a sieve. Return the puréed soup to the saucepan and stir in the soured cream. Heat through gently without boiling.

Pour the soup into a warmed tureen or individual soup bowls and sprinkle over the crumbled bacon. Serve hot.
Serves 6-8

Mushroom soup

25g/1oz butter
1 small onion, finely chopped
3 Tbsp flour
salt and black pepper
¼ tsp dried oregano
pinch cayenne pepper
900ml/1½ pints chicken stock
500g/1lb mushrooms, sliced
1 bay leaf
150ml/5floz double cream

Melt the butter in a saucepan. Add the onion and fry until it is soft but not brown. Sprinkle over the flour, salt and pepper to taste, the oregano and cayenne. Cook, stirring, for 1 minute. Remove from the heat and gradually stir in the stock. Stir in

Mushroom Soup – a creamy delight for a chilly winter day.

the mushrooms and bay leaf.

Return to the heat and bring to the boil, stirring. Cover and simmer for 30 minutes.

Stir in the cream and heat through gently without boiling. Remove the bay leaf and serve.

Serves 4-6

Split pea soup

1 x 700g/1½lb ham hock, soaked
overnight, rinsed and drained
2.4l/4 pints water
500g/1lb dried split peas, soaked overnight
and drained
1 bay leaf
salt and black pepper
50g/2oz butter
2 medium onions, chopped
2 celery stalks, chopped
2 carrots, scraped and thinly sliced
2 leeks, cut into 1cm/½in pieces

Put the ham hock in a saucepan and pour over the water. Bring to the boil, then simmer for 1 hour.

Add the split peas, bay leaf and salt and pepper to taste and continue to simmer for 1 hour.

Meanwhile, melt the butter in a frying pan. Add the vegetables and fry until they are just beginning to soften. Add to the saucepan and stir well. Cover and simmer for a further 45 minutes.

Remove from the heat and allow the soup to cool. Skim off any fat from the surface. Remove the ham hock and cut the meat from the bone. Chop the meat and return to the saucepan. Bring the soup back to the boil, then serve.

Serves 6-8

Oyster soup

600ml/1 pint single cream
300ml/10floz milk
24 oysters, shelled and liquid from the
shells reserved
250g/8oz prawns (shelled weight), deveined
and chopped
salt and white pepper
½ tsp paprika

Scald the cream and milk in a saucepan. Remove from the heat and keep hot.

Put the oysters and their liquid in another saucepan. Add the prawns and cook, stirring, for 2 to 3 minutes, or until the shellfish are heated through. Remove from the heat and stir in the cream and milk mixture, salt and pepper to taste and the paprika.

Serve hot.

Serves 4-6

Main Dishes

Cullen skink

500g/1lb smoked haddock
water, boiling
2 onions, finely chopped
3 large potatoes, sliced
white pepper
450ml/15floz milk
15g/½oz butter

Place the haddock in a heatproof basin. Pour over enough boiling water to cover and leave for 10 to 15 minutes. Strain the liquid and pour 300ml/10floz into a saucepan. Add the onions, potatoes and pepper to taste. Cover and cook for 20 minutes or until the potatoes are tender.

Meanwhile, remove the skin and bones from the haddock and flake the flesh into large pieces.

Remove the pan from the heat and mash the potatoes with the onions and cooking liquid. Gradually stir in the milk. Return to the heat and add the flaked haddock and butter. Heat through gently. Taste and add salt if necessary.

Serve hot.
Serves 4

Plaice fillets with mushroom sauce

300ml/10floz dry white wine
125ml/4floz water
1 Tbsp lemon juice
1 bay leaf
6 black peppercorns
1 small onion, thinly sliced
salt
8 plaice fillets
50g/2oz butter
500g/1lb button mushrooms, thickly sliced
2 Tbsp flour
4 Tbsp double cream
1½ tsp dried chervil
pinch cayenne pepper
50g/2oz Cheddar cheese, grated

Mix together the wine, water, lemon juice, bay leaf, peppercorns, onion and salt to taste in a baking dish. Place the fillets in the dish and turn to coat them with the wine mixture. Cover the dish and bake in a moderate oven (180°C/350°F or Gas Mark 4) for 25 to 30 minutes or until the fish is cooked. Test with a fork: the flesh should flake easily.

Transfer the fish to a flameproof serving dish. Keep hot. Strain the cooking liquid and reserve 300ml/10floz.

Melt 40g/1½oz of the butter in a saucepan. Add the mushrooms and cook for 3 minutes. Remove from the heat and keep hot.

Melt the remaining butter in another saucepan. Stir in the flour and cook, stirring, for 1 minute. Remove from the heat and gradually stir in the reserved cooking liquid. Return to the heat and bring to the boil, stirring. Simmer, stirring, until thickened and smooth. Remove from the heat and stir in the cream, chervil, cayenne and salt to taste. Stir in the mushrooms.

Pour the mushroom sauce over the fish and sprinkle over the cheese. Grill for 5 minutes or until the cheese has melted and is lightly browned.

Serve hot.
Serves 4

Fish pie

300ml/10floz milk
1 shallot, sliced
½ tsp dried marjoram
¼ tsp dried dill
1 bay leaf
salt and black pepper
500g/1lb cod or other white fish fillets
25g/1oz butter
25g/1oz flour
8 Tbsp parsley, freshly chopped
1 tsp lemon juice
PASTRY
350g/12oz flour
¼ tsp salt
350g/12oz unsalted butter, chilled
6 Tbsp iced water
1 egg yolk
2 Tbsp milk

First make the pastry. Sift the flour and salt into a mixing bowl. Add one-third of the butter and cut into small pieces. Rub the butter into the flour until the mixture resembles breadcrumbs. Stir in enough of the water to bind the mixture and knead to a dough. Chill for 15 minutes. Form the remaining butter into a slab about 2cm/¾in thick.

Roll out the dough to a rectangle about 6mm/¼in thick. Place the slab of butter in the centre and fold the dough over it to make a parcel. Chill for 10 minutes.

Place the dough, folds down, on a floured surface and roll out into a rectangle. Fold the rectangle in three, then turn so the open end is facing you. Roll out again, fold and chill for 15 minutes. Repeat the rolling and folding twice more and leave to chill while making the filling.

Put the milk, shallot, marjoram, dill, bay leaf and salt and pepper to taste in a

Opposite above : Economical, warming and filling, Cullen Skink is a traditional Scottish dish of smoked haddock and potatoes. Opposite below : A light, tasty main meal, Plaice Fillets with Mushroom Sauce may be served with croquette or creamed potatoes and a well-chilled white wine.

Mushrooms and parsley are just two of the ingredients in the delicious, Beef, Kidney and Oyster Pie.

saucepan. Infuse over low heat for 10 minutes. Strain.

Poach the cod fillets in the strained milk for about 15 minutes. Test with a fork: the flesh should flake easily. Drain, then remove the skin. Flake the fish into large pieces.

Melt the butter in a saucepan. Add the flour and cook, stirring, for 1 minute. Remove from the heat and gradually stir in the strained milk. Return to the heat and simmer, stirring, until thickened and smooth. Remove from the heat and stir in the flaked fish, parsley and lemon juice.

Roll out the dough to a square about 6mm/¼in thick. Trim the edges to straighten them. Lift the dough onto a greased baking sheet. Spoon the fish filling into the centre of the dough over the filling. Pinch them together in the centre to seal. Mix together the egg yolk and milk and brush over the dough.

Bake in a fairly hot oven (190°C/375°F or Gas Mark 5) for 30 to 40 minutes or until the pastry is golden brown.

Serve hot.
Serves 4

Pike or perch fillets with mustard and green peppercorn sauce

1kg/2lb pike or perch fillets, skinned
juice of 1 lemon
salt and white pepper
175g/6oz butter
1 onion, finely chopped
1 tsp green peppercorns, crushed
1 Tbsp prepared German mustard
2 Tbsp double cream
1 Tbsp parsley, freshly chopped

Put the fillets in a shallow dish and sprinkle with the lemon juice. Leave for 10 minutes, then pat dry with kitchen paper towels. Rub the fillets with salt and pepper.

Melt 50g/2oz of the butter in a frying pan. Add the fillets and fry for 5 minutes on each side or until cooked. Test with a fork: the flesh should flake easily. Transfer the fillets to a warmed serving dish and keep hot.

Add the remaining butter to the cleaned-out frying pan. When it has melted, add the onion. Fry until it is soft but not brown. Stir in the peppercorns and mustard and cook for 2 minutes. Stir in the cream. Remove from the heat and pour this sauce over the fillets. Sprinkle with the parsley and serve hot.
Serves 4-6

Beef, kidney and oyster pie

25g/1oz flour
salt and black pepper
¼ tsp dry mustard
1kg/2lb lean stewing beef, cut into
2.5cm/1in cubes
250g/8oz kidney, skinned, cored and cut
into small pieces
4 Tbsp vegetable oil
2 medium onions, chopped
250ml/8floz beef stock
150ml/5floz sherry or Madeira
1 tsp Worcestershire sauce
1 bouquet garni
125g/4oz mushrooms, quartered
2 Tbsp parsley, freshly chopped
12 oysters, removed from the shells
PASTRY
175g/6oz flour
pinch salt
125g/4oz butter
3-4 Tbsp iced water
1 egg, lightly beaten

First make the pastry. Sift the flour and salt into a mixing bowl. Add the butter and cut into small pieces, then mix in enough of the water to bind the mixture to a dough which should be lumpy. Roll out the dough to an oblong and fold in three. Turn so that the open end faces you and roll out again. Fold and turn twice more, then wrap the dough in greaseproof paper and put it in the refrigerator to chill for 15 minutes.

Mix together the flour, salt and pepper and the mustard in a polythene bag. Add the beef cubes and kidney pieces and shake the bag so they become well coated with the flour mixture.

Heat the oil in a frying pan. Add the beef and kidney and fry until they are browned on all sides. Transfer to a deep pie dish, using a slotted spoon.

Add the onions to the frying pan and fry until they are soft but not brown. Stir in the stock, sherry or Madeira, salt and pepper to taste, the Worcestershire sauce and bouquet garni. Bring to the boil and pour over the meat in the pie dish. Stir in the mushrooms, parsley and oysters. Leave to cool.

Place a pie funnel, or an up-turned egg cup, in the centre of the pie dish. Roll out the pastry to 6mm/¼in thick. Cut a long strip 2.5cm/1in wide and place around the edge of the pie dish. If it is not long enough, cut another and join. Brush with beaten egg. Roll out the remaining pastry to fit the top of the dish. Lift on with a rolling pin. Press the edges together, trim and knock up with the blade of a knife. Crimp edges. Brush pastry with beaten

egg. Make leaves with the dough trimmings and stick in place.

Bake in a fairly hot oven (200°C/400°F or Gas Mark 6) for 1 hour or until the pastry is golden brown.

Serve hot.

Serves 4-6

Italian beef braised in red wine

1.2kg/2½lb top rump of beef, rolled and tied
2 garlic cloves, halved
salt and black pepper
25g/1oz plus 1 Tbsp butter
1 Tbsp vegetable oil
1 medium onion, thinly sliced
3 celery stalks, chopped
4 small carrots, scraped and sliced
3 large tomatoes, skinned, seeded and chopped
¼ tsp ground cloves
300ml/10floz dry red wine
1 Tbsp flour

Rub the beef all over with the cut sides of the garlic, then discard the garlic. Rub the beef with salt and pepper.

Melt all but 1 tablespoon of the butter with the oil in a flameproof casserole. Add the beef and brown it on all sides. Remove the beef from the casserole and put it to one side.

Add the onion, celery and carrots to the casserole and fry until the onion is soft but not brown. Stir in the tomatoes and cloves and return the beef to the casserole. Pour over the wine and bring to the boil. Cover and transfer to a moderate oven (180°C/350°F or Gas Mark 4). Braise for 3 hours or until the meat is very tender when pierced with the point of a knife.

Transfer the meat to a warmed serving dish. Keep hot. Skim any fat from the surface of the liquid in the casserole. Strain into a saucepan, pressing down well on the vegetables to extract the juices. Bring the strained liquid to the boil and boil for 3 minutes.

Blend the flour with the remaining butter to make a paste. Add to the cooking liquid, in small pieces, and simmer, stirring, until thickened and smooth. Pour this sauce into a sauceboat and serve with the meat.

Serves 4

Italian Beef Braised in Red Wine is a simple, succulent dish, perfect for a dinner party.

Well worth the time and trouble spent in preparation, Spiced Brisket of Beef tastes really fabulous.

Spiced brisket of beef

75g/3oz soft brown sugar
1 x 2.75kg/6lb brisket or silverside of beef
15g/½oz saltpetre
100g/4oz sea salt or rock salt
2 Tbsp black peppercorns
2 Tbsp juniper berries
1 Tbsp allspice berries
300ml/10floz water

Rub the sugar all over the beef. Place the beef in a heavy earthenware pot, cover with muslin and leave in a cool place for 2 days.

Crush the saltpetre, salt, peppercorns, juniper berries and allspice berries using a pestle and mortar. Each day for the next 10 days, rub the sugared beef with the salt mixture.

Shake any excess sugar and salt mixture off the beef and place it in a heavy casserole. Add the water and cover the pot with three layers of greaseproof paper and then the lid. Bake in a very cool oven (140°C/275°F or Gas Mark 1) for 5 hours.

Remove from the oven and leave to cool for 2 hours. Remove and discard the greaseproof paper.

Remove the beef from the casserole and wrap it in foil. Place a plate with a heavy weight on top. Leave for 24 hours before slicing thinly and serving.

Serves 12

Russian meat and potato pie

1kg/2lb potatoes
50g/2oz butter
4 Tbsp milk
salt and black pepper
2 eggs, lightly beaten
2 Tbsp vegetable oil
2 medium onions, thinly sliced
125g/4oz mushrooms, sliced
500g/1lb minced beef
½ tsp caraway seeds
50g/2oz Cheddar cheese, grated

Cook the potatoes in boiling salted water until they are tender. Drain well. Return to the saucepan and add half of the butter, the milk and salt and pepper to taste. Mash well until smooth. Allow to cool for 10 minutes.

Stir half the beaten egg into the potato mixture, beating briskly until the mixture is smooth and slightly stiff. Set aside while you cook the pie filling.

Melt the remaining butter with the oil in a frying pan. Add the onions and fry until they are soft but not brown. Add the mushrooms and fry for 3 minutes. Add the meat, salt and pepper to taste and the caraway seeds and cook until the meat is browned.

Cover the bottom of a baking dish with

half the potato mixture. Spoon over the meat mixture and cover with the remaining potato mixture. Brush the top with the remaining beaten egg. Sprinkle over the cheese.

Bake in a moderate oven (180°C/350°F or Gas Mark 4) for 30 to 40 minutes or until the top is golden brown.

Serve hot.

Serves 4-6

Beef stew with chick-peas

3 streaky bacon rashers, chopped
1.5kg/3lb lean stewing beef, cut into
2.5cm/1in cubes
2 Tbsp vegetable oil
2 large onions, thinly sliced
2 garlic cloves, crushed
1 Tbsp flour
1.2l/2 pints water
2 Tbsp tomato purée
375g/12oz tomatoes, peeled and quartered
1 tsp dried basil
½ tsp dried chervil
salt and black pepper
175g/6oz dried chick-peas, soaked
overnight, cooked and drained

Fry the bacon in a frying pan until it is crisp and golden brown and has rendered most of its fat. Transfer the bacon to a large, ovenproof casserole using a slotted spoon. Set aside.

Add the meat cubes to the frying pan, in batches, and brown on all sides. Transfer to the casserole. Add the oil to the frying pan and when it is hot add the onions and garlic. Fry until the onions are golden brown. Sprinkle over the flour and stir the flour into the onion mixture to form a smooth paste. Cook, stirring, until the mixture becomes a deep golden brown.

Transfer to an ovenproof casserole dish and gradually stir in the water. Set over medium heat and bring to the boil, stirring. Stir in the tomato purée, tomatoes, basil, chervil and salt and pepper to taste. Pour into the casserole and stir well.

Cover the casserole and bake in a warm oven (170°C/325°F or Gas Mark 3) for 2 hours.

Add the chick-peas, stir well and continue cooking for 30 minutes or until the meat is tender. Serve hot, from the casserole.

Serves 6

Beef Stew with Chick peas is a delicious, economical stew.

Allspice veal roll

50g/2oz fresh white breadcrumbs
1 Tbsp raisins
grated rind of 1 orange
1 Tbsp parsley, freshly chopped
1 tsp sage, freshly chopped
1 tsp thyme, freshly chopped
1 Tbsp onion, finely chopped
salt and black pepper
1kg/2lb breast of veal (boned weight)
40g/1½oz butter, cut into small pieces
1 Tbsp ground allspice
75g/3oz butter
3 Tbsp orange juice
watercress and orange slices, to garnish

Mix together the breadcrumbs, raisins, orange rind, parsley, sage, thyme, onion and salt and pepper to taste. Lay the veal out flat and cover with the breadcrumb mixture. Dot with the pieces of butter. Roll up like a Swiss roll and tie at 2.5cm/1in intervals with string.

Cream together the allspice and 25g/1oz of the butter. Spread this mixture all over the rolled veal. Melt the remaining butter and pour it into a roasting tin. Place the veal roll in the tin and turn to coat it with the butter. Pour over the orange juice. Roast in a moderate oven (180°C/350°F or Gas Mark 4) for 1¼ hours or until the veal is cooked through.

Transfer to a warmed serving dish and remove the string. Garnish with the watercress and orange slices.
Serves 4

Osso Buco

75g/3oz flour
salt and black pepper
1.5kg/3lb veal knuckle or shank, sawn into
8cm/3in pieces
125g/4oz butter
1 large onion, thinly sliced
400g/14oz can tomatoes
2 Tbsp tomato purée
175ml/6floz dry white wine
1 tsp sugar
GREMOLADA
1 Tbsp finely grated lemon rind
2 garlic cloves, crushed
1½ Tbsp parsley, freshly chopped

Mix together the flour and salt and pepper and use to coat the veal pieces. Melt the butter in a flameproof casserole. Add the veal pieces and brown on all sides. Remove from the casserole.

Add the onion to the casserole and fry until it is soft but not brown. Stir in the tomatoes with the can juice, the tomato purée, wine and sugar. Bring to the boil.

The juice and grated rind of orange give this Allspice Veal Roll a really individual flavour.

*Pork Chops with Mushrooms and
Parsley Stuffing will grace any table.
Serve with carrots and onions.*

Melt 25g/1oz of the remaining butter in
the same pan. Add the pork rolls and brown
on all sides. Transfer the rolls to a flameproof casserole and pour over the cider.
Cover and bake in a moderate oven (180°C/
350°F or Gas Mark 4) for 1 hour or until
the pork is tender.

Transfer the pork rolls to a warmed
serving dish. Remove the string. Keep hot.

Place the casserole over heat on top of
the stove and bring to the boil. Blend
together the remaining butter and the
flour to make a smooth paste. Add in small
pieces to the cooking liquid and simmer,
stirring, until thickened and smooth. Pour
this sauce over the pork rolls and serve.
Serves 4

Pork chops with mushroom and parsley stuffing

4 double loin pork chops
1 Tbsp parsley, freshly chopped
25g/1oz fresh white breadcrumbs
¼ tsp cayenne pepper
salt and black pepper
25g/1oz butter
1 small onion, finely chopped
1 garlic clove, crushed
50g/2oz mushrooms, finely chopped
1 Tbsp vegetable oil
MAITRE D'HÔTEL BUTTER
50g/2oz butter
2 tsp parsley, freshly chopped
1 tsp lemon juice
salt and white pepper

First make the maitre d'hôtel butter.
Cream the butter until it is soft and beat in
the remaining ingredients with salt and
pepper to taste. Form into a roll. Wrap in
greaseproof paper and chill.

Make a slit in the meaty part of each chop
to make a pocket. Mix together the parsley,
breadcrumbs, cayenne and salt and pepper
to taste.

Melt the butter in a saucepan. Add the
onion and garlic and fry until the onion is
soft but not brown. Stir in the mushrooms
and fry for 3 minutes. Remove from the
heat and stir in the parsley mixture. Stuff
the chops with this mixture and secure the
opening with wooden cocktail sticks.

Place the chops in a baking dish and
brush with the oil. Cover and bake in a
warm oven (170°C/325°F or Gas Mark 3)
for 1 hour. Uncover the dish and bake for
a further 30 minutes.

Cut the chilled butter into slices.

Transfer the chops to a warmed serving
dish. Discard the cocktail sticks and top
each chop with pats of maitre d'hôtel
butter. Serve immediately.
Serves 4

Return the veal pieces to the casserole with
salt and pepper to taste and stir well. Cover
and simmer for 1½ to 2 hours or until the
veal is so tender it is almost falling off the
bone.

Meanwhile, make the gremolada. Mix
together the lemon rind, garlic and parsley.

Stir the gremolada into the veal mixture
and cook for a further 1 minute. Serve hot,
from the casserole.
Serves 6

Normandy pork

65g/2½oz butter
1 large onion, finely chopped
1 small apple, peeled, cored and finely
chopped
125g/4oz pork sausagemeat
50g/2oz fresh breadcrumbs
1 Tbsp parsley, freshly chopped
1 tsp sage, freshly chopped
salt and black pepper
1 egg, lightly beaten
8 pork escalopes
300ml/10floz cider
2 Tbsp flour

Melt 25g/1oz of the butter in a frying pan.
Add the onion and fry until it is soft but
not brown. Transfer the onion to a mixing
bowl using a slotted spoon.

Add the apple, sausagemeat, breadcrumbs, parsley, sage, salt and pepper to
taste and the egg to the onion and mix
well. Lay the pork pieces flat and spoon this
stuffing onto them. Roll up and tie each
roll with string.

Loin of pork with dried fruit

16 dried stoned prunes
16 dried apricot halves
½ tsp mixed spice
juice and grated rind of ½ orange
juice and grated rind of ½ lemon
600ml/1 pint dry white wine
1 x 2.5kg/5lb loin of pork (boned weight),
rolled and tied
salt and black pepper
1 Tbsp sage, freshly chopped
25g/1oz butter
1 Tbsp soft brown sugar
1 garlic clove, crushed
2 cooking apples, peeled and sliced
2 tsp cornflour

Put the prunes and apricots in a mixing bowl. Sprinkle with the spice, orange juice and rind, lemon juice and rind and half the wine. Cover and leave to soak overnight.

Rub the pork with salt and pepper and the sage. Melt the butter in a flameproof casserole. Add the pork and brown on all sides. Pour in the soaked fruit mixture. Sprinkle over the brown sugar and garlic and add all but 1 tablespoon of the remaining wine. Bring to the boil, cover and cook for 2 hours.

Skim off any fat from the surface of the cooking liquid. Add the apple slices, re-cover and cook for a further 20 minutes.

Transfer the pork to a carving board. Carve into thick slices and arrange on a warmed serving dish. Keep hot.

Dissolve the cornflour in the remaining tablespoon of wine. Stir a little of the hot liquid into the cornflour mixture and then stir into the casserole and simmer, stirring, for 5 minutes. Pour the sauce over the meat and serve.

Serves 6

Loin of Pork with Dried Fruit is a succulent and fruity casserole and makes an attractive main course.

Pork chilli

15g/½oz butter
1 Tbsp vegetable oil
2 medium onions, thinly sliced
1 green pepper, pith and seeds removed
and chopped
1kg/2lb pork shoulder (boned weight),
trimmed of excess fat and cut into
2.5cm/1in cubes
400g/14oz can condensed tomato soup
1 large celery stalk, finely chopped
¼ tsp hot chilli powder
400g/14oz can red kidney beans, drained
salt and black pepper

Melt the butter with the oil in a saucepan.
Add the onions and fry until they are golden
brown. Stir in the green pepper and pork
cubes and fry until the pork cubes are
browned on all sides. Cover and cook
gently for 35 minutes.

Stir in the soup (undiluted), celery and
chilli powder and continue to cook,
covered, for 15 minutes or until the pork is
tender.

Stir in the kidney beans with salt and
pepper to taste. Cook, uncovered, for 5
minutes. Serve hot.
Serves 4

Pork fillets with red wine

125g/4oz butter
4 Tbsp olive oil
1.5kg/3lb pork fillets, cut into thick slices
2 large onions, chopped
salt and black pepper
350ml/12floz dry red wine
275g/10oz mushrooms, sliced
2 Tbsp flour
350ml/12floz double cream

Melt half the butter with the oil in a
frying pan. Add the pork slices and fry
until they are browned on all sides. Transfer the pork to a flameproof casserole, using
a slotted spoon.

Add the onions to the frying pan and
fry until they are soft but not brown.
Transfer the onions to the casserole and
sprinkle over salt and pepper to taste. Pour
in the wine.

Place the casserole in a moderate oven
(180°C/350°F or Gas Mark 4) and cook for
1½ hours or until the pork is tender.

Fifteen minutes before the pork is ready,
melt the remaining butter in a saucepan.
Add the mushrooms and cook for 3
minutes. Transfer the mushrooms to the
casserole with a slotted spoon. Continue
cooking for 10 minutes.

Remove the pork slices from the
casserole and keep hot. Mix together the
flour and cream, adding a little cream at a
time. Stir a little of the hot cooking liquid
into the mixture. Place the casserole over
low heat. Add the cream mixture a little at
a time, stirring constantly until thickened.
Return the meat to the casserole and serve,
from the casserole.
Serves 6

Knackwurst and lentil casserole

500g/1lb red lentils
1.2l/2 pints beef stock
salt and black pepper
1 large onion
1 bouquet garni
25g/1oz butter
6 bacon slices, chopped
2 garlic cloves, chopped
6 Knackwurst, cut into 2.5cm/1in thick
slices
125g/4oz Cheddar cheese, grated

Put the lentils, stock, salt to taste, the
skinned, whole onion and bouquet garni in
a saucepan. Bring to the boil, then simmer
for 1 hour or until the lentils are tender.
Drain the lentils, reserving any cooking
liquid. Discard the onion and bouquet
garni.

Melt the butter in a frying pan. Add the
bacon and garlic and fry until the bacon is
lightly browned. Add the knackwurst and
fry for 5 minutes. Remove from the heat
and drain the bacon and knackwurst on
kitchen paper towels.

Cover the bottom of a baking dish with
half the lentils. Add the knackwurst and
bacon and sprinkle with pepper. Top with
the remaining lentils. Pour in the reserved
lentil cooking liquid. Sprinkle the cheese
on top and bake in a moderate oven
(180°C/350°F or Gas Mark 4) for 45
minutes to 1 hour or until the cheese is
golden brown. Serve hot, from the dish.
Serves 6

Ham cooked in beer

600ml/1 pint light beer
600ml/1 pint dark beer
175g/6oz light brown sugar
1 x 4.5kg/10lb ham, soaked, drained and
cooked
15g/½oz butter
2 Tbsp flour

Bring the beers and sugar to the boil in a
roasting tin, stirring to dissolve the sugar
Remove from the heat.

Peel the skin and excess fat from the ham
and place it in the roasting tin. Baste with
the beer mixture. Bake in a moderate oven

(180°C/350°F or Gas Mark 4) for 2 hours.

Transfer the ham to a warmed serving dish. Keep hot.

Strain the cooking liquid into a saucepan. Blend the butter with the flour to make a paste. Add this in small pieces to the cooking liquid, stirring, and bring to the boil. Simmer, stirring, until thickened and smooth. Pour this sauce into a warmed sauceboat and serve with the ham.

Serves 10-15

Stuffed cabbage leaves

700g/1½lb lean lamb, minced
4 shallots, finely chopped
3 tomatoes, peeled, seeded and chopped
65g/2½oz long-grain rice, cooked
salt
¼ tsp cayenne pepper
¼ tsp grated nutmeg
1 medium cabbage, parboiled and
separated into leaves
1 Tbsp vegetable oil
300ml/10floz dry white wine
juice of 1 lemon
1 Tbsp flour

Mix together the lamb, shallots, tomatoes, rice, salt to taste, the cayenne and nutmeg. Form into a thick sausage shape. Wrap the cabbage leaves around the sausage to enclose it completely. If necessary, tie with string at 5cm/2in intervals.

Heat the oil in a flameproof casserole.

Put the cabbage roll in the casserole and pour over the wine. Bring to the boil, then cover and simmer for 1 hour.

Transfer the cabbage roll to a warmed serving dish. Keep hot. Mix together the lemon juice and flour, stir in 2 tablespoons of the hot liquid from the casserole and then stir into the casserole. Simmer, stirring, until thickened and smooth. Pour this sauce into a sauceboat and serve with the stuffed cabbage. Serve hot or cold.

Serves 4-6

Roast leg of lamb coated with mustard

125g/4oz prepared French mustard
3 Tbsp soy sauce
2 garlic cloves, crushed
1½ Tbsp rosemary, freshly chopped
1 Tbsp olive oil
1 x 2.5kg/5lb leg of lamb
salt and black pepper

Mix together the mustard, soy sauce, garlic and rosemary. Beat in the oil. Place the lamb on a rack in a roasting tin and rub it with salt and pepper. Brush over the mustard mixture. Roast in a moderate oven (180°C/350°F or Gas Mark 4) for 1½ hours or until the juices run only faintly pink when the lamb is pierced with a skewer. Transfer to a carving board and serve.

Serves 4-6

Knackwurst and Lentil Casserole is a tasty and filling family meal, ideal for cold winter days.

Country-style lamb

1 x 1kg/2lb best end of lamb
25g/1oz butter
3 Tbsp vegetable oil
1 cooking apple, peeled, cored and chopped
3 medium potatoes, cut into 6mm/¼in thick slice
1 medium onion, thinly sliced
175ml/6floz beef stock
2 tsp tomato purée
½ tsp dried marjoram
salt and black pepper

Cut the loose flap, or chine, of bones from the lamb and cut the meat into strips. Put the butter and 1 tablespoon of the oil in a roasting tin. Add the meat, strips of meat and the apple. Roast on a rack in a fairly hot oven (190°C/375°F or Gas Mark 5) for about 20 minutes, basting occasionally, or until the meat is well browned.

Heat the remaining oil in a frying pan. Add the potatoes and onion and fry until the potatoes are lightly browned and almost tender. Remove from the heat.

Remove the meat from the oven. When it is cool enough to handle, cut it between the rib bones into chops. Place about one-third of the potatoes and onion in a baking dish. Cover with half the chops and then another layer of potatoes and onion. Add the remaining chops with the apple and cooking liquid, and remaining potatoes and onion.

Mix together the stock, tomato purée, marjoram and salt and pepper to taste. Pour into the baking dish. Cover and bake for 15 minutes or until the meat is tender. Serve hot, from the dish.
Serves 3-4

Braised oxtail

1 oxtail, skinned and cut into pieces
salt and black pepper
¼ tsp mixed spice
1 Tbsp brandy
25g/1oz butter
2 medium onions, chopped
2 medium carrots, scraped and chopped
1 bouquet garni
175ml/6floz brown stock
175ml/6floz dry red wine
2 Tbsp tomato purée

Rub the oxtail pieces with salt and pepper and the spice. Sprinkle with the brandy and leave for 20 minutes.

Melt the butter in a flameproof casserole. Add the oxtail pieces and brown on all sides. Remove the oxtail pieces from the pot. Add the onions and carrots to the casserole and fry until the onions

are soft but not brown. Return the oxtail pieces to the casserole with the bouquet garni, stock, wine and tomato purée. The liquid should almost cover the meat so add a little more stock if necessary.

Bring to the boil, skimming off any scum that rises to the surface. Cover and simmer for 4 hours or until the meat is very tender and falling off the bones. Remove from the heat and allow to cool. Remove the bouquet garni.

Chill for at least 8 hours or overnight.

Remove the fat from the surface. Bring to the boil again and simmer for 10 minutes. Transfer the oxtail pieces to a warmed serving dish and keep hot.

Boil the braising liquid until it has reduced by about one-third. Pour a little over the oxtail pieces and the remainder into a sauceboat. Serve immediately.
Serves 4

Devilled liver

50g/2oz flour
salt and black pepper
½ tsp cayenne pepper
1 tsp dry mustard
1kg/2lb calf's or lamb's liver, sliced 6mm/¼in thick
50g/2oz butter
1 Tbsp olive oil
SAUCE
2 Tbsp Worcestershire sauce
2 tsp paprika
1 Tbsp red wine vinegar
1 tsp dry mustard
2 tomatoes, peeled, seeded and chopped
1 Tbsp castor sugar
1 Tbsp onion, minced
1 Tbsp chutney
75ml/3floz dry red wine
1 garlic clove, crushed
75ml/3floz single cream

First make the sauce. Put all the ingredients, except the cream, in a saucepan. Bring to the boil, then simmer for 5 minutes. Remove from the heat.

Mix together the flour, salt and pepper, the cayenne, and mustard. Coat the liver slices in this seasoned flour.

Melt the butter with the oil in a frying pan. Add the liver slices and cook for 2 to 3 minutes on each side, or until spots of blood appear on the surface. Transfer the liver to a warmed serving dish. Keep hot.

Stir any leftover flour into the fat in the frying pan. Gradually stir in the sauce and bring to the boil. Simmer, stirring, for 3 minutes. Stir in the cream and heat through without boiling. Spoon the sauce over the liver and serve hot.
Serves 4-6

Chicken and leek pie

1 x 2.5kg/5lb chicken
2 medium onions, halved
2 celery stalks, quartered
1 bouquet garni
salt
2.4l/4 pints water
1kg/2lb leeks, cut into 1cm/½in slices
1 tsp sugar
125g/4oz cooked ham, thinly sliced
1 Tbsp parsley, freshly chopped
4 Tbsp double cream
PASTRY
175g/6oz flour
pinch salt
150g/5oz butter, cut into pieces
3-4 Tbsp iced water
1 egg, lightly beaten

Put the chicken, onions, celery, bouquet garni and salt in a saucepan. Add the water. The chicken should be completely covered, so if necessary add more water. Bring to the boil, skimming off any scum that rises to the surface. Cover and simmer for 1 to 1½ hours or until the chicken is tender.

Meanwhile, make the pastry. Sift the flour and salt into a mixing bowl. Add the butter and the water and mix quickly to a lumpy dough. Roll out the dough into an oblong and fold it in three. Turn so the open end faces you and roll out again into an oblong. Fold, turn and roll out twice more, then chill for 30 minutes.

Transfer the chicken to a carving board. Strain the cooking liquid and return 500ml/16floz of it to the saucepan. Add the leeks and return to the heat. Bring to the boil, then partly cover and simmer for 15 to 20 minutes or until the leeks are tender. Remove from the heat.

Skin the chicken and remove the meat from the bones. Cut the meat into bite-size pieces and put them in a deep pie dish. Pour the leeks and stock into the dish. Sprinkle with salt and the sugar. Cover with a layer of ham slices, leaving a small gap in the centre, and sprinkle over the parsley.

Roll out the dough and use to cover the pie dish, crimping the edges to seal. Cut a cross in the centre. Brush the dough with the beaten egg. Use the dough trimmings to decorate the top.

Bake in a fairly hot oven (200°C/400°F or Gas Mark 6) for 1 hour or until the pastry is golden brown.

Heat the cream gently in a saucepan. Open the cross in the pastry and pour in the cream. Serve hot or cold.
Serves 6

An economical idea for mid-week cooking, Braised Oxtail may be served with vegetables, sausages and buttered noodles for a really satisfying meal.

Chicken and Peanut Butter Stew – a spicy and colourful dish to brighten up those winter days.

Chicken and peanut butter stew

2 Tbsp peanut oil
1 medium onion, chopped
1 garlic clove, crushed
1 green pepper, pith and seeds removed and chopped
1 x 2kg/4lb chicken, cut into serving pieces
250g/8oz peanut butter
600ml/1 pint chicken stock
salt and black pepper
1 tsp turmeric
1 Tbsp ground coriander
1 tsp ground cumin
¼ tsp hot chilli powder

Heat the oil in a saucepan. Add the onion, garlic and green pepper. Fry until the onion is soft but not brown. Add the chicken pieces and brown on all sides. Remove from the heat.

Mix together the peanut butter, 125ml/4floz of the stock, salt and pepper to taste, the turmeric, coriander, cumin and chilli powder. Stir into the saucepan containing the chicken and cook, stirring, for 5 minutes. Stir in the remaining stock and simmer for 30 minutes.

Uncover and cook for a further 15 minutes or until tender. Serve hot.
Serves 4

Orange chicken with rosemary

4 large chicken quarters
salt and black pepper
75g/3oz butter
2 large onions, thinly sliced
500ml/16floz orange juice
1 Tbsp rosemary, freshly chopped
1 Tbsp grated orange rind
1½ Tbsp cornflour
1 Tbsp water

Rub the chicken pieces with salt and pepper. Melt 50g/2oz of the butter in a flameproof casserole. Add the chicken pieces and brown on all sides. Remove from the casserole.

Add the remaining butter to the casserole with the onions. Fry until they are soft but not brown. Stir in the orange juice and bring to the boil. Return the chicken pieces to the casserole with the rosemary and orange rind. Cover and simmer for 30 to 40 minutes or until the chicken is tender.

Transfer the chicken pieces to a warmed serving dish. Keep hot.

Dissolve the cornflour in the water and stir gradually, into the liquid in the casserole. Simmer, stirring, until thickened. Pour this sauce over the chicken and serve.
Serves 4

Stuffed boned turkey with chestnuts

25g/1oz butter
1 large onion, finely chopped
1.5kg/3lb pork sausagemeat
4 Tbsp fresh white breadcrumbs
1 Tbsp thyme, freshly chopped
salt and black pepper
1 tsp celery salt
¼ tsp grated nutmeg
2 eggs, lightly beaten
4 Tbsp milk
75ml/3floz port
1 x 4.5kg/10lb turkey, boned
125g/4oz butter, melted
1kg/2lb chestnuts
600ml/1 pint water
2 tsp dark brown sugar

Melt half the butter in a saucepan. Add the onion and fry until it is golden brown. Add the sausagemeat and cook, stirring, until it loses its pinkness. Stir in the breadcrumbs, thyme, pepper to taste, the celery salt and nutmeg. Cook for a further 5 minutes, then remove from the heat.

Mix together the eggs, milk and port. Stir into the sausagemeat mixture. Return to the heat and cook, stirring, for 5 minutes. Remove from the heat.

Rub the turkey all over with salt and pepper. Lay it out flat and cover with the sausagemeat mixture. Form into a roll, securing where necessary with a trussing needle and string.

Place the turkey in a roasting tin and dot with the remaining butter, cut into small pieces. Roast in a fairly hot oven (190°C/375°F or Gas Mark 5) for 2 to 2½ hours. Baste occasionally with the melted butter.

Meanwhile, split the skins of the chestnuts at the pointed end and put in a saucepan. Cover with water and bring to the boil. Boil for 30 seconds, then drain and peel.

Put the measured water and brown sugar in the saucepan and stir over gentle heat to dissolve the sugar. Add the peeled chestnuts and bring to the boil. Cover and simmer for 20 minutes or until the chestnuts are tender but still firm. Drain and refresh under cold running water. Drain again and dry with kitchen paper towels.

Ten minutes before the turkey is cooked, arrange the chestnuts around it in the roasting tin. Baste well with the cooking juices and continue roasting.

Transfer the turkey to a warmed serving dish. Remove the trussing string. Drain the chestnuts and arrange around the turkey. Serve hot.
Serves 8-10

Duck with port and cherries

1 x 2.5kg/5lb duck
salt and black pepper
25g/1oz butter
1 medium onion, chopped
2 small apples, peeled, cored and grated
125g/4oz muesli
1 egg, lightly beaten
75ml/3floz port
425g/15oz can Morello cherries, stoned, drained and juice reserved
2 tsp cornflour
1 tsp water

Prick the duck all over. Rub the cavity with salt and pepper.

Melt the butter in a saucepan. Add the onion and fry until lightly browned. Stir in the apples and muesli. Remove from the heat and stir in the egg. Spoon the stuffing into the duck and secure the opening with a skewer or trussing needle and string.

Place the duck on a rack in a roasting tin and roast in a moderate oven (180°C/350°F or Gas Mark 4) for 1½ to 2 hours or until the juices run clear when the thigh is pierced with a skewer. Baste occasionally with the fat in the tin.

Transfer the duck to a warmed serving dish. Remove the skewer or string and keep hot.

Skim the fat from the surface of the cooking liquid in the tin. Pour the liquid into a saucepan and stir in the port and reserved cherry juice. Dissolve the cornflour in the water and stir into the port mixture. Bring to the boil and simmer, stirring, until thickened and smooth. Stir in the cherries and heat through gently.

Arrange the cherries around the duck and pour the sauce into a sauceboat. Serve immediately.
Serves 4

Rabbit hot pot

40g/1½oz flour
salt and black pepper
2kg/4lb rabbit, cut into serving pieces
2 large onions, thinly sliced
3 carrots, scraped and sliced
2 Tbsp parsley, freshly chopped
1 tsp thyme, freshly chopped
500g/1lb potatoes, thickly sliced
500ml/16floz chicken stock

Mix the flour with salt and pepper and use to coat the rabbit pieces. Place half the sliced onion in a casserole. Cover with half the carrots, then with all the rabbit pieces. Sprinkle with the parsley and thyme and cover with the remaining onion and carrot slices. Arrange the potatoes on top, slightly

Usually chestnuts form part of a stuffing but here they are used to accompany Stuffed Boned Turkey.

overlapping, to cover completely. Pour in the stock.

Cover the casserole and bake in a warm oven (170°C/325°F or Gas Mark 3) for 2 hours or until the rabbit is tender. Increase the temperature to moderate (180°C/350°F or Gas Mark 4). Uncover the casserole and bake for a further 30 minutes or until the potatoes are lightly browned. Serve hot, from the casserole.
Serves 4-6

Pheasant casserole

500g/1lb chestnuts
2 young pheasants
salt and black pepper
2 Tbsp grated orange rind
1 Tbsp thyme, freshly chopped
4 streaky bacon slices
50g/2oz butter
2 Tbsp vegetable oil
1 medium onion, finely chopped
2 garlic cloves, crushed
175g/6oz button mushrooms, sliced
250ml/8floz chicken stock
2 Tbsp orange juice
1 bay leaf
2 Tbsp port
1 Tbsp flour

Split the skins of the chestnuts at the pointed end and put in a saucepan. Cover with water and bring to the boil. Boil for 30 seconds, then drain and peel.

Rub the pheasants inside and out with salt and pepper. Mix together the orange rind and thyme and place in the cavities in the pheasants. Cover the breasts with the bacon slices and truss the birds.

Melt half the butter with the oil in a frying pan. Add the pheasants and brown on all sides. Transfer to a flameproof casserole. Add the onion and garlic to the frying pan and fry until the onion is soft but not brown. Stir in the mushrooms and chestnuts and fry for 5 minutes. Remove from the heat.

Arrange the vegetables around the pheasants in the casserole. Pour in the stock and orange juice and add the bay leaf. Place the casserole over the heat on top of the stove and bring to the boil. Cover and simmer for 1 hour or until the pheasants are cooked. (The juices should run clear when the thigh is pierced.)

Transfer the pheasants to a warmed serving dish. Untruss and discard the bacon. Arrange the vegetables and chestnuts around the birds. Keep hot.

Strain the cooking liquid into a saucepan. Stir in the port and bring to the boil. Blend the remaining butter with the flour to form a smooth paste. Add in small pieces to the cooking liquid and simmer, stirring, until thickened and smooth. Pour this sauce over the pheasants and serve.
Serves 4

Roast pheasant

2 young pheasants
salt and black pepper
4 streaky bacon slices (optional)
25g/1oz butter, melted
watercress, to garnish

Rub the pheasants all over with salt and pepper. Truss them. If they have not been larded, cover the breasts with the bacon. Place in a roasting tin and roast in a moderate oven (180°C/350°F or Gas Mark 4) for 1 hour or until the pheasants are cooked. Baste frequently with the melted butter.

Transfer the pheasants to a warmed serving dish and garnish with the watercress. Serve hot, with game chips and cranberry and bread sauces.
Serves 4

Roast stuffed goose

1 x 3.5-4kg/8-9lb goose, liver reserved
salt and black pepper
4 Tbsp clear honey
STUFFING
25g/1oz butter
2 medium onions, finely chopped
500g/1lb pork sausagemeat
75g/3oz fresh white breadcrumbs
50g/2oz black olives, stoned and chopped
2 Tbsp red wine
salt and black pepper
1 Tbsp thyme, freshly chopped

Prick the goose all over and rub with salt and pepper. Chop the goose liver.

To make the stuffing, melt the butter in a saucepan. Add the onions and fry until they are soft but not brown. Add the sausagemeat and fry, stirring, until it is well browned. Add the goose liver and cook for a further 2 to 3 minutes. Remove from the heat and stir in the remaining ingredients with salt and pepper to taste.

Stuff the goose with this mixture and secure the opening with a skewer or trussing needle and string. Place the goose, on its breast, on a rack in a roasting tin. Roast in a very hot oven (230°C/450°F or Gas Mark 8) for 15 minutes. Reduce the temperature to moderate (180°C/350°F or Gas Mark 4) and continue roasting for 2½ to 3 hours or until the goose is cooked. (The juices should be clear when the thigh is pierced with a skewer.) Turn the goose onto its back halfway through the cooking.

Tender Roast Pheasant with the traditional accompaniment of game chips is an ideal dinner party-dish.

Remove all the fat from the roasting tin. Increase the oven temperature to very hot (230°C/450°F or Gas Mark 8). Coat the goose with the honey and return to the oven. Roast for a further 8 to 10 minutes or until the skin is glazed and crisp. Untruss and serve the goose immediately.
Serves 4-6

Hare chasseur

2 saddles of hare, cut into fillets
salt and black pepper
1 Tbsp lemon juice
25g/1oz flour
50g/2oz butter
2 large shallots, finely chopped
2 slices cooked ham, cut into strips
250ml/8floz dry white wine
125g/4oz mushrooms
250ml/8floz double cream
1 Tbsp parsley, freshly chopped

Rub the fillets with salt and pepper and the lemon juice. Coat them with the flour. Melt the butter in a frying pan. Add the shallots and ham. Fry until the shallots are soft but not brown.

Put the hare fillets in the pan and brown on all sides. Pour over the wine and bring to the boil. Simmer gently for 10 minutes.

Transfer the fillets to a baking dish using a slotted spoon.

Add the mushrooms and cream to the frying pan and stir well. Heat through gently without boiling. Pour this sauce over the fillets. Bake in a moderate oven (180°C/350°F or Gas Mark 4) for 20 minutes.

Sprinkle over the parsley and serve, from the dish.
Serves 6

Guinea fowl with cherry sauce

2 x 700g/1½lb guinea fowl
salt and black pepper
125g/4oz salt pork, diced
1 medium onion, finely chopped
1 tsp sage, freshly chopped
2 tsp grated orange rind
65g/2½oz long-grain rice, cooked
250ml/8floz chicken stock
500g/1lb can Morello cherries, stoned
and drained
4 Tbsp double cream
1 Tbsp brandy

Rub the guinea fowl inside and out with salt and pepper. Fry the pork fat in a flameproof casserole until golden brown and it has rendered most of its fat. Transfer the dice to a mixing bowl.

Add the onion to the casserole and fry until it is soft but not brown. Remove from the heat. Add the onion to the pork dice, using a slotted spoon. Stir the sage, orange rind, rice and salt and pepper to taste into the pork dice mixture. Stuff the guinea fowl with this mixture. Secure the opening with a skewer or trussing needle and string.

Reheat the pork fat in the casserole. Add the guinea fowl and brown on all sides. Pour in the stock and bring to the boil. Cover and cook for 50 minutes to 1 hour or until the birds are tender.

Transfer the guinea fowl to a warmed serving dish and keep hot.

Bring the liquid in the casserole to the boil and boil until it has reduced to about half the original quantity. Stir in the cherries, cream and brandy and heat through gently without boiling. Pour this sauce over the guinea fowl and serve.
Serves 4

Venison chops with soured cream and horseradish sauce

4 venison chops
salt and black pepper
2 garlic cloves, halved
4 Tbsp vegetable oil
175ml/6floz soured cream
1 tsp horseradish, grated
MARINADE
125ml/4floz dry white wine
4 Tbsp olive oil
1 onion, thinly sliced
1 garlic clove, crushed
6 black peppercorns
1 Tbsp thyme, freshly chopped

Mix together the marinade ingredients in a shallow dish. Add the venison chops and leave to marinate for 24 hours, basting occasionally.

Remove the chops from the marinade and pat dry with kitchen paper towels. Reserve the marinade. Rub the chops with salt and pepper and the cut sides of the garlic cloves. Discard the garlic.

Heat the oil in a frying pan. Add the chops and brown on each side. Pour in the reserved marinade and bring to the boil. Cover and simmer for 20 minutes or until the chops are tender.

Remove from the heat and allow to cool. Leave to marinate for a further 24 hours.

Return the pan to the heat and bring to the boil. Simmer for 15 minutes. Transfer the chops to a warmed serving dish. Keep hot. Strain the cooking juices into a saucepan and bring to the boil. Reduce the heat and stir in the soured cream and horseradish. Heat through gently without boiling. Pour the sauce over the chops and serve.
Serves 4

Guinea Fowl with Cherry Sauce makes a lovely rich meal certain to impress dinner guests.

Vegetables

Gratin dauphinois

1 garlic clove, halved
25g/1oz butter
1kg/2lb potatoes, cut into 6mm/¼in thick slices
salt and black pepper
175g/6oz Cheddar cheese, grated
1 egg, lightly beaten
300ml/10floz milk, scalded
pinch grated nutmeg

Rub a baking dish with the cut sides of the garlic. Discard the garlic. Grease the dish thickly with half the butter. Place about one-third of the potato slices in the dish and sprinkle with the salt and pepper and 25g/1oz of the cheese. Add another layer in this way and top with the remaining potato slices.

Put the egg, milk and nutmeg in a saucepan and bring to the boil, stirring. Pour into the baking dish. Sprinkle over the remaining cheese and dot with the remaining butter, cut into small pieces.

Bake in a fairly hot oven (190°C/375°F or Gas Mark 5) for 45 to 50 minutes or until the potatoes are tender. Serve hot.
Serves 6

This appetizing dish, Gratin Dauphinois, is a classic French recipe and is especially good served with roast lamb or veal.

Turnip, potato and carrot hash

1 large turnip, peeled and chopped
3 medium carrots, scraped and chopped
1 large onion, chopped
3 medium potatoes, peeled and chopped
250ml/8floz can beef consommé
salt and black pepper
15g/½oz butter, cut into small pieces

Put the vegetables in a saucepan with the consommé and salt to taste. Bring to the boil, then simmer for 20 to 30 minutes or until the vegetables are tender and most of the liquid has evaporated.

Remove from the heat and pour off any excess liquid. Add pepper to taste and mash the vegetables to form a smooth, thick purée. Transfer the purée to a baking dish, smoothing the top. Dot with the pieces of butter and bake in a fairly hot oven (200°C/400°F or Gas Mark 6) for 10 to 15 minutes or until the top is golden brown.

Serve hot, from the baking dish.
Serves 6

Onions with lemon and marjoram sauce

6 medium onions
salt and black pepper
1 bouquet garni
450ml/15floz milk
½ tsp dried marjoram
finely grated rind of 1 lemon
25g/1oz butter
2 Tbsp flour
1 Tbsp lemon juice
1 Tbsp parsley, freshly chopped
lemon wedges, to serve

Blanch the onions in boiling water for 2 minutes. Drain well. Return to the saucepan and cover with fresh water. Add salt and the bouquet garni. Bring to the boil, then cover and simmer for 25 to 30 minutes or until the onions are tender.

Meanwhile, put the milk, marjoram and lemon rind in a saucepan. Infuse over low heat for 10 minutes. Strain the milk.

Melt the butter in a saucepan. Stir in the flour and cook, stirring, for 1 minute. Remove from the heat and gradually stir in the milk. Return to the heat and cook, stirring, until thickened and smooth. Stir in salt and pepper to taste and the lemon juice and remove from the heat.

Drain the onions and place on a warmed serving dish. Pour over the sauce and sprinkle with the parsley. Garnish with the lemon wedges and serve.
Serves 4-6

Brussels sprouts with chestnuts

700g/1½lb Brussels sprouts
salt and black pepper
24 chestnuts
2 Tbsp arrowroot
1 Tbsp port or water
450ml/15floz beef stock
100g/4oz butter

Cook the sprouts in boiling salted water for 6 to 8 minutes or until they are almost tender. Drain and refresh under cold running water, then drain again.

Split the skins of the chestnuts at the pointed end and put in a saucepan. Cover with water and bring to the boil. Boil for 30 seconds, then drain and peel.

Put the peeled chestnuts in a flameproof casserole. Mix together the arrowroot and port or water, then stir in the stock. Pour this mixture over the chestnuts. Add 40g/1½oz of the butter. Put the casserole over the heat and bring to the boil. Cover and transfer to a warm oven (170°C/325°F or Gas Mark 3). Cook for 45 to 60 minutes or until the chestnuts are tender.

Drain the chestnuts and return to the casserole. Add the Brussels sprouts, remaining butter and salt and pepper to taste. Cover the casserole with buttered greaseproof paper and bake for a further 20 minutes. Serve hot.
Serves 6

Sweet potato and marshmallow bake

700g/1½lb sweet potatoes
salt
2 tsp clear honey
25g/1oz butter
juice of 1 orange
2 eggs, well beaten
250g/8oz marshmallows

Bake the sweet potatoes in a moderate oven (180°C/350°F or Gas Mark 4) for 1 hour or until they are tender. Remove from the oven, cool, then peel the skins.

Put the sweet potatoes, salt to taste, the honey, butter, orange juice and eggs in a mixing bowl. Mash together until a thick, smooth purée is formed. Transfer to a greased baking dish and smooth the top. Bake in the moderate oven for 10 minutes.

Remove from the oven and arrange the marshmallows over the top. Increase the temperature to fairly hot (200°C/400°F or Gas Mark 6) and bake for a further 10 minutes or until the marshmallow topping is lightly browned. Serve hot.
Serves 4

Cauliflower bread

2 cauliflowers, broken into flowerets
700g/1½lb potatoes, quartered
15g/½oz butter
salt and white pepper
¼ tsp cayenne pepper
6 eggs
150g/5oz Gruyère cheese, grated

Cook the cauliflowers in boiling salted water for 15 minutes or until tender. Meanwhile, cook the potatoes in boiling salted water for 15 minutes or until tender. Drain the potatoes and cauliflowers and place in a mixing bowl. Add the butter, salt and pepper to taste and the cayenne. Mash together to form a purée.

Beat the eggs into the purée, one at a time, then stir in all but 2 tablespoons of the cheese. Spoon into a greased 2.5l/4 pint mould and place the mould in a roasting tin. Pour enough boiling water into the tin to come halfway up the sides of the mould. Cover the mould tightly with foil and bake in a moderate oven (180°C/350°F or Gas Mark 4) for 1 hour.

Remove the foil and turn the cauliflower bread out onto a warmed heatproof serving dish. Sprinkle over the remaining cheese and bake for a further 5 minutes or until the cheese is lightly browned. Serve hot.
Serves 4-6

Braised celeriac

125g/4oz streaky bacon, chopped
1 large celeriac, peeled and sliced
15g/½oz butter
1 small onion, chopped
300ml/10floz beef stock
175ml/6floz dry white wine or additional stock
salt and black pepper
1 Tbsp parsley, freshly chopped

Blanch the bacon in boiling water for 10 minutes. Meanwhile, blanch the celeriac in boiling salted water for 5 minutes. Drain the bacon and celeriac.

Melt the butter in a flameproof casserole. Add the bacon and onion. Fry until the onion is soft but not brown. Remove the bacon and onion from the casserole with a slotted spoon.

Add the celeriac to the casserole and spoon the onion and bacon on top. Pour in the stock and wine and add salt and pepper to taste. Bring to the boil, cover and transfer to a moderate oven (180°C/350°F or Gas Mark 4). Braise for 1 hour.

Sprinkle over the parsley and serve, from the casserole.
Serves 6

The sweet potato is an edible tuber native to South America. It has a floury texture and tastes sweet, hence its name.

Salads

Chicory, almond and pepper salad

4 heads chicory, sliced
150g/5oz blanched almonds, lightly toasted
2 red chilli peppers, seeded and finely chopped
1 red pepper, pith and seeds removed and thinly sliced
DRESSING
6 Tbsp olive oil
2 Tbsp red wine vinegar
1 tsp lemon juice
salt and black pepper

Put the chicory, almonds, chilli peppers and red pepper in a salad bowl. Put all the dressing ingredients, with salt and pepper to taste, in a screwtop jar. Shake well and pour over the salad ingredients. Toss together and serve.

Serves 4

Beetroot and orange salad

6 medium beetroots, cooked and peeled
2 large oranges
2 bunches watercress
DRESSING
4 Tbsp olive oil
1½ Tbsp wine vinegar
1 tsp prepared mustard
¼ tsp dried tarragon
salt and black pepper
½ tsp sugar

Slice the beetroots. Grate the rind of one orange. Peel the oranges, removing all the white pith. Slice the oranges.

Arrange the watercress on a serving dish. Place the orange and beetroot slices alternately, slightly overlapping, in circles on the watercress.

Put all the dressing ingredients, with salt and pepper to taste, in a screwtop jar. Add the orange rind and shake well. Pour this dressing over the beetroot and orange slices and serve.

Serves 4

An unusual combination, Beetroot and Orange Salad has both colour and flavour.

Breakfasts

Egg and bacon with sherry sauce

25g/1oz butter
1 Tbsp flour
175ml/6floz milk
175ml/6floz double cream
salt and white pepper
50g/2oz Cheddar cheese, grated
4 Tbsp dry sherry
2 egg yolks, lightly beaten
4 slices hot buttered toast
4 eggs
4 bacon slices
1 tsp paprika

Put the eggs in a saucepan and cover with water. Bring to the boil, then remove from the heat and leave to soft-cook for 5 minutes. While the eggs are cooking, grill the bacon until it is crisp.

Meanwhile, make the sauce. Melt the butter in a saucepan. Stir in the flour and cook, stirring, for 1 minute. Remove from the heat and gradually stir in the milk. Return to the heat and simmer, stirring, until thickened and smooth. Stir in the cream, salt and pepper to taste, the cheese and sherry. Heat through gently without boiling until the cheese melts. Remove from the heat and beat in the egg yolks.

Place a slice of hot toast on each of four warmed serving plates. Top each with a slice of bacon and an egg. Spoon over the sauce and sprinkle with paprika. Serve immediately.
Serves 4

Herrings in rolled oats

4 large herrings, filleted and halved
1 lemon, quartered
125g/4oz rolled oats
salt and black pepper
1 egg, lightly beaten
125g/4oz butter

Rub the herring fillets all over with the lemon quarters. Discard the lemon. Mix together the rolled oats and salt and pepper. Coat the herrings first in the beaten egg and then in the rolled oats.

Melt the butter in a frying pan. Add the herrings, in batches, and fry for 2 to 3 minutes on each side or until the fish is cooked. Test with a fork: the flesh should flake easily.

Transfer to a warmed serving dish and serve hot.
Serves 6-8

Buttermilk pancakes with maple syrup

275g/10oz flour
½ tsp salt
2 tsp baking powder
1 Tbsp castor sugar
2 eggs, separated
500ml/16floz buttermilk
50g/2oz butter, melted
4 Tbsp vegetable oil
250ml/8floz maple syrup

Sift the flour, salt, baking powder and sugar into a mixing bowl. Add the egg yolks, buttermilk and melted butter and beat well until smooth. Beat the egg whites until they will hold a soft peak and fold into the buttermilk mixture.

Lightly grease a frying pan with a little of the oil. Drop tablespoonsful of the batter onto the pan, well spaced, and cook for about 1 minute or until the pancakes bubble on the surface. Turn over and cook the other sides for 30 seconds or until lightly browned. Transfer the pancakes to a warmed dish and keep hot while you cook the remaining pancakes in the same way.

Meanwhile, gently heat the maple syrup.

Serve the pancakes hot, with the maple syrup.
Serves 4-6

Sand waffles

50g/2oz cornflour
250g/8oz flour
½ tsp salt
½ tsp ground cinnamon
125g/4oz butter
50g/2oz castor sugar
2 eggs
4 Tbsp soured cream
350ml/12floz milk
grated rind of ½ lemon

Sift together the cornflour, flour, salt and cinnamon. Cream the butter with the sugar. Beat in the eggs, one at a time, then fold in the flour mixture. Stir in the soured cream and milk to form a fairly thick but pouring batter. Stir in the lemon rind. Heat a waffle iron.

Spoon a few tablespoonsful of the batter into the hot waffle iron and press the lid down firmly. Bake until the waffle is golden brown and crisp. Transfer to a warmed serving dish and keep hot while you make the remaining waffles.

Serve hot with maple syrup or honey, according to taste.
Serves 4-6

A tasty mixture of cooked fish, rice and hard-boiled eggs, Kedgeree is a traditional British breakfast dish of Anglo-Indian origin that makes a good start to a winter's day.

Kidney and mushroom croûtes

4 large slices of bread cut 2cm/¾in thick, crusts removed
5 eggs
150ml/5floz milk
50g/2oz butter
4 lean bacon slices, chopped
4 lambs' kidneys, skinned, cored and chopped
250g/8oz mushrooms, chopped
1 Tbsp lemon juice
salt and black pepper
4 Tbsp vegetable oil

Slightly hollow out the centres of the bread slices, making a 1cm/½in deep indentation in each one. Mix together one of the eggs and the milk in a shallow dish. Put the bread slices in the dish and leave to soak. Set aside.

Melt 25g/1oz of the butter in a frying pan. Add the bacon and fry until it is crisp and brown. Add the kidney pieces and cook for 5 minutes. Stir in the mushrooms and cook for 3 minutes. Stir in the lemon juice and salt and pepper to taste and simmer gently for 2 minutes. Remove from the heat and keep hot.

Poach the remaining four eggs.

Meanwhile, melt the remaining butter in another frying pan. Add the bread slices and fry for 4 minutes, turning once, or until they are golden brown and crisp. Drain on kitchen paper towels.

Place the bread croûtes on warmed serving dishes and fill with the kidney mixture. Top each with a poached egg and serve hot.
Serves 4

Kedgeree

125g/4oz butter
275g/10oz cooked smoked haddock, skinned, boned and flaked
275g/10oz long-grain rice, cooked
2 eggs, hard-boiled and finely chopped
salt and black pepper
¼ tsp cayenne pepper
2 Tbsp single cream
1 Tbsp parsley, freshly chopped

Melt 75g/3oz of the butter in a frying pan. Add the fish, rice, eggs, salt and pepper to taste and the cayenne. Stir in the cream. Heat through gently without boiling, then pile onto a warmed serving dish. Cut the remaining butter into small pieces and dot over the top. Sprinkle with parsley and serve immediately, accompanied by crisp, buttered toast.
Serves 4

Light Dishes

Broccoli soufflé

700g/1½lb broccoli, cut into small pieces
salt and black pepper
1 garlic clove
25g/1oz butter
50g/2oz flour
250ml/8floz double cream
4 eggs, separated
50g/2oz Parmesan cheese, grated

Cook the broccoli in boiling salted water, with the garlic, for 15 minutes. Drain well and discard the garlic. Finely chop the broccoli.

Melt the butter in a saucepan. Stir in the flour and cook, stirring, for 1 minute. Remove from the heat and gradually stir in the cream. Return to the heat and cook, stirring, until thickened. Remove from the heat and allow to cool slightly.

Lightly beat the egg yolks and stir into the cream sauce. Add salt and pepper to taste, then stir in the broccoli. Beat the egg whites until they hold a stiff peak. Fold into the broccoli mixture. Spoon into a greased ring mould. Place the mould in a roasting tin and add enough boiling water to come halfway up the sides of the mould.

Bake in a moderate oven (180°C/350°F or Gas Mark 4) for 35 to 40 minutes or until the soufflé is puffed and set. Turn out onto a warmed serving dish and fill the centre with cooked carrot slices or any hot cooked vegetable. Sprinkle over the cheese. Serve hot.
Serves 6

Chef's salad

1 medium lettuce
75g/3oz cooked chicken, cut into strips
75g/3oz cooked tongue, cut into strips
75g/3oz Gruyere cheese, cut into strips
1 egg, hard-boiled and thinly sliced
1 Tbsp onion, finely chopped
3 Tbsp black olives, stoned and chopped
75ml/3floz olive oil
2 Tbsp red wine vinegar
½ tsp lemon juice
¼ tsp prepared French mustard
salt and black pepper

Break the lettuce into leaves and arrange in a large salad bowl. Add the chicken, tongue, cheese, egg, onion and olives. Chill for 10 minutes.

Put the remaining ingredients, with salt and pepper to taste, in a screwtop jar. Shake well. Just before serving, pour this dressing over the salad ingredients.
Serves 4

An unusual and colourful vegetable dish, Broccoli Soufflé is delicious decorated with parsley and served with new potatoes.

Top: Spaghetti Carbonara – one of the great Italian pasta dishes is excellent served with a green salad and a glass of Valpolicella.

Above: Omelet Arnold Bennett – one of the classics of French cookery – is a meal in itself; light yet satisfying.

Omelet Arnold Bennett

40g/1½oz butter
125g/4oz smoked haddock, cooked and flaked
150ml/5floz double cream
6 eggs, separated
3 Tbsp Parmesan cheese, grated
salt and black pepper
1 Tbsp parsley, freshly chopped

Melt 25g/1oz of the butter in a frying pan. Add the haddock and 2 tablespoons of the cream. When the cream is hot, remove from the heat and allow to cool.

Beat the egg yolks with half the cheese, salt and pepper to taste and the parsley. Stir in the haddock mixture. Beat the egg whites until they will hold a stiff peak. Fold into the haddock mixture.

Melt the remaining butter in a frying pan or omelet pan. Pour in the haddock mixture and cook for 2 minutes or until the bottom is set and lightly browned.

Sprinkle over the remaining cheese and pour over the remaining cream. Transfer the pan to the grill and grill for 30 seconds. Slide the omelet onto a warmed serving dish and serve.

Serves 2-3

Spaghetti carbonara

500g/1lb spaghetti
40g/1½oz butter
125g/4oz lean bacon, rinds removed and chopped
3 Tbsp double cream
3 eggs
125g/4oz Parmesan cheese, grated
salt and black pepper

Cook the spaghetti in boiling salted water for 8 to 12 minutes or until it is *al dente* (just tender to the bite).

Meanwhile, melt 15g/½oz of the butter in a frying pan. Add the bacon and fry until it is crisp and golden brown. Remove from the heat and stir in the cream. Keep hot.

Beat the eggs and 50g/2oz of the cheese together until the mixture is well blended. Stir in salt and pepper to taste.

Drain the spaghetti and transfer it to a warmed mixing bowl. Add the remaining butter and toss well to coat the strands. Stir in the bacon mixture, then the egg mixture, tossing the spaghetti thoroughly to coat well.

Serve at once, with the remaining cheese.
Serves 4

Desserts

Spotted Dick

250g/8oz flour
1 tsp salt
2 Tbsp sugar
2 tsp baking powder
pinch ground cloves
75g/3oz shredded suet
125g/4oz currants
50g/2oz sultanas
6-8 Tbsp water
6 Tbsp strawberry jam
3 Tbsp milk

Sift the flour, salt, sugar, baking powder and cloves into a mixing bowl. Stir in the suet, currants and sultanas. Stir in enough water to bind the mixture and knead to a dough. Roll out the dough to a rectangle about 6mm/¼in thick. Brush the edges with milk. Spread over the jam and roll up the dough like a Swiss roll. Press the edges together to seal.

Wrap the roll loosely in foil or muslin, making a pleat to allow for expansion. Steam for 2½ hours, replenishing the boiling water when necessary.

Remove the pan from the heat, unwrap the pudding and transfer to a warmed serving dish.

Serves 6-8

Apples baked in brandy and vermouth

4 cooking apples, cored
65g/2½oz butter
2 Tbsp castor sugar
125ml/4floz dry white vermouth
125ml/4floz water
75ml/3floz brandy
4 white bread slices, crusts removed
2 Tbsp redcurrant jelly

Make a shallow slit all around the skin of the apples. Put 1 teaspoon of butter in the cavity of each and place in a flameproof baking dish. Sprinkle over the sugar, vermouth, water and 2 tablespoons of the brandy. Bake in a moderate oven (180°C/350°F or Gas Mark 4) for 30 to 35 minutes or until the apples are tender.

Meanwhile, cut the bread slices into circles about 8cm/3in in diameter. Melt the remaining butter in a frying pan. Add the bread slices and fry until crisp and golden brown on both sides. Drain the bread slices on kitchen paper towels and arrange on a warmed serving dish. Place an apple on each slice and keep hot.

Place the baking dish over the heat on top of the stove and stir in the remaining brandy and redcurrant jelly. Bring to the boil and boil until reduced to about half the original quantity. Pour this sauce over the apples and serve.

Serves 4

This traditional British dessert, Spotted Dick, made with suet, dried fruits and filled with strawberry jam is a great favourite. Served steaming hot with custard, it is a perfect choice for a cold winter's day.

Rhubarb and orange pie

PASTRY
275g/10oz flour
¼ tsp salt
175g/6oz butter
6 Tbsp iced water
2 Tbsp milk
2 Tbsp castor sugar
FILLING
750g/1½lb rhubarb, cut into 5cm/2in pieces
juice and finely grated rind of 2 oranges
2 Tbsp cornflour
175g/6oz soft brown sugar

Sift the flour and salt into a mixing bowl. Add the butter and cut into small pieces, then rub the fat into the flour until the mixture resembles breadcrumbs. Stir in enough water to bind the mixture, then knead to a dough. Chill for 30 minutes.

Put the rhubarb in a mixing bowl and pour over the orange juice. Leave to marinate for 30 minutes.

Roll out two-thirds of the dough and use to line a 23cm/9in pie dish. Drain the rhubarb, discarding the orange juice. Arrange half the rhubarb in the pie dish and sprinkle with half the orange rind, half the cornflour and half the brown sugar. Add the remaining rhubarb, orange rind, cornflour and brown sugar. Roll out the remaining dough and use to cover the pie dish. Press the edges together to seal and cut a cross in the centre.

Brush the pie with the milk and sprinkle over the sugar. Bake in a fairly hot oven (190°C/375°F or Gas Mark 5) for 30 to 40 minutes or until the pastry is golden brown. Serve hot or cold.
Serves 4-6

Guards' pudding

250g/8oz fresh white breadcrumbs
250g/8oz shredded suet
175g/6oz dark brown sugar
4 Tbsp strawberry or raspberry jam
2 eggs
1½ tsp bicarbonate of soda

Mix together the breadcrumbs, suet and sugar. Stir in the jam. Beat the eggs with the soda and stir into the breadcrumb mixture. Spoon into a greased 1.8l/3 pint pudding basin. Cover with a lid of greased greaseproof paper and foil and tie on securely with string, making a pleat across the centre to allow for expansion.

Steam for 3 hours, adding more boiling water when necessary.

Turn the pudding out onto a warmed serving dish and serve hot.
Serves 4-6

Dried fruit compôte

750g/1½lb mixed dried fruit (apples, apricots, raisins, prunes, etc.)
425ml/14floz water
175ml/6floz dry red wine
250g/8oz sugar
5cm/2in cinnamon stick
finely pared rind of 1 lemon, cut into thin strips

Soak the fruit in cold water to cover for 12 hours or overnight. Drain well and discard the water in which the fruit was soaked. Set aside.

Put the water, wine, sugar, cinnamon and lemon rind in a saucepan and heat gently, stirring to dissolve the sugar. Bring to the boil. Add the fruit and simmer for 10 to 15 minutes or until the fruit is tender.

Transfer the fruit to a serving dish using a slotted spoon. Keep hot if serving the compôte hot by covering the dish with a piece of aluminium foil.

Remove the cinnamon stick from the liquid and return to the boil. Boil for 30 minutes or until reduced and slightly thickened. Pour the syrup over the fruit and serve. Alternatively, allow to cool and chill well before serving.
Serves 6-8

Steamed chocolate pudding

125g/4oz dark cooking chocolate, broken into small pieces
2 Tbsp strong black coffee
125g/4oz butter
150g/5oz castor sugar
5 eggs, separated
125g/4oz walnuts, chopped

Melt the chocolate with the coffee gently in a saucepan. Remove from the heat and allow to cool.

Cream the butter and the sugar together until the mixture is light and fluffy. Beat in the egg yolks, one at a time. Stir in the chocolate mixture, then the walnuts. Beat the egg whites until they will hold a stiff peak. Fold into the chocolate mixture using a metal spoon.

Spoon into a greased 900ml/1½ pint pudding basin and cover with a lid of greased greaseproof paper and foil. Make a pleat in the centre to allow for expansion. Tie the lid onto the basin securely with string.

Steam the pudding for 1 to 1¼ hours, replenishing the boiling water when necessary. Remove the pudding from the pan and serve hot, from the basin.
Serves 4

Above: Cooked in red wine with a delicate, aromatic flavour this original winter fruit salad – Compote of Dried Fruits – makes an attractive dessert. Below: This rich chocolate steamed pudding from Germany – Schokoladen Pudding is made with chocolate, walnuts, eggs and coffee and is especially good served with whipped cream.

Mincemeat and apple crumble

500g/1lb cooking apples, peeled, cored and sliced
2 Tbsp sugar
250g/8oz mincemeat
2 tsp grated lemon rind
½ tsp ground allspice
2 Tbsp brandy
TOPPING
175g/6oz flour
75g/3oz butter
125g/4oz sugar
2 tsp grated lemon rind
½ tsp ground allspice

Put the apples and sugar in a saucepan and add enough water just to cover. Bring to the boil, then poach gently until the apples are tender but still firm. Drain the apple slices and mix with the mincemeat, lemon rind, allspice and brandy. Spoon into a greased baking dish.

To make the topping, sift the flour into a mixing bowl. Add the butter and cut into small pieces, then rub into the flour until the mixture resembles breadcrumbs. Stir in the remaining ingredients. Spoon the topping over the mincemeat mixture and smooth the top.

Bake in a fairly hot oven (200°C/400°F or Gas Mark 6) for 30 to 40 minutes or until the topping is browned and crisp. Serve hot with cream or custard sauce.
Serves 4

Cranberry mousse

250g/8oz cranberries
75g/3oz sugar
2 Tbsp water
4 egg yolks
1 Tbsp orange juice
2 egg whites
150ml/5floz double cream

Put the cranberries, 25g/1oz of the sugar and the water in a saucepan. Cook gently until the fruit is just tender. Remove from the heat. Drain the cranberries, reserving the juice. Add enough bottled or canned cranberry juice to make up to 125ml/4floz, if necessary.

Put the egg yolks in the top of a double saucepan or heatproof bowl over a pan of hot water and whisk with the remaining sugar over heat until they are thick and pale. Whisk in the cranberry juice. Continue whisking until the mixture will make a ribbon trail on itself when the whisk is lifted. Remove from the heat and stir in the cranberries and orange juice. Chill for 30 minutes.

Beat the egg whites until they will hold a stiff peak. Whip the cream until it is thick. Fold the cream into the cranberry mixture, then fold in the egg whites. Spoon into a serving dish or individual dishes and chill for at least 6 hours.
Serves 4

German cheesecake

175g/6oz digestive biscuits, crushed
75g/3oz butter, melted
125g/4oz sugar
1 tsp ground cinnamon
2 eggs, lightly beaten
¼ tsp salt
juice and grated rind of ½ lemon
125ml/4floz single cream
250g/8oz cottage cheese
75g/3oz mixed chopped nuts

Mix together the biscuit crumbs, melted butter, 25g/1oz of the sugar and the cinnamon. Press into the bottom and sides of a greased 20cm/8in cake tin, reserving 2 tablespoons of the crumb mixture.

Beat the eggs, salt, lemon juice and rind together until well mixed. Stir in the cream, cottage cheese and half the nuts. Spoon into the crumb shell and sprinkle over the reserved crumb mixture and remaining nuts.

Bake in a moderate oven (180°C/350°F or Gas Mark 4) for 35 to 45 minutes or until the filling is set. Turn off the oven and leave the cake inside, with the door open, for 10 minutes.

Remove from the oven and allow to cool completely. Serve cold.
Serves 6-8

Bananas baked in rum and cream

6 bananas
1 Tbsp castor sugar
6 Tbsp white rum
125g/4oz macaroons, crushed
15g/½oz butter, melted
300ml/10floz double cream

Put the bananas in a greased baking dish. Sprinkle with the sugar and rum. Bake in a moderate oven (180°C/350°F or Gas Mark 4) for 15 minutes.

Remove from the oven and allow to cool for 10 minutes.

Reset the oven to warm (170°C/325°F or Gas Mark 3). Mix the macaroons with the butter. Pour the cream over the bananas and sprinkle over the macaroon mixture. Bake for a further 20 minutes. Serve hot, in the baking dish.
Serves 4

Above : Cranberry Mousse, a refreshing cold dessert with a difference, is best made during Christmas when cranberries are readily available and makes a superb sweet for a special dinner party.
Below : A traditional German cheesecake, Kasekuchen has a crunchy cinnamon biscuit base with a smooth cream, egg, lemon, cheese and nut filling.

Drinks

Hot toddy

300ml/10floz water
150ml/5floz whisky or brandy
1 tsp lemon juice
2 strips lemon rind
pinch ground allspice
2 Tbsp light brown sugar

Put all the ingredients in a saucepan and stir over gentle heat to dissolve the sugar. Heat through without boiling. Discard the lemon rind and pour into a jug. Serve immediately.
Serves 4

Festive and spicy, Mulled Wine is guaranteed to warm up any winter party and will prove highly popular with the guests.

Mulled wine

1 bottle dry red wine
juice and thinly pared rind of 1 lemon
½ tsp grated nutmeg
5cm/2in cinnamon stick
3 Tbsp sugar
1 lemon, thinly sliced

Put the wine, lemon rind and juice, grated nutmeg, cinnamon stick and sugar in a saucepan. Stir over gentle heat to dissolve the sugar. Heat through without boiling, then strain into a jug. Garnish with the lemon slices and serve.
Serves 6-8

Archbishop

1 Seville orange
20 whole cloves
1 Tbsp brown sugar
1 bottle medium dry sherry

Stud the orange with the cloves. Bake in a moderate oven (180°C/350°F or Gas Mark 4) for 30 minutes or until the orange is brown.

Cut the orange in half and sprinkle with the sugar. Put the halves in the bottom of a heatproof punch bowl.

Warm the sherry in a saucepan until it is hot but not boiling. Pour into the punch bowl and serve hot.
Serves 4-6

Hot apple drink

450ml/15floz apple juice
2 Tbsp orange-flavoured liqueur
2 strips lemon rind
1 Tbsp light brown sugar
pinch grated nutmeg

Put all the ingredients in a saucepan and stir over gentle heat to dissolve the sugar. Heat through without boiling, then strain into a jug and serve.
Serves 4

Hot buttered rum

175ml/6floz boiling cider or water
1 Tbsp butter
4 Tbsp dark rum
1 tsp castor sugar
pinch grated nutmeg

Mix together 4 tablespoons of the cider or water and the butter in a mug. Stir to melt the butter. Stir in the rum and sugar, then the remaining cider or water. Sprinkle the nutmeg on top and serve.
Serves 1

Marmalades

Marmalade

Marmalade is a preserve made with citrus fruit—oranges, lemons, limes, grapefruit and tangerines—and the best time to make it is in winter when the bitter Seville oranges have their short season. Other fruit, such as apples, pineapples and pears, may be added to give a pleasant combination, and the marmalade may be flavoured with ginger and other spices.

Marmalade is made in the same way as jam (see Summer section), with one difference—because the peel of citrus fruit is tough, it has to be softened either by soaking or cooking. The softening of the peel also releases the pectin, which is contained in the pith and pips.

There are three basic methods of making marmalade. One is to squeeze the juice into a pan and add the chopped peel (with pith) and the pips tied in a piece of muslin. Acid (lemon juice or citric or tartaric acid) and a measured amount of water are stirred in and the mixture is simmered for 2 hours. The bag of pips is discarded and sugar stirred in. When it has dissolved, the marmalade is boiled until setting point is reached.

For the second method, the fruit is finely pared and the rind is shredded. The rind, acid and half the water are simmered together for 2 hours. Meanwhile, the fruit pulp is cooked with the pith in the remaining water for 2 hours. The fruit pulp is drained and all pips, pith and coarse tissue discarded. The remaining pulp is sieved and added to the rind mixture with sugar, and the marmalade is boiled until setting point is reached.

The third method uses whole fruit. They are put in the pan with the water and simmered for 2 hours or until tender. The fruit is then removed from the pan and chopped and the pips are returned to the pan tied in muslin. After a further simmering of 15 minutes, the pips are discarded and the chopped fruit returned to the pan. Sugar is stirred in and the marmalade boiled until setting point is reached.

To bottle marmalade, remove from the heat and skim off the scum. Allow to cool slightly until a skin forms on top, then ladle into warmed jars. Cover with waxed paper discs and when cold, seal with jam covers. Label and store in a cool, dry, dark place.

The following recipes include only the ingredients and information in addition to that given above.

Seville orange marmalade

1.5kg/3lb Seville oranges
juice of 2 lemons
2.4-3.6l/4-6 pints water
2.75kg/6lb sugar

Scrub the fruit and use either method one, two or three.
Makes about 4.5kg/10lb

Five fruit marmalade

1 orange
1 grapefruit
1 lemon
1.5l/2½ pints water
1 large cooking apple, peeled, cored and diced
1 pear, peeled, cored and diced
1.5kg/3lb sugar

Scrub the orange, grapefruit and lemon and prepare according to either method one, two or three. Add the apple and pear and continue as specified.
Makes about 2.25kg/5lb

Grapefruit marmalade

1.5kg/3lb grapefruit
2 tsp citric acid
3.6l/6 pints water
2.75kg/6lb sugar

Scrub the grapefruit and proceed as method one, two or three.
Makes about 4.5kg/10lb

An interesting variation, Five Fruit Marmalade made from orange, grapefruit, lemon, apple and pear, has a distinctive, delicate flavour of its own.

Feast Days

When agriculture, and the consequent provision of food, were more closely linked to the seasons of the calendar, special days of fasting and feasting were as much a matter of practical necessity as of spiritual celebration. Although the seasons have become extended and blurred, religious and historical feast days and festivals are still celebrated, however, and enjoyed, throughout the world. The Lenten feast and the harvest festival, for example, remind us of the cycle of nature but are now more closely linked to religion than the scarcity or abundance of fresh food.

Each country and religion has its own celebrations and special days set aside to remember great events, no matter what seasonal calendar they follow. By trying to understand the meaning behind them and enjoying the food traditionally eaten on those days we can all enjoy them no matter what our religion or nationality.

January 1 - New Year's Day

On the stroke of midnight, on the 31st of December, the New Year begins, and with it our hopes for prosperity, health and happiness. As the clock chimes, and "Auld Lang Syne" is sung, thoughts turn to family and friends gathered together. An ideal centrepiece for the New Year's Day buffet table would be a baked ham glazed with bourbon whisky.

Bourbon-glazed ham

4.5kg/10lb smoked ham, well scrubbed,
soaked overnight and drained
1 bouquet garni
8 peppercorns
1 onion, quartered
1 carrot, scraped and quartered
1 celery stalk, quartered
375g/12oz dark brown sugar
2 tsp dry mustard
150ml/5floz bourbon whisky
12 whole cloves
2 oranges, peeled and segmented

Put the ham in a saucepan and cover with water. Add the bouquet garni, peppercorns, onion, carrot and celery. Bring to the boil, then simmer for 4½ hours.

Remove from the heat and leave the ham to cool in the liquid.

Mix together the brown sugar, mustard and 4 tablespoons of the bourbon. Drain the ham and cut away the rind. Score the fat in a diamond pattern, making cuts all the way through the fat to the meat. Put the ham on a rack in a roasting tin and coat with the remaining bourbon. Spread over the sugar mixture. Push the cloves into the fat and arrange the orange segments on top, securing each segment with a wooden cocktail stick.

Bake in a moderate oven (180°C/350°F or Gas Mark 4) for 45 minutes to 1 hour. Serve hot or cold.
Serves 10-12

January 6 - Twelfth Night

Twelfth Night, or the Feast of the Epiphany, commemorates the visit of the Magi to the infant Jesus. In Mexico, for instance, children put out shoes to receive gifts from the passing kings. In France, and other Catholic European countries, a fruit bread or cake is baked with a dried bean inside. Whoever finds the bean is king or queen for the evening's festivities.

Twelfth night cake

375g/12oz butter
375g/12oz sugar, castor
6 eggs, standard
375g/12oz flour
½ tsp grated nutmeg
1 tsp ground cinnamon
1 tsp ground ginger
375g/12oz sultanas
375g/12oz currants
75g/3oz ground almonds
250g/8oz mixed candied peel, chopped
3 Tbsp whisky

Cream the butter and sugar together in a mixing bowl until the mixture is light and fluffy. Beat in the eggs, one at a time, adding a little flour with each egg to prevent curdling. Sift together the remaining flour and spices and fold into the creamed mixture with the fruit. Stir in the whisky.

Spoon the cake mixture into a deep 23cm/9in diameter cake tin which has been lined with greased greaseproof paper. Bake in a cool oven (150°C/300°F or Gas Mark 2) for 4 to 4½ hours·or until a skewer inserted into the centre comes out clean.

Leave to cool in the tin for 1 hour, then

Twelfth Night Cake is a traditional British cake served on the 12th day after Christmas as the celebrations for the festive season come to an end.

turn out onto a wire rack to cool completely. Store in an airtight tin.
Makes one 23cm/9in cake

January 25 - Burn's Night

Scottish people throughout the world celebrate the birth of the famous Scottish poet, Robert Burns, born on January 25, 1759, with a banquet. The celebration begins with the famous grace:

'Somehae meat that canna eat,
And some wad eat that want it,
But we hae meat, and we can eat,
And sae the Lord be thankit.'

"The Skirl o' the Pipes" then announces the arrival of the haggis, the highlight of the meal, at the table and it is slit open with a *skean d'hu* (ceremonial knife) while Burns' salutation to a haggis is recited.

Traditional haggis recipes call for the savoury meat mixture to be boiled in a sheep's paunch, but as this is difficult for modern cooks, we give a version of haggis steamed in a basin. Haggis is traditionally served with chappit (mashed) potatoes and bashed neeps (mashed swedes) and washed down with Scotch whisky.

Haggis

250g/8oz liver
175g/6oz oatmeal
2 medium onions
250g/8oz lean minced beef
175g/6oz shredded beef suet
salt and black pepper
pinch grated nutmeg

Put the liver in a saucepan and cover with cold water. Bring to the boil and boil for 5 minutes. Drain the liver, reserving 4 tablespoons of the water.

Toast the oatmeal under the grill or in the oven until it is golden brown. Allow to cool slightly. Meanwhile, mince the liver with the onions. Add the oatmeal, beef, suet, salt and pepper to the taste, nutmeg and the reserved liver cooking liquid to the minced mixture and combine thoroughly. Spoon into a greased pudding basin and tie a lid of greased greaseproof paper and foil on top. Make a pleat in the lid to allow for expansion.

Steam the haggis for 3 hours, replenishing the boiling water when necessary. Serve hot with bagpipes and plenty of Scotch whisky.
Serves 6-8

Fresh root ginger is a common ingredient in Chinese dishes and can be bought from most delicatessens.

January/February – Chinese New Year (Yüan Tan)

The renewal of the Chinese lunar calendar falls between January 21 and February 19 on the Gregorian calendar. This colourful and exciting two-week celebration ends with the Lantern Festival (Yüan Hsiao) when children parade with beautiful lighted lanterns. Rice is a symbol of life and fertility, and in some parts of China it is customary to 'present the New Year's rice', that is to place a wooden bowl of rice on the altar dedicated to the family ancestors. One day of the New Year festivities commemorates the first planting of rice, five thousand years ago.

Feng kuo (crabmeat dumplings)

6 dried Chinese mushrooms, soaked for 30
minutes and drained
2 Tbsp sesame or vegetable oil
1 Tbsp spring onions, chopped
1 tsp root ginger, peeled and finely
chopped
250g/8oz crabmeat, flaked
salt and black pepper
¼ tsp sugar
1 tsp soy sauce
1 Tbsp dry sherry
DUMPLING DOUGH
250g/8oz flour
125ml/4floz boiling water

Remove and discard the mushroom stalks. Finely chop the caps. Heat the oil in a frying pan. Add the mushrooms, spring onions, ginger and crabmeat. Fry, stirring, for 3 minutes. Stir in salt and pepper to taste, the sugar, soy sauce and sherry and cook, stirring, for 1 minute. Remove from the heat.

Sift the flour into a mixing bowl and gradually stir in the boiling water. Knead the dough for 5 minutes or until smooth and elastic. Return to the bowl, cover and leave for 30 minutes.

Roll the dough into a sausage about 2.5cm/1in in diameter. Cut into slices 2.5cm/1in thick. Flatten the slices until they are about 8cm/3in in diameter. Place a teaspoonful of the crabmeat filling on one half of each dough circle and fold over the other half to make half-moon shapes. Press the edges together to seal.

Steam the dumplings, in batches if necessary, for about 10 minutes. Serve hot.
Serves 4

Chinese fried rice

250g/8oz long-grain rice, soaked in cold
water for 30 minutes and drained
500ml/16floz water
salt
2 Tbsp vegetable oil
2 medium onions, finely chopped
250g/8oz cooked ham, finely chopped
2 Tbsp peas or petits pois, cooked
2 medium tomatoes, peeled and quartered
250g/8oz shrimps (shelled weight),
deveined
1 Tbsp soy sauce
1 egg, lightly beaten

Put the rice, water and 1 teaspoon salt in a saucepan and bring to the boil. Cover and simmer for 15 minutes or until all the water has been absorbed. Remove from the heat.

A classic Chinese dish –Hung Shao Chu Jo is also one of the most popular. The skin of the pork is considered to be an integral part of the delicacy of the dish.

Heat the oil in another saucepan. Add the onions and cook, stirring, for 2 minutes. Add the ham, peas, tomatoes, shrimps and salt to taste and cook, stirring, for 1 minute.

Stir in the rice and cook, stirring, for 2 minutes. Add the soy sauce and egg and cook, stirring, for a further 2 minutes.

Transfer the fried rice mixture to a warmed serving bowl and serve immediately or keep warm until required.

Serves 4

Hung shao chu jo (Red-cooked pork)

2kg/4lb belly of pork
75ml/3floz vegetable oil
7 Tbsp soy sauce
1 Tbsp sugar
150ml/5floz chicken or beef stock
150ml/5floz red wine

Cut the pork into twelve pieces. Heat the oil in a flameproof casserole. Add the pork pieces and brown on all sides. Remove from the heat and pour off the oil. Add 4 tablespoons of the soy sauce, half the sugar and 75ml/3floz each of the stock and wine. Turn the meat over in this sauce several times.

Return to the heat and bring to the boil. Transfer to a warm oven (170°C/325°F or Gas Mark 3) and bake for 1 hour, turning the meat once.

Add the remaining soy sauce, sugar, stock and wine to the casserole. Turn the meat over several times, then return to a cool oven (150°C/300°F or Gas Mark 2). Continue baking for 1 hour, turning the meat once.

Remove the casserole from the oven and serve hot, straight from the dish.

Serves 4

February 14 - St. Valentine's Day

The origins of this day may be traced to the old Roman feast, Lupercalia, in February, at which young men and maidens drew partners by lot. A later festival custom was associated with the Christian bishop, Valentine, who was martyred on February 14, 271 AD. Another idea relates this holiday to the mating season for birds! Whatever its origin, it is a day for exchanging promises of love, in the form of anonymous greetings cards, chocolates, flowers—or a heart-shaped cake.

This superbly, decorative Valentine Cake would make a delightful present for someone special on St. Valentine's Day. The cake takes some time and effort to prepare, but the result is very rewarding.

Valentine cake

CAKE

300g/10oz castor sugar
8 eggs, at room temperature
½ tsp vanilla essence
250g/8oz flour
250g/8oz unsalted butter, melted

FILLING AND ICING

185g/6oz strawberry jam
700g/1½lb sugar
500ml/16floz water
pinch cream of tartar
½ tsp red food colouring
250g/8oz icing sugar

To make the cake, put the sugar, eggs and vanilla in a heatproof bowl over a pan of hot water. Beat until the mixture is pale and thick and will make a ribbon trail on itself when the beater is lifted. (If using an electric beater, no heat is required.) Remove from the heat and sift the flour into the bowl. Fold it in, then gradually stir in the melted butter. Pour into a greased and floured deep heart-shaped cake tin (20cm/8in across at its widest point) or two shallow heart-shaped cake tins.

Bake in a fairly hot oven (190°C/375°F or Gas Mark 5) for 20 to 30 minutes or until the cake springs back when lightly pressed in the centre. Allow to cool in the tin for 5 minutes, then turn out onto a wire rack and leave to cool completely.

If baked in a deep cake tin, slice the cake into two layers. Spread one layer with the jam and place the other layer on top.

Set the cake aside while you prepare the icing.

Put 500g/1lb of the sugar and 225ml/7floz of the water in a saucepan. Stir over gentle heat to dissolve the sugar, then bring to the boil. When the mixture boils, sprinkle over the cream of tartar and boil until the mixture reaches 115°C/240°F on a sugar thermometer (the soft ball stage).

Remove from the heat and pour the fondant onto a marble or enamel surface which has been sprinkled lightly with water. Do not scrape out the pan as sugar crystals will have formed and will make the icing uneven. Sprinkle the surface of the fondant with water and leave to cool for 3 minutes.

Using a metal spatula or a sugar scraper, start working the fondant by bringing the mixture in from the edges to the middle and form it into a large ball shape. When the fondant 'turns' or goes white and opaque, knead it with your hands to make it smooth.

Put the remaining sugar and 250ml/8floz of the remaining water in a saucepan. Stir over gentle heat to dissolve the sugar, then bring to the boil. Boil until the mixture reaches 105°C/220°F on a sugar thermometer. Remove from the heat and allow the sugar syrup to cool slightly.

Cut off one-quarter of the fondant and roll it out to about 3mm/⅛in thick. Cut out three small heartshapes and a long strip. Twist the strip into a ribbon bow.

Put the remaining fondant into a heatproof bowl over a pan of hot water. Heat until the fondant is very soft (do not let the water boil). Beat in 8 tablespoons of the sugar syrup, a tablespoon at a time. Stir in the food colouring, adding more if necessary to make the icing a deep red.

Remove from the heat and spread the icing over the top and sides of the cake. When the cake is covered with icing, dip a knife in boiling water and use to make the icing smooth. Arrange the hearts and ribbon bow on top.

Dissolve the icing sugar in enough of the remaining water to make a stiff mixture. Pipe in small rosettes around the top and bottom edges of the cake.

Makes one heart-shaped cake

February/March - Shrove Tuesday

Shrove Tuesday, or Fastnacht, Carnival or Mardi Gras, is a day of feasting before the Lenten fast begins on Ash Wednesday. Eggs, milk and other food not permitted during the fast are to be used up. In England, these are made into pancake batter and the pancakes are most often served simply with sugar and lemon juice, on 'Pancake Day'. A well-known and very delicious pancake recipe is Crêpes Suzette.

Crêpes Suzette

BATTER
150g/5oz flour
1 Tbsp castor sugar
3 egg yolks
65g/2½oz butter, melted
125ml/4floz milk
125ml/4floz cold water
2 Tbsp vegetable oil
FILLING
4 sugar lumps
2 medium oranges
4 Tbsp castor sugar
185g/6oz unsalted butter, softened
75ml/3floz orange juice
5 Tbsp orange-flavoured liqueur
3 Tbsp brandy

To make the batter, sift the flour and sugar into a mixing bowl. Make a well in the centre and add the egg yolks and melted butter. Mix together, then gradually draw in the flour. Stir in the milk and water and beat to a smooth dough.

Grease a crêpe pan or frying pan with a little of the oil. Pour in a few tablespoonsful of the batter and tilt the pan so the bottom is evenly covered. Cook the pancake for about 1 minute, then turn it over and cook the other side for about 30 seconds. Slide the pancake out of the pan and keep hot while you cook the remaining pancakes in the same way. Interleave the pancakes with greaseproof paper. Keep hot.

Rub the sugar lumps over the rind of the oranges so they absorb the zest (oil). Put the sugar lumps in a mixing bowl and mash them with a wooden spoon. Peel the oranges, removing all the white pith from the rind. Finely chop the orange rind and add to the sugar lumps with half the sugar and the softened butter. Cream the mixture together until it is light and fluffy. Stir in the orange juice and 3 tablespoons of the organge-flavoured liqueur.

Melt the orange butter in a frying pan. Dip the pancakes in, one at a time, until well soaked, then fold into quarters. Arrange in a warmed shallow serving dish. Sprinkle the remaining sugar over the pancakes and pour over any remaining orange butter.

Warm the remaining orange-flavoured liqueur and brandy in a small saucepan. Pour over the pancakes and ignite. Shake the dish gently and serve when the flames have died away.
Serves 4-6

This decorative Valentine's Cake makes a unique present for someone special on St. Valentine's Day.

Mothering Sunday

Falling on the fourth Sunday in Lent, this is named for the custom of the faithful attending the mother church in which they had been baptized. Gifts were offered at the altar to the church, and to their mothers as tokens of love and gratitude.

In Britain, in the days when many girls worked in service, often away from home, Mothering Sunday was one of their few days holiday. Traditionally they baked a Simnel Cake as a present for their mothers, but today it is more often baked at Easter. The cake is topped by eleven marzipan balls said to represent the Apostles. However, in ancient Rome also, Roman matrons honoured Juno and her son Mars during the festival of Matronalia by baking ball-topped cakes.

The cake has a central layer of marzipan which is cooked with the cake mixture. The top is decorated with another layer of marzipan which is grilled or baked until a little of the sugar caramelizes and turns golden brown.

Simnel cake

185g/6oz flour
25g/1oz rice flour
1 tsp baking powder
185g/6oz castor sugar
185g/6oz butter
3 eggs
185g/6oz sultanas
185g/6oz currants
125g/4oz glacé cherries, chopped
grated rind of 1 lemon
2 Tbsp candied lemon peel, finely chopped
1 tsp grated orange rind
MARZIPAN
500g/1lb ground almonds
375g/12oz icing sugar
125g/4oz sugar
2-3 egg yolks
½ tsp almond essence
APRICOT GLAZE
4 Tbsp apricot jam
75ml/3floz water
1 tsp lemon juice

Sift the flour, rice flour and baking powder into a mixing bowl. In another bowl, cream the sugar and butter together until the mixture is light and fluffy. Beat in the eggs, one at a time, with a tablespoon of the flour mixture between each. Fold in half the remaining flour. Mix the remaining flour with the sultanas, currants, glacé cherries, lemon rind, candied lemon peel and grated orange rind, stirring to coat the fruit well. Fold the flour and fruit mixture into the batter.

To make the marzipan, sift the almonds, icing sugar and sugar into a mixing bowl. Add two of the egg yolks and the almond essence and mix together with your fingertips. Add the remaining egg yolk if the mixture is too dry. Turn the marzipan out onto a surface dusted with icing sugar or cornflour and knead for 5 minutes or until very smooth.

Cut off one-third of the marzipan and shape into a 16cm/6½in circle. Spoon half the cake mixture into a deep 18cm/7in diameter cake tin that has been lined with greased greaseproof paper. Smooth the surface of the cake mixture and place the marzipan circle on top. Cover with the remaining cake mixture and smooth the surface. Bake in a moderate oven (180°C/350°F or Gas Mark 4) for 1½ hours. Reduce the temperature to cool (150°C/300°F or Gas Mark 2) and continue baking for 1 to 1¼ hours or until a skewer inserted into the centre comes out clean.

Allow the cake to cool in the tin for 5 minutes, then turn out onto a wire rack and leave to cool completely.

Meanwhile, make the apricot glaze. Put the jam and water in a saucepan and cook gently for 5 minutes. Stir in the lemon juice, then remove from the heat and strain.

Brush the top of the cake with most of the apricot glaze. Cut off half the remaining marzipan and roll out to a circle the same diameter as the top of the cake. Lay on top of the cake. Roll the remaining marzipan into 11 balls. Brush the balls with the remaining apricot glaze and press around the edge of the marzipan top.

Place the cake on an ovenproof dish and bake in a hot oven (220°C/425°F or Gas Mark 7) for 5 to 8 minutes or until the tops of the balls are golden brown. Allow to cool before serving. Place the cake on a serving dish and serve.
Makes one 18cm/7in cake

*Opposite : Simnel Cake – a traditional British cake originally given to mothers by girls in service as a gift on Mothering Sunday, although nowadays often served at Easter.
Left : Each of the eleven glazed marzipan balls represents one of the Apostles.*

Passover

This Jewish festival runs in the lunar month Nisan. It gives thanks for the 'passing over' of the plagues of Egypt and the consequent deliverance of the Hebrews from Egyptian bondage in the thirteenth century BC. On the first and second nights of Passover, there is a ceremony called a Seder with unleavened bread, or matzo, and bitter herbs symbolizing the Exodus. Matzo Brei and the carrot sweets, Ingber, are made with ingredients symbolically linked to the Passover.

Ingber (carrot sweets)

450g/14oz sugar
3 Tbsp water
500g/1lb carrots, scraped and grated
½ tsp root ginger, peeled and finely chopped
50g/2oz walnuts, finely chopped
2 Tbsp lemon juice

Dissolve the sugar in the water in a saucepan over low heat. Stir in the carrots, then bring to the boil. Boil for 30 minutes or until the mixture is very thick.

Remove from the heat and stir in the ginger, walnuts and lemon juice. Pour into a greased 15cm/6in square cake tin. Allow to cool, then cut into 2.5cm/1in squares. When the sweets are completely cold and set, remove from the tin.
Makes about 20

Matzo brei (scrambled eggs with matzos)

2 matzos, broken into 5cm/2in pieces
125ml/4floz milk
2 eggs, lightly beaten
salt
pinch grated nutmeg
25g/1oz vegetable fat

Put the matzo pieces in a mixing bowl and pour over the milk. Leave to soak for 5 minutes. Pour off any excess milk and stir in eggs, salt to taste and the nutmeg.

Melt the butter in a saucepan. Pour in the matzo mixture and cook, stirring occasionally, until the eggs are lightly scrambled. Serve hot.
Serves 2

April/May - Good Friday

The cross on the Hot Cross Bun, traditionally baked for this holy day, is said to symbolize Christ's cross. Yet, the Greeks and Romans had similar cakes for festivals, with the sun symbol—a circle—divided into quarters by a cross, to represent the four seasons.

Hot cross buns

15g/½oz fresh yeast
250ml/8floz lukewarm milk
500g/1lb flour
½ tsp salt
1 tsp mixed spice
1 tsp ground cinnamon
50g/2oz sugar
2 eggs
50g/2oz butter, melted
50g/2oz raisins
50g/2oz mixed candied peel, chopped
CROSSES
15g/½oz butter
25g/1oz flour
1 tsp cold water
GLAZE
2 Tbsp milk
1 tsp sugar

Mash the yeast to a paste with 2 tablespoons of the milk. Set aside in a warm, draught-free place until frothy. Sift the flour, salt, spice, cinnamon and sugar into a mixing bowl. Make a well in the centre and add the yeast mixture, remaining milk, eggs and melted butter. Gradually draw the flour mixture into the liquids and continue mixing until all the flour is incorporated and the dough comes away from the sides of the bowl.

Turn out of the bowl and knead for 10 minutes or until the dough is smooth and elastic. Return to a greased bowl, cover and leave to rise in a warm, draught-free place for 1 hour or until almost doubled in bulk.

Knock back the dough and knead again. Knead in the raisins and candied peel. Divide the dough into sixteen pieces and form into bun shapes. Place on two greased baking sheets, leaving 5cm/2in space between each bun, and let rise for 15 to 20 minutes.

Meanwhile, make the dough for the crosses. Rub the butter into the flour until the mixture resembles breadcrumbs. Stir in the cold water to bind the mixture, then knead to a dough. Roll out to a rectangle about 3mm/⅛in thick and cut into 32 strips 5cm/2in long. Press two strips, in a cross, on the top of each bun.

Mix together the milk and sugar for the glaze and brush over the buns. Bake in a very hot oven (230°C/450°F or Gas Mark 8) for 15 minutes or until the buns are a deep golden brown. Allow to cool.
Makes 16

Above right : Traditionally eaten during the Passover, Ingber or Ingberlach are unusual carrot and walnut sweets. Old carrots are best for this recipe.
Below right : Decorated with a cross, Hot Cross Buns are a traditional British treat eaten on Good Friday.

April/May - Easter Sunday

A moveable feast day, Easter Sunday falls on the first Sunday after Good Friday, when Christ is supposed to have risen from the dead. Called Ostern in Germany, Pasqua in Italy, Pâques in France, Pasha in Greece and Paske in Norway, it is, along with Christmas, the most important Christian religious festival. The recipes given are traditional for Easter—Cassata alla Siciliana, an Italian chocolate cake, Greek Easter Lamb, Russian Kulich (a fruit bread) and Easter bunny-shaped biscuits from the USA.

Cassata alla Siciliana (Italian chocolate cake)

1 Madeira cake, 23cm/9in long and 8cm/3in wide
500g/1lb ricotta (cottage) cheese
2 Tbsp double cream
50g/2oz sugar
2½ Tbsp orange-flavoured liqueur
2 Tbsp mixed candied fruit, chopped
1 Tbsp pistachio nuts, chopped
50g/2oz dark cooking chocolate, grated
CHOCOLATE ICING
375g/12oz dark cooking chocolate, broken into small pieces
175ml/6floz black coffee
250g/8oz unsalted butter, cut into small pieces and chilled

Cut the cake lengthways into 1cm/½in slices. Press the ricotta through a sieve into a mixing bowl. Beat until it is smooth, then beat in the cream, sugar and liqueur. Fold in the candied fruit, nuts and grated chocolate.

Place one slice of cake on a flat plate and spread with one-third of the ricotta mixture. Place another slice of cake on top and spread with another third of the ricotta mixture. Make another layer in this way and finish with the last slice of cake. Gently press the loaf together. Wrap the cake in foil and chill for 3 hours.

Melt the chocolate with the coffee in a heatproof bowl over a pan of hot water. Remove from the heat and beat in the butter, a piece at a time. Continue beating until the mixture is smooth, then allow to cool until the icing is thick enough to spread.

Cover the top and sides of the cake with the icing, reserving a little for decoration. Pipe the reserved icing on top in swirls. Chill the cake for at least 12 hours before serving.

Serves 8-10

Kulich (Russian Easter bread)

40g/1½oz fresh yeast
225ml/7floz lukewarm milk
50g/2oz raisins
3 Tbsp rum
700g/1½lb flour
275g/9oz icing sugar
½ tsp salt
½ tsp vanilla essence
9 egg yolks
250g/8oz unsalted butter, softened
½ tsp saffron powder
1 Tbsp hot water
50g/2oz blanched almonds, slivered
50g/2oz candied peel, chopped
ICING
250g/8oz icing sugar
3 Tbsp cold water
1 tsp lemon juice

Mash the yeast and 1 tablespoon of the milk to make a paste. Leave in a warm, draught-free place until frothy. Meanwhile, soak the raisins in the rum for 15 minutes.

Sift the flour, icing sugar and salt into a mixing bowl. Make a well in the centre and add the yeast mixture and remaining milk. Gradually mix the flour into the liquid. Beat in the vanilla, then the egg yolks, one at a time. Gradually beat in the softened butter.

Dissolve the saffron in the hot water and stir into the dough. Turn out of the bowl and knead for 10 minutes or until smooth and elastic. Return to a greased bowl and leave to rise in a warm place for 1 to 1½ hours or until doubled in bulk.

Toast the almonds under the grill until they are golden brown. Add to the soaked raisins with the candied peel. Knock back the dough. Add the fruit and nuts and knead to distribute them evenly. Put the dough into a greased and lined coffee tin or tall cylindrical mould that is about 15cm/6in in diameter and 18cm/7in tall. Leave to rise in a warm place for 30 minutes.

Bake in a fairly hot oven (200°C/400°F or Gas Mark 6) for 40 minutes. Reduce the temperature to moderate (180°C/350°F or Gas Mark 4) and continue baking for 1 hour.

Cool in the tin for 10 minutes, then cool completely, standing upright, on a wire rack.

To make the icing, sift the icing sugar into a mixing bowl. Add the water and lemon juice and mix to a thin paste. Pour this icing over the top of the cooled bread and allow it to trickle down the sides.

Makes one 1.5kg/3lb bread

Left : Topped with icing, Kulich is one of the traditional foods cooked for the Russian Orthodox Easter celebrations and is rich with rum, almonds, eggs and fruit.
Above : Eggs are universal symbols of creation. Decorating them for gifts and festive occasions is a traditional and favourite pastime with children at Easter.

Easter bunnies

90g/3oz butter
50g/2oz plus 1 Tbsp castor sugar
1 egg, separated
175g/6oz flour
1½ tsp baking powder
¼ tsp salt
2 Tbsp warm milk

Cream the butter and all but 1 tablespoon of the sugar together until the mixture is light and fluffy. Beat in the egg yolk. Sift together the flour, baking powder and salt and fold into the creamed mixture. Stir in the milk. Chill the dough for 1 hour or until it is fairly firm.

Roll out the dough to 6mm/¼in thick. Cut out ten 5cm/2in circles, ten 2.5cm/1in circles, twenty 2cm/¾in circles and ten 1cm/½in circles. Make up the bunnies on a greased baking sheet, using the 5cm/2in circles for the bodies, the 2.5cm/1in circles for the heads and the 1cm/½in circles for the tails. Shape the 2cm/¾in circles into ovals for the ears.

Bake the bunnies in a fairly hot oven (200°C/400°F or Gas Mark 6) for 10 minutes. Coat the bunnies with the lightly beaten egg white and sprinkle with the remaining sugar. Bake for a further 10 minutes or until the bunnies are golden brown. Cool on a wire rack.
Makes 10

Greek Easter lamb

1 x 2.5kg/5lb leg of lamb
2 garlic cloves, cut into slivers
2 rosemary sprigs
salt and black pepper
50g/2oz butter
250g/8oz broad beans (shelled weight)
4 small onions
6 medium potatoes, peeled and thinly sliced
600ml/1 pint chicken stock

Make several incisions in the lamb and insert the garlic slivers in them. Rub the meat with the salt and pepper and lay the rosemary sprigs over the fat. Put the meat on a rack in a roasting tin and cover with the butter. Roast in a very hot oven (230°C/450°F or Gas Mark 8) for 10 minutes.

Baste the lamb with the fat in the tin and arrange the beans, onions and potatoes around the meat. Pour the stock over the vegetables. Return to a moderate oven (180°C/350°F or Gas Mark 4) and continue roasting for 2 to 2¼ hours or until the lamb is cooked.

Serve hot.
Serves 6

July 4 - Independence Day, U.S.A

On July 4, 1776, the Continental Congress adopted the Declaration of Independence, thereby severing the ties between England and the American colonies. Every year on this day, Americans celebrate with fireworks, parades and patriotic fervour. Why not celebrate by making two typically American recipes, Southern-fried Chicken and Devil's Food Cake.

Devil's food cake

125g/4oz dark cooking chocolate
250ml/8floz milk
185g/6oz light brown sugar
3 egg yolks
300g/10oz flour
1 tsp bicarbonate of soda
pinch salt
125g/4oz butter
185g/6oz castor sugar
4 Tbsp water
1 tsp vanilla essence
2 egg whites
CHOCOLATE FUDGE FROSTING
250ml/8floz single cream
500g/1lb sugar
pinch salt
50g/2oz dark cooking chocolate, grated
45g/1½oz butter
½ tsp vanilla essence
50g/2oz walnuts, chopped

Put the chocolate, milk, brown sugar and one egg yolk in the top of a double saucepan or in a heatproof bowl placed over a pan of hot water. Heat gently, stirring, until the chocolate melts and the sugar dissolves. Remove from the heat. Sift the flour, soda and salt into a mixing bowl.

Cream the butter and sugar together in another mixing bowl until the mixture is light and fluffy. Beat in the remaining egg yolks, one at a time. Mix in one-third of the flour, then half the water. Add the remaining flour and water and beat until the batter is smooth. Stir in the vanilla essence and chocolate mixture.

Beat the egg whites until they will hold a stiff peak. Fold into the chocolate batter. Spoon into three greased shallow 20cm/8in sandwich cake tins. Bake in a moderate oven (180°C/350°F or Gas Mark 4) for 25 minutes or until a skewer inserted into the centres comes out clean. Turn the cake layers out onto a wire rack and allow to cool.

To make the frosting, scald the cream in a saucepan. Remove from the heat and stir in the sugar, salt and grated chocolate. Return to the heat and stir to melt the chocolate, then cover and cook for 3 minutes. Uncover the pan and boil until the mixture reaches 115°C/238°F on a sugar thermometer (the soft ball stage). Remove from the heat and place the bottom of the pan in cold water.

When the mixture has cooled to 43°C/110°F, beat in the butter and vanilla. Continue beating until the frosting is thick and of a spreading consistency. Stir in the walnuts.

Sandwich the three cake layers together with three-quarters of the frosting and cover the tops and sides with the remainder.

Serves 8-10

Southern fried chicken

350ml/12floz milk
5 Tbsp flour
salt and black pepper
4 chicken breasts
1 egg
1 tsp water
75g/3oz fresh white breadcrumbs
125g/4oz butter
3 Tbsp vegetable oil
½ tsp sugar

Put 3 tablespoons of milk in a saucer. Mix together 4 tablespoons of the flour with salt and pepper on a plate. Dip the chicken breasts in the milk and then in the seasoned flour. Leave to dry for 10 minutes.

Lightly beat the egg with the water on a plate. Put the breadcrumbs on another plate. Dip the chicken breasts in the egg and then in the breadcrumbs, coating well.

Melt three-quarters of the butter with the oil in a frying pan. Add the chicken breasts and cook, turning occasionally, for 20 minutes. Drain the chicken on kitchen paper towels and transfer to a warmed serving dish. Keep hot.

Melt the remaining butter in a saucepan. Stir in the sugar and cook, stirring, until the mixture turns dark brown. Stir in the remaining flour and cook, stirring, for 1 minute. Remove from the heat and gradually stir in the remaining milk. Return to the heat and bring to the boil. Simmer, stirring, until thickened and smooth. Pour this sauce into a sauceboat and serve with the chicken.

Serves 4

This famous American dish has almost as many 'correct' versions as there are states. Here, Southern Fried Chicken is served with fried bananas, bacon rolls and horseradish sauce although other accompaniments may include corn fritters, potato pancakes, boiled rice, or mashed potatoes – so its up to you to choose!

The pumpkin is an autumn fruit which is traditionally served on Thanksgiving Day in the United States of America.

September 29 - Michaelmas Day

Michaelmas is the feast day of the archangel St. Michael. It marked the end of the agricultural hire year when men were free to look for fresh employment—and when tenants had to pay their quarterly rent. To appease the landlord, it was the custom to give a fat goose which had fed on the corn stubble after the harvest. In Ireland there is also an old saying that if you eat goose on Michaelmas Day, you will never want for money all the year round! So here to help you celebrate Michaelmas, is a recipe for a succulent stuffed goose.

Michaelmas goose

1 x 3.5-4kg/8-9lb goose
1 lemon, quartered
salt and black pepper
STUFFING
6 large potatoes, peeled
1 medium onion, chopped
4 streaky bacon slices, finely diced
salt and black pepper
375g/12oz pork sausagemeat
1 Tbsp parsley, freshly chopped
1 tsp thyme, freshly chopped
1 tsp sage, feshly chopped
ONION SAUCE
4 medium onions, chopped
150ml/5floz water
150ml/5floz milk
2.5cm/1in thick slice of turnip
50g/2oz butter
1 tsp grated nutmeg
salt and black pepper
4 Tbsp single cream
APPLE SAUCE
2 large cooking apples, peeled, cored and chopped
125ml/4floz water
25g/1oz butter
2 Tbsp sugar
1 tsp lemon juice
pinch salt

Prick the goose all over and rub the skin with three of the lemon quarters. Squeeze the juice from the remaining lemon quarter into the cavity in the goose. Rub the skin with salt and pepper.

To make the stuffing, cook the potatoes in boiling salted water for 15 to 20 minutes or until they are tender. Drain well and mash to a smooth purée. Allow to cool, then stir in the remaining stuffing ingredients with salt and pepper to taste. Spoon the stuffing into the goose and close the opening with a skewer or trussing needle and string.

Place the goose, on its breast, on a rack in a roasting tin. Roast in a very hot oven (230°C/450°F or Gas Mark 8) for 30 minutes. Reduce the temperature to moderate (180°C/350°F or Gas Mark 4) and continue roasting for 3 hours 20 minutes. Remove the fat from the tin occasionally. To test if the goose is cooked, pierce the thigh with a skewer: the juices should be clear.

Meanwhile, prepare the sauces. To make the onion sauce, put the onions, water, milk and turnip in a saucepan and bring to the boil. Simmer for 20 minutes or until the onions are very soft and beginning to pulp. Remove from the heat and beat in the butter, nutmeg and salt and pepper to taste. When the mixture is smooth, stir in the cream. Keep hot.

To make the apple sauce, put the apples and water in a saucepan and cook until the apples are soft and pulpy. Remove from the heat and purée in a foodmill or by pushing through a sieve. Stir in the remaining sauce ingredients and keep hot.

Transfer the goose to a carving board and serve with the onion and apple sauces. *Serves 6-8*

November 5 - Guy Fawkes' Day

In 1605, the hapless Guy Fawkes and his fellow Roman Catholic conspirators attempted to blow up Parliament. The Gunpowder Plot, as it became known, was discovered, and Guy Fawkes is still being punished today—once a year, on November 5, he is burned as a straw effigy at the top of the garden bonfire. Gingerbread, often in the shape of a man—Guy Fawkes again?—and toffee are enjoyed during the festivities.

Gingerbread

250g/8oz flour
½ tsp bicarbonate of soda
1½ tsp ground ginger
¼ tsp ground cloves
½ tsp ground cinnamon
¼ tsp salt
75g/3oz butter, softened
125g/4oz sugar
1 egg
175ml/6floz treacle
250ml/8floz soured cream

Sift the flour, soda, ginger, cloves, cinnamon and salt into a mixing bowl. Cream the butter and sugar together in another bowl until the mixture is light and fluffy. Beat in the egg and treacle, then stir in the soured cream. Gradually stir the flour mixture into the treacle mixture.

Pour into a greased 1kg/2lb loaf tin. Bake in a moderate oven (180°C/350°F or Gas Mark 4) for 1¼ hours or until a skewer inserted into the centre comes out clean. Allow to cool on a wire rack.

Makes one 1kg/2lb bread

Toffee

375g/12oz soft brown sugar
90g/3oz butter
1 Tbsp golden syrup
2 tsp malt vinegar
3 Tbsp water

Put all the ingredients in a saucepan and stir over gentle heat to dissolve the sugar. Bring to the boil and boil until the mixture reaches 163°C/325°F on a sugar thermometer (the hard crack stage). Alternatively, test by dropping a little of the mixture into cold water. If it sets and is hard and crunchy, the toffee is ready. Remove from the heat and allow to cool for 10 minutes.

Pour the toffee into a greased 15cm/6in square baking tin. Leave until cool but not set. Cut into 2.5cm/1in squares with an oiled knife. Leave until completely cold, then remove from the tin and break into pieces. Wrap each in a piece of grease-proof paper and store in an airtight tin.

Makes 60

November - Thanksgiving

On the fourth Thursday in November, Americans celebrate the feast of Thanksgiving, which harks back to the first harvest feast enjoyed by the Pilgrims, having survived their first winter in the New World. Foods that are traditional Thanksgiving fare were eaten then—turkey, corn, sweet potatoes, pumpkins—and here are recipes for a delicious roast stuffed turkey and pumpkin pie.

Pumpkin pie

PASTRY
185g/6oz flour
¼ tsp salt
90g/3oz butter
2-3 Tbsp iced water
FILLING
125g/4oz brown sugar
pinch salt
1½ tsp ground cinnamon
½ tsp ground ginger
¼ tsp ground cloves
700g/1½lb can puréed pumpkin
3 eggs, lightly beaten
300ml/10floz single cream

To make the pastry, sift the flour and salt into a mixing bowl. Add the butter and cut into small pieces, then rub the fat into the flour until the mixture resembles breadcrumbs. Stir in enough of the water to bind the mixture, then knead to a dough. Chill for 30 minutes.

Roll out the dough and use to line a 23cm/9in pie or flan dish.

Mix together all the ingredients for the filling. Pour into the dough-lined dish. Bake in a fairly hot oven (190°C/375°F or Gas Mark 5) for 45 to 50 minutes or until a knife inserted into the filling comes out clean.

Allow to cool completely before serving.
Serves 6-8

A favourite with children, and many adults too, toffee is easy to make, but it is important to use a large saucepan, as the syrup boils up quickly.

Roast turkey with pumpkin and pork and cranberry stuffings

1 x 4.5kg/10lb turkey, liver reserved and
finely chopped
salt and black pepper
125g/4oz butter, melted
4 Tbsp apricot jam
150ml/5floz white wine
2 Tbsp flour
15g/½oz butter

PUMPKIN STUFFING
50g/2oz butter
2 medium onions, finely chopped
300g/10oz pumpkin, peeled, seeded and
grated
2 large carrots, scraped and grated
salt and black pepper
2 tsp sugar
½ tsp grated nutmeg
4 Tbsp double cream

PORK AND CRANBERRY STUFFING
25g/1oz butter
1 medium onion, finely chopped
300g/10oz pork sausagemeat
125g/4oz cranberry jelly
1½ tsp dried basil
salt and black pepper
50g/2oz blanched almonds, chopped

Rub the turkey, inside and out, with salt and pepper and set it to one side while you make the stuffings.

To make the pumpkin stuffing, melt the butter in a saucepan. Add the onions, pumpkin and carrots and fry until the onions are soft but not brown. Stir in salt and pepper to taste, the sugar, nutmeg and cream. Cook gently for 10 minutes or until the pumpkin is tender and most of the liquid has evaporated. Remove from the heat and allow to cool while you prepare the second stuffing.

To make the pork and cranberry stuffing, melt the butter in a frying pan. Add the onion and fry until it is soft but not brown. Stir in the sausagemeat and fry until the meat loses its pinkness. Add the turkey liver, cranberry jelly, basil, salt and pepper to taste and the almonds. Cook for a further 3 minutes. Remove from the heat and allow to cool.

Fill the neck end of the turkey with as much of the pumpkin stuffing as it will hold. Secure the flap with a skewer or trussing needle and string. Put any remaining pumpkin stuffing in the vent end and follow with the pork and cranberry stuffing. Secure that opening with a skewer or trussing needle and string.

Brush the turkey with some of the melted butter. Place it, breast side down, in a roasting tin. Pour over the remaining melted butter. Roast in a hot oven (220°C/425°F or Gas Mark 7) for 15 minutes.

Reduce the temperature to moderate (180°C/350°F or Gas Mark 4) and continue roasting for 2¼ hours, basting occasionally with the butter in the tin.

Turn the turkey onto its back and brush with the jam. Pour over the wine and roast for a further 30 minutes or until the skin is golden brown and the turkey is cooked. To test, pierce the thigh with a skewer or the point of a sharp knife: the juices should be clear.

Transfer the turkey to a carving board and remove the skewers or string. Pour 350ml/12floz of the liquid from the tin into a saucepan. Bring to the boil and boil for 5 minutes. Blend the flour and butter together to make a paste and add in small pieces to the cooking liquid. Simmer, stirring, until thickened and smooth. Pour into a sauceboat and serve this sauce with the turkey.
Serves 8-10

Below, left : This mouth-watering recipe for Roast Turkey will certainly turn a Thanksgiving dinner into a feast. It should be served with sweet potatoes and is delicious with chilled white wine.
Below, right : Corn dollies, made as long ago as 5000 years, were generally made as fertility symbols. After the last sheaf of harvest was cut it would be made into a corn dolly and great feasting and celebration would take place.

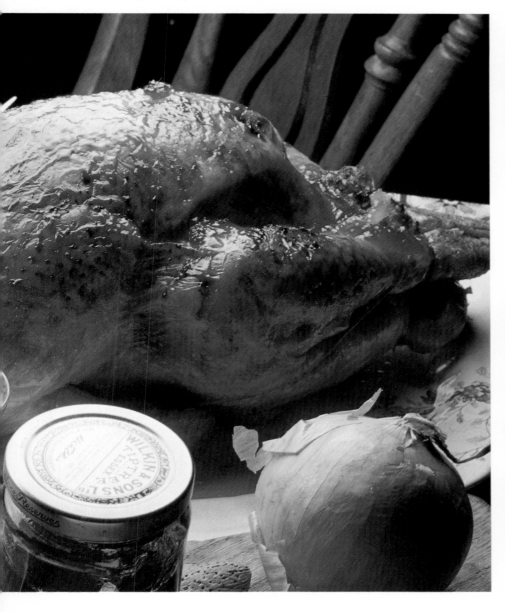

December 25 - Christmas Day

Christmas is surely the happiest and most meaningful of all Christian celebrations. All over the Christian world, the Christmas Day feasting is long and joyous. From Britain we have a recipe for steamed christmas pudding, from Germany a rich yeast fruit cake, from the West Indies a spicy meat mould, and, enjoyed everywhere mincemeat pies and a wassail bowl. The wassail bowl takes its name from the Saxon toast, 'Waes Hael'—Good Health.

It is traditional, when making a Christmas Pudding, for each member of the family to take a turn stirring the pudding mixture, wishing for health and prosperity for the family. The stirring must be done clockwise as that is the direction the sun moves around earth at the centre of the universe—to stir 'widdershins' invites trouble. Tokens may be added to the mixture—a silver coin signifying wealth, a ring for marriage, a thimble for spinsterhood, a button for bachelorhood. Whoever finds a token when eating the pudding has his future predicted!

Christmas pudding

250g/8oz self-raising flour
1 tsp salt
1 tsp grated nutmeg
1 tsp ground cinnamon
1 tsp ground cloves
375g/12oz fresh breadcrumbs
375g/12oz shredded beef suet
500g/1lb light brown sugar
500g/1lb currants
500g/1lb sultanas
1kg/2lb raisins
125g/4oz candied peel, chopped
50g/2oz glacé cherries, chopped
50g/2oz blanched almonds, slivered
2 medium cooking apples, peeled, cored and grated
finely grated rind and juice of 1 orange
finely grated rind and juice of ½ lemon
6 eggs
150ml/5floz milk
75ml/3floz brandy (optional)

Sift the flour, salt, nutmeg, cinnamon and cloves into a mixing bowl. Add the breadcrumbs, suet, sugar, currants, sultanas, raisins, candied peel, cherries and almonds. Mix well, then stir in the apples and lemon and orange rinds.

Lightly beat the eggs, milk, orange juice and lemon juice together. Stir into the dry ingredients until they are thoroughly moistened. Spoon into two greased 1.8l/3 pint pudding basins, packing down well and slightly doming the tops.

Cover the basins with a lid of greased greaseproof paper and foil, making a pleat in the centre to allow for expansion. Tie on securely with string. Steam for 6 hours, replenishing the boiling water when necessary.

Allow the puddings to cool, then recover with fresh greaseproof paper and foil. Store in a cool, dry place until Christmas.

To prepare for serving, steam the puddings for a further 3 hours, replenishing the boiling water when necessary. Turn out the puddings onto a warmed serving dish and pour over the brandy, if you are using it. Set alight and serve while still flaming.

Makes two large puddings

Stollen (German fruit bread)

15g/½oz fresh yeast
1 Tbsp lukewarm water
175ml/6floz milk
125g/4oz butter
500g/1lb flour
1 tsp salt
½ tsp ground cinnamon
¼ tsp ground mace
¼ tsp ground cardamom
185g/6oz sugar
2 eggs, lightly beaten
175g/6oz candied peel, chopped
75g/3oz sultanas
65g/2½oz walnuts, chopped
ICING
25g/1oz butter, melted
250g/8oz icing sugar
2 Tbsp water
¼ tsp vanilla essence
DECORATION
16 walnut halves

Mash the yeast and water to a paste and set aside in a warm, draught-free place until the mixture is frothy. Meanwhile, scald the milk. Remove from the heat and add the butter. When it has melted, set aside to cool to lukewarm.

Sift the flour, salt and spices into a mixing bowl. Make a well in the centre and add the sugar, yeast mixture, milk mixture and eggs. Mix well, gradually drawing the flour into the liquid. Turn the dough out of the bowl and knead for 10 minutes or until it is smooth and elastic. Return to a greased bowl and leave to rise in a warm place for 1 to 1½ hours or until doubled in bulk.

Knock back the dough and knead for 4

Above : Evergreen trees are traditionally set up at Christmas and hung with candles, presents and decorations.
Left : This delicious spicy fruit bread – Stollen – is a German speciality and is traditionally served at Christmas.

minutes. Knead in the candied peel, sultanas and walnuts to distribute them evenly. Shape the dough into a rounded crescent and place on a greased baking sheet. Leave in a warm place for 30 to 45 minutes to rise.

Bake in a fairly hot oven (200°C/400°F or Gas Mark 6) for 15 minutes. Reduce the temperature to moderate (180°C/350°F or Gas Mark 4) and continue baking for 30 minutes. To test if the stollen is cooked, rap the bottom with your knuckles: it should sound hollow like a drum. Allow to cool on a wire rack.

To make the icing, beat all the ingredients together until the mixture is smooth. Spread the icing over the top of the stollen and allow it to drip down the sides. Decorate the top with the walnut halves.
Makes one 1.5kg/3lb loaf

Wassail bowl

1.8l/3 pints beer
300ml/10floz medium sweet sherry
¼ tsp grated nutmeg
pinch ground cinnamon
pinch ground ginger
pared rind of 2 lemons
125g/4oz soft brown sugar
4 red-skinned apples, baked for 10 minutes
and kept warm
4 Tbsp brandy

Put the beer, sherry, nutmeg, cinnamon, ginger, lemon rind and brown sugar in a saucepan and stir over gentle heat to dissolve the sugar. Bring to just below boiling point, then remove from the heat.

Put the apples in a heatproof punch bowl. Warm the brandy in a ladle and ignite it. Pour it flaming over the apples, then pour over the beer mixture. Serve hot.
Serves 18-20

Mince pies

500-700g/1-1½lb mincemeat
3 Tbsp milk
2 Tbsp sugar
PASTRY
375g/12oz flour
¼ tsp salt
90g/3oz butter
90g/3oz vegetable fat
2-3 Tbsp iced water

To make the pastry, sift the flour and salt into a mixing bowl. Add the butter and vegetable fat and cut into small pieces, then rub the fat into the flour until the mixture resembles breadcrumbs. Stir in enough water to bind the mixture and knead to a dough. Chill for 30 minutes.

Roll out two-thirds of the dough to about 6mm/¼in thick. Cut out sixteen 8cm/3in circles. Use to line sixteen patty tins. Place a spoonful of mincemeat in each dough-lined tin. Roll out the remaining dough to 6mm/¼in thick and cut out sixteen 6cm/2½in circles. Use these as lids and press the edges to seal.

Brush the pies with milk and bake in a fairly hot oven (200°C/400°F or Gas Mark 6) for 20 minutes or until the pastry is golden brown. Sprinkle with the sugar and serve warm or cold.
Makes 16

Mincemeat

125g/4oz beef suet, minced or finely
chopped
125g/4oz sultanas
125g/4oz currants
125g/4oz raisins
1 medium cooking apple, peeled, cored
and grated
2 Tbsp mixed candied peel, chopped
½ tsp grated orange rind
½ tsp grated lemon rind
1 Tbsp orange juice
1 tsp lemon juice
3 Tbsp dry sherry
pinch grated nutmeg
pinch ground cinnamon
pinch ground allspice
pinch ground mace
1½ Tbsp ground almonds
1½ Tbsp brandy

Mix together all the ingredients except the brandy. Spoon the mincemeat into clean dry jam jars, filling them to within 2.5cm/1in of the tops. Sprinkle a little brandy over each and cover the jars. Leave in a cool, dark, dry place for at least 1 month before using.
Makes about 700g/1½lb

December 31-Hogmanay

The last day of the year is called Hogmanay in Scotland and some parts of the North of England, and as may be expected is observed with much sampling of Scotland's fine whisky. Also traditional on this day are Black Bun, a rich fruit cake encased in pastry, and Shortbread.

Shortbread is often formed into shapes in special shortbread moulds. These are made of wood and have a thistle pattern on the bottom, which leaves an imprint on the shortbread when it is turned out.

Black bun

PASTRY

350g/12oz flour

¼ tsp salt

75g/3oz butter

2 Tbsp sugar

2 small eggs, lightly beaten

4-6 Tbsp iced water

FILLING

250g/8oz flour

1 tsp bicarbonate of soda

1½ tsp baking powder

125g/4oz soft brown sugar

1 tsp mixed spice

½ tsp ground cinnamon

½ tsp ground ginger

¼ tsp ground mace

350g/12oz sultanas

350g/12oz currants

125g/4oz almonds, chopped

125g/4oz walnuts, chopped

125g/4oz mixed candied peel, chopped

grated rind and juice of 1 lemon

175ml/6floz milk

1 Tbsp brandy

1 egg, lightly beaten

First make the pastry. Sift the flour and salt into a mixing bowl. Add the butter and cut into small pieces, then rub the fat into the flour until the mixture resembles breadcrumbs. Stir in the sugar. Stir in the eggs with enough of the water to bind the mixture and knead to a dough. Chill for 30 minutes.

Roll out just over two-thirds of the dough to a circle about 1cm/½in thick. Use to line a deep 18cm/7in diameter cake tin. Chill while you make the filling.

Sift the flour, soda and baking powder into a mixing bowl. Stir in the brown sugar, spices, sultanas, currants, almonds, walnuts, candied peel and lemon rind and juice. Mix in the milk and brandy. Spoon into the dough-lined cake tin and smooth the top.

Roll out the remaining piece of dough to a circle large enough to cover the top of the tin. Place over the filling and press the edges together to seal. Cut a cross in the centre of the dough top and brush with the beaten egg. Bake in a fairly hot oven (200°C/400°F or Gas Mark 6) for 15 minutes. Cover with foil and reduce the temperature to warm (170°C/325°F or Gas Mark 3). Continue baking for 3½ hours or until a skewer inserted into the centre cross comes out clean.

Turn the cake out of the tin and cool on a wire rack. Wrap in foil and leave for at least 1 week before serving.
Makes one 18cm/7in cake

A Scottish speciality, this unusual, rich fruit cake encased in a sweet crisp pastry is a great favourite at Hogmonay.

Shortbread is another favourite at Hogmonay, which is offered to every guest in a Scottish home on New Year's Eve along with a glass of whisky.

Shortbread

250g/8oz butter
125g/4oz plus 1 Tbsp castor sugar
250g/8oz flour
125g/4oz rice flour
salt

Place the butter and sugar in a bowl and cream together with a wooden spoon until thoroughly blended. Sift the flour and rice, with a pinch of salt, into a second bowl. Then gradually work into the butter mixture until all the flour is incorporated and a smooth dough is formed.

Divide the dough in half and form each piece into a circle about 1cm/½in thick and 20cm/8in in diameter. Transfer the circles to a greased baking sheet. Crimp the edges to make a decorative effect and prick the top with a fork. Chill for 20 minutes.

Bake the shortbread in a moderate oven (180°C/350°F or Gas Mark 4) for 10 minutes. Reduce the temperature to cool (150°C/300°F or Gas Mark 2) and continue baking for 30 to 40 minutes or until the shortbread is crisp and lightly browned.

Cut the shortbread circles into triangles and allow to cool slightly on the baking sheet. Sprinkle with the sugar and cool completely on a wire rack.

Makes two 20cm/8in circles

Index

Pictures supplied by:
Bernard Alfieri: 118T; 199T
Heather Angel: 94B
Rex Bamber: 107
Steve Bicknell: 193
Pat Brindley: 57T
Barry Bullough: 87L
Camera Press: 195
Patrick Cocklin: 178
Delu/PAF International: 18; 37; 62;
72; 103
Alan Duns: 9; 12; 17; 22; 26; 31;
34L; 34R; 39T; 46; 49; 59TR;
66L; 68; 69; 75B 78; 81B; 82T;
88; 99; 105; 109; 116; 117R;
118B; 119B; 121; 123; 127; 129;
138T; 138B; 146/147; 161; 181;
197T&B
V Finnis: 23
P Hunt: 86
George Hyde: 171
Paul Kemp: 13; 16; 27; 31B;
38; 44; 55; 56; 67; 154; 185
Don Last: 14; 102; 125; 126
Michael Leale: 80
John Lee: 81
Max Logan: 76; 167T
David Meldrum: 19; 35; 42/3; 73;
75T; 104; 162
M. Nimmo: 155
Stanli Opperman: 53; 149
Roger Phillips: FC; 6/7; 10; 11;
20/1; 28; 30; 32; 33; 40; 47; 48; 50;
57B; 58; 60/1; 63; 66R; 70; 74; 77;
79T; 79B; 82B; 83; 85; 87R; 89;
90/1; 93; 95; 96; 97; 100; 101; 111;
112; 114; 115; 117; 120; 124; 128;
131; 132/3; 135; 139; 141; 144; 145;
153; 156; 158/9; 164; 165; 166T&B;
168B; 170T; 172; 173; 174/5;
176/7; 178/9; 182; 185B; 186; 191;
191; 192/3; 194; 198
Iain Reid: 25; 45; 64; 106; 110;
137; 140; 151; 167; 170B; 189
David Smith: 140T; 148; 190
Harry Smith: 130
Jerry Tubby: 187
John Turner: 136
Unwins Limited: 65
George Wright: 94T